Compulsory
Mis-education

AND

The Community
of Scholars

by

PAUL GOODMAN

VINTAGE BOOKS
A Division of Random House • New York

VINTAGE BOOKS

are published by Alfred A. Knopf, Inc.

and Random House, Inc.

Library of Congress Catalog Card Number: 66-13013

Acknowledgments are made to the publications in which some chapter of *Compulsory Mis-education* appeared in an earlier form: *The American Child* (National Committee on the Employment of Youth); *Harvard Educational Review; The School Dropout,* Daniel Schreiber, ed. (NEA Project: School Dropouts); *Channels* (Western Michigan University); *Commonweal; Orientation/1964,* a subsidiary of *motive* magazine (The Division of Higher Education of The Methodist Church, © 1964); *Playboy.*

Compulsory Mis-education is reprinted by arrangement with Horizon Press.

Compulsory Mis-education   *1*

The Community of Scholars   *155*

Compulsory
Mis-education

For Mabel

CONTENTS

for Compulsory Mis-education

Preface   7

Part One   Primary Grades

  1   The universal trap   15
  2   Visiting a school   35
  3   The present moment in progressive education   40

Part Two   High School

  4   A proposal to extend compulsory schooling   51
  5   The universe of discourse
              in which they grow up   64
  6   Programmed   80
  7   Teaching science   92

Part Three   College

  8   "I don't want to work—why should I?"   105
  9   An unteachable generation   113
  10   Two simple proposals   122
  11   A usual case—nothing fancy   131

"One had to cram all this stuff into one's mind, whether one liked it or not. This coercion had such a deterring effect that, after I had passed the final examination, I found the consideration of any scientific problems distasteful to me for an entire year. . . . It is in fact nothing short of a miracle that the modern methods of instruction have not yet entirely strangled the holy curiosity of inquiry; for this delicate little plant, aside from stimulation, stands mainly in need of freedom; without this it goes to wrack and ruin without fail. It is a very grave mistake to think that the enjoyment of seeing and searching can be promoted by means of coercion and a sense of duty. To the contrary, I believe that it would be possible to rob even a healthy beast of prey of its voraciousness, if it were possible, with the aid of a whip, to force the beast to devour continuously, even when not hungry —especially if the food, handed out under such coercion, were to be selected accordingly."

—Albert Einstein
(quoted in *Examining in Harvard College*)

PREFACE

i

In these remarks on the schools, I do not try to be generous or fair, but I have seen what I am talking about and I hope I am rational. This case is that we have been swept on a flood-tide of public policy and popular sentiment into an expansion of schooling and an aggrandizement of school-people that is grossly wasteful of wealth and effort and does positive damage to the young. Yet I do not hear any fundamental opposition in principle, nor even prudent people (rather than stingy people) saying, go warily. The dominance of the present school auspices prevents any new thinking about education, although we face unprecedented conditions.

It is uncanny. When, at a meeting, I offer that perhaps we already have too much formal schooling and that, under present conditions, the more we get the less education we will get, the others look at me oddly and proceed to discuss how to get more money for schools and how to upgrade the schools. I realize suddenly that I am confronting a mass superstition.

In this little book, I keep resorting to the metaphor school-monks: the administrators, professors, academic sociologists, and licensees with diplomas who have proliferated into an invested intellectual class worse than anything since the time of Henry the Eighth. Yet I am convinced—as they get their grants and buildings and State laws that give them sole competence—that the monks are sincere in their bland faith in the school. The schools provide the best preparation for everybody for a complicated world, are the logical haven for unemployed youth, can equalize opportunity for the underprivileged, administer research in all fields, and be the indispensable mentor for creativity, business-practice, social work, mental hygiene, genuine literacy—name it, and there are credits for it leading to a degree. The schools offer very little evidence of their unique ability to perform any of these things—there is plenty of evidence to the contrary—but they do not need to offer evidence, since nobody opposes them or proposes alternatives.

A major pressing problem of our society is the defective structure of the economy that advantages the upper middle-class and excludes the lower class. The school-people and Ph.D. sociologists loyally take over also this problem, in the war on poverty, the war against delinquency, retraining those made jobless, training the Peace Corps, and so forth. But as it turns out, just by taking over the problem, they themselves gobble up the budgets and confirm the defective structure of the economy.

And inevitably, expanding and aggrandizing, becoming the universal trainer, baby-sitter, and fix-it, the schools are losing the beautiful academic and community functions that by nature they do have.

ii

The ideas in this book were called up for specific busy occasions. The remarks on the drop-outs were the substance of a contribution to a national conference on the problem, called by the National Education Association. The notes on psychosomatic education were, first, the report of a school visit when I was a member of a local school board in New York; the note on progressive education was a recruiting talk for a Summerhill-variant school of which I am a trustee. The remarks on the Secretary of Labor's proposal and on the hang-ups of getting a job were asked for by the National Committee on Employment of Youth, and printed in *The American Child*. The discussion of adolescent difficulties in communication was commissioned for a freshman course at the University of Western Michigan; and the discussion of unteachability was commissioned by the Methodists for a freshman-orientation program. The critique of programmed instruction was part of a controversy in the *Harvard Educational Review*. The analysis of teaching science was the gist (as I saw it) of a couple of seminars with people from the government science institutes that I attended at the Institute for Policy Studies in Washington. And the proposals for the liberal arts colleges were the gist of a section at the 1964 meeting of the Association for Higher Education.

(At that meeting, I asked the A.H.E. to urge society to find various other means of coping with youth unemployment, rather than putting the entire burden on the colleges. Not surprisingly, this modest resolution went crashingly nowhere.)

Re-writing, I have kept in evidence these busy and polemical contexts. For this is where my story is. John Dewey somewhere makes the remarkable observation that the essential part of philosophy is the philosophy of education, the rest being the subject of special sciences. But I am not able, or prepared, to write such a philosophy. What I can, and do, write is this fighting recall to plain sense, holding action, attempt to lay the groundwork of a decent future.

iii

The immediate future of our country seems to me to have two looming prospects, both gloomy. If the powers-that-be proceed as stupidly, timidly, and "politically" as they have been doing, there will be a bad breakdown and the upsurge of a know-nothing fascism of the right. Incidentally, let me say that I am profoundly unimpressed by our so-called educational system when, as has happened, Governor Wallace comes from the South as a candidate in Northern states and receives his highest number of votes (in some places a majority) in suburbs that have had the *most* years of schooling, more than 16.

The other prospect—which, to be frank, seems to me to be the goal of the school-monks themselves—is a progressive regimentation and brainwashing, on scientific principles, directly toward a fascism-of-the-center, 1984. Certainly this is not anybody's deliberate purpose; but given the maturing of automation, and the present dominance of the automating spirit in schooling, so that all of life becomes geared to the automatic system, that is where we will land.

Therefore in this book I do not choose to be "generous" and "fair."

iv

Underlying the present superstition, however, is an objective fact. Major conditions of modern life *are* unprecedented and we do not know how to cope with them. Confused, people inevitably try to ward off anxiety by rigidifying the old methods of dominant economic and intellectual groups. Omitting the changed international conditions, let me just mention some unprecedented domestic developments that are crucial for even primary education.

Within the United States, we have reached a point of productivity when it becomes absurd to use the rate of growth and the Gross National Product as measures of economic health. To be useful, new production must be much more narrowly qualified, e.g. serve the public sector or eliminate grinding poverty. Unqualified growth already does more harm than good. Thus, we must consider concepts like "work" and "leisure" and "unemployment" in a new way, and we must begin to distinguish between economic well-being and mere affluence. Yet only a handful of economists are thinking along these lines, and almost no one escapes the mesmerism of the GNP. We cannot expect educators to be far ahead.

Correspondingly, the social valuation of scientific technology and science must change. Up to now, the emphasis has been on the products, including the research products, the Knowledge Explosion. But these become diminishingly useful, and the more they flood the environment, the less skillful the average man becomes. The problem for general education, rather, is to learn to *live* in a high technology. The emphasis ought to be on the moral virtues of science itself, both austere and liberating; on its humane beauty; on the selectivity and circumspect reasonableness of sciences like ecology and psychosomatic medicine. These are very different values from the present gearing of general education to the processing of Ph.D.'s.

Urbanization is almost total; independent farming, farming as "a way of life," is at the point of extinction. Yet this development is unexamined and uncontrolled. The disastrous pattern of blighted center, suburbs, and conurbation is taken for granted, and highway, tax, housing, and schooling policies serve only to intensify it. Then astoundingly, we come to suffer from what looks like a population explosion, even though, in this country, vast and beautiful regions are being depopulated. One weeps to see it, yet nothing is done to find possible principles of rural recovery and better balance. Or, in the dense cities, to find functional equivalents for the lost self-reliance, extended family, and community.

There is anomie and an alarming rate of urban mental illness. My own view is that an important factor in these is powerlessness; it is impossible to become engaged or usefully to identify when one cannot initiate and have a say in deciding. If this is so, we should be studying new patterns of decentralizing while we centralize. But there are no such studies and, in my opinion, the bureaucratic methods of social psychiatry probably worsen the social diseases. Certainly we are in a political crisis, for, though the forms of democracy are intact, the content is vanishing. Such political vitality as there is finds its expression in paralegal ways; but these will eventually either renovate the constitution or degenerate into violence and gross injustice. Meantime, there is a proliferation of media of communication and messages communicated, for people need to be informed and want to be informed; yet, partly just because of the communications, there is brainwashing and conformity.

Such are some of the extraordinary conditions for which our schooling fails to educate. It is essential to find alternative ways of educating.

North Stratford, New Hampshire
July 1964

PART ONE

Primary Grades

Chapter 1

THE UNIVERSAL TRAP

i

A conference of experts on school drop-outs will discuss the background of poverty, cultural deprivation, race prejudice, family and emotional troubles, neighborhood uprooting, urban mobility. It will explore ingenious expedients to counteract these conditions, though it will not much look to remedying them—that is not its business. And it will suggest propaganda—e.g. no school, no job—to get the youngsters back in school. It is axiomatic that they ought to be in school.

After a year, it proves necessary to call another conference to cope with the alarming fact that more than 75% of the drop-outs who have been cajoled into returning, have dropped out again. They persist in failing; they still are not sufficiently motivated. What curricular changes must there be? how can the teachers learn the life-style of the underprivileged?

Curiously muffled in these conferences is the question that puts the burden of proof the other way: What are they drop-outs from? Is the schooling really good for them, or much good for anybody? Since, for many, there are such difficulties with the present arrangements, might not some better arrangements be invented? Or bluntly, since schooling undertakes to be compulsory, must it not continually review its claim to be useful? Is it the only means of education? Isn't it unlikely that *any* single type of social institution could fit almost every youngster up to age 16 and beyond? (It is predicted that by 1970, 50% will go to college.)

But conferences on drop-outs are summoned by school professionals, so perhaps we cannot hope that such elementary questions will be raised. Yet neither are they raised by laymen. There is a mass superstition, underwritten by additional billions every year, that adolescents must continue going to school. The middle-class *know* that no professional competence—i.e. status and salary—can be attained without many diplomas; and poor people have allowed themselves to be convinced that the primary remedy for their increasing deprivation is to agitate for better schooling. Nevertheless, I doubt that, *at present or with any reforms that are conceivable under present school administration,* going to school is the best use for the time of life of the majority of youth.

ii

Education is a natural community function and occurs inevitably, since the young grow up on the old, toward their activities, and into (or against) their institutions; and the old foster, teach, train, exploit, and abuse the young. Even neglect of the young, except physical neglect, has an educational effect—not the worst possible.

Formal schooling is a reasonable auxiliary of the inevitable process, whenever an activity is best learned by singling it out or special attention with a special person to teach it. Yet it by no means follows that the complicated artifact of a school system has much to do with education, and certainly not with good education.

Let us bear in mind the way in which a big school system might have nothing to do with education at all. The New York system turns over $700 millions annually, not including capital improvements. There are 750 schools, with perhaps 15 annually being replaced at an extra cost of $2 to $5 millions each. There are 40,000 paid employees. This is a vast vested interest, and it is very probable that—like much of our economy and almost all of our political structure, of which the public schools are a part—it goes on for its own sake, keeping more than a million people busy, wasting wealth, and pre-empting time and space in which something else could be going on. It is a gigantic market for textbook manufacturers, building contractors, and graduate-schools of Education.

The fundamental design of such a system is ancient, yet it has not been altered although the present operation is altogether different in scale from what it was, and therefore it must have a different meaning. For example, in 1900, 6% of the 17-year-olds graduated from high school, and less than ½% went to college; whereas in 1963, 65% graduated from high school and 35% went on to something called college. Likewise, there is a vast difference between schooling intermitted in life on a farm or in a city with plenty of small jobs, and schooling that is a child's only "serious" occupation and often his only adult contact. Thus, a perhaps outmoded institution has become almost the only allowable way of growing up. And with this pre-empting, there is an increasing intensification of the one narrow experience, e.g. in the shaping of the curriculum and testing according to the increasing requirements of graduate schools far off in time and place. Just as our American society as a whole is more and more tightly organized, so its school system is more and more regimented as part of that organization.

In the organizational plan, the schools play a non-educational and an educational role. The non-educational role is very important. In the tender grades, the schools are a baby-sitting service during a period of collapse of the old-type family and during a time of extreme urbanization and urban mobility. In the junior and senior high school grades, they are an arm of the police, providing cops and concentration camps paid for in the budget under the heading "Board of Education." The educational role is, by and large, to provide —at public and parents' expense—apprentice-training for corporations, government, and the teaching professions itself, and also to train the young, as New York's Commissioner of Education has said (in the Worley case), "to handle constructively their problems of adjustment to authority."

The public schools of America have indeed been a powerful, and beneficent, force for the democratizing of a great mixed population. But we must be careful to keep reassessing them when, with changing conditions, they become a universal trap and democracy begins to look like regimentation.

iii

Let me spend a page on the history of the compulsory nature of the school systems. In 1961, in *The Child, the Parent, and the State,* James Conant mentions a possible incompatibility between "individual development" and "national needs"; this, to my mind, is a watershed in American philosophy of education and puts us back to the ideology of Imperial Germany, or on a par with contemporary Russia.

When Jefferson and Madison conceived of compulsory schooling, such an incompatibility would have been unthinkable. They were in the climate of the Enlightenment, were strongly influenced by Congregational (town-meeting) ideas, and were of course makers of a revolution. To them, "citizen" meant society-*maker*, not one "participating in" or "adjusted to" society. It is clear that they regarded themselves and their friends as citizens existentially, so to speak; to make society was their breath of life. But obviously such conceptions are worlds removed from, and diametrically opposed to, our present political reality, where the ground rules and often the score are pre-determined.

For Jefferson, people had to be taught in order to multiply the sources of citizenly initiative and to be vigilant for freedom. Everybody had to become literate and study history, in order to make constitutional innovations and be fired to defend free institutions, which was presumably the moral that history taught. And those of good parts were to study a technological natural philosophy, in order to make inventions and produce useful goods for the new country. By contrast, what are the citizenly reasons for which we compel everybody to be literate, etc.? To keep the economy expanding, to understand the mass-communications, to choose between indistinguishable Democrats and Republicans. Planning and decision-making are lodged in top managers; rarely, and at most, the electorate serves as a pressure-group. There is a new emphasis on teaching science—we will discuss this in another context—but the vast majority will never use this knowledge and will forget it; they are consumers.

Another great impulse for compulsory education came from the new industrialism and urbanism during the three or four decades after the Civil War, a time also of maximum immigration. Here the curricular demands were more mundane: in the grades, literacy and

arithmetic; in the colleges, professional skills to man
the expanding economy. But again, no one would have
spoken of an incompatibility between 'individual development" and "national needs," for it was considered to
be an open society, abounding in opportunity. Typically,
the novels of Horatio Alger, Jr., treat schooling as
morally excellent as well as essential for getting ahead;
and there is no doubt that the immigrants saw educa-
tion-for-success as also a human value for their children. Further, the school-system was not a trap. The
94% who in 1900 did not finish high school had other
life opportunities, including making a lot of money and
rising in politics. But again, by and large this is not our
present situation. There is plenty of social mobility,
opportunity to rise—except precisely for the ethnic
minorities who are our main concern as drop-outs—but
the statuses and channels are increasingly stratified,
rigidified, cut and dried. Most enterprise is parceled out
by feudal corporations, or by the state; and these determine the requirements. Ambition with average talent
meets these rules or fails; those without relevant talent,
or with unfortunate backgrounds, cannot even survive
in decent poverty. The requirements of survival are
importantly academic, attainable only in schools and
universities; but such schooling is ceasing to have an
initiating or moral meaning.

We do not have an open economy; even when jobs
are not scarce, the corporations and state dictate the
possibilities of enterprise. General Electric swoops down
on the high schools, or IBM on the colleges, and skims
off the youth who have been pre-trained for them at
public or private expense. (Private college tuition runs
upward of $6000, and this is estimated as a third or
less of the actual cost for "education and educational
administration.") Even a department store requires a
diploma for its salespeople, not so much because of the

skills they have learned as that it guarantees the right character: punctual and with a smooth record. And more generally, since our powers-that-be have opted for an expanding economy with a galloping standard of living, and since the powers of the world are in an arms and space race, there *is* a national need for many graduates specifically trained. Thus, even for those selected, the purpose is irrelevant to citizenly initiative, the progress of an open society, or personal happiness, and the others have spent time and effort in order to be progressively weeded out. Some drop out.

iv

It is said that our schools are geared to "middle-class values," but this is a false and misleading use of terms. The schools less and less represent *any* human values, but simply adjustment to a mechanical system.

Because of the increasing failure of the schools with the poor urban mass, there has developed a line of criticism—e.g. Oscar Lewis, Patricia Sexton, Frank Riessman, and even Edgar Friedenberg—asserting that there is a "culture of poverty" which the "middle-class" schools do not fit, but which has its own virtues of spontaneity, sociality, animality. The implication is that the "middle class," for all its virtues, is obsessional, prejudiced, prudish.

Pedagogically, this insight is indispensable. A teacher must try to reach each child in terms of what he brings, his background, his habits, the language he understands. But if taken to be more than technical, it is a disastrous conception. The philosophic aim of education must be to get each one out of his isolated class and into the one humanity. Prudence and responsibility are not middle-class virtues but human virtues; and spontaneity and sexuality are not powers of the simple but of human health. One has the impression that our social-psychologists are looking not to a human community but to a future in which the obsessionals will take care of the impulsives!)

In fact, some of the most important strengths that have historically belonged to the middle class are flouted by the schools: independence, initiative, scrupulous honesty, earnestness, utility, respect for thorough scholarship. Rather than bourgeois, our schools have become petty-bourgeois, bureaucratic, time-serving, gradgrind-practical, timid, and *nouveau riche* climbing. In the upper grades and colleges, they often exude a cynicism that belongs to rotten aristocrats.

Naturally, however, the youth of the poor and of the middle class respond differently to the petty bourgeois atmosphere. For many poor children, school is orderly and has food, compared to chaotic and hungry homes, and it might even be interesting compared to total deprivation of toys and books. Besides, the wish to improve a child's lot, which on the part of a middle-class parent might be frantic status-seeking and pressuring, on the part of a poor parent is a loving aspiration. There is here a gloomy irony. The school that for a poor Negro child might be a great joy and opportunity is likely to be dreadful; whereas the middle-class child might be better off *not* in the "good" suburban school he has.

Other poor youth, herded into a situation that does not fit their disposition, for which they are unprepared by their background, and which does not interest them, simply develop a reactive stupidity very different from their behavior on the street or ball field. They fall behind, play truant, and as soon as possible drop out. If the school situation is immediately useless and damaging to them, their response must be said to be life-preservative. They thereby somewhat diminish their chances of a decent living, but we shall see that the usual propaganda—that schooling is a road to high salaries—is for most poor youth a lie; and the increase in security is arguably not worth the torture involved.

The reasonable social policy would be not to have these youth in school, certainly not in high school, but to educate them otherwise and provide opportunity for a decent future in some other way. How? I shall venture some suggestions later; in my opinion, the wise thing would be to have our conferences on *this* issue, and omit the idea of drop-out altogether. But the brute fact is that our society isn't really interested; the concern for the drop-outs is mainly because they are a nuisance and a threat and can't be socialized by the existing machinery.

Numerically far more important than these overt drop-outs at 16, however, are the children who conform to schooling between the ages of 6 to 16 or 20, but who drop out internally and day-dream, their days wasted, their liberty caged and scheduled. And there are many such in the middle class, from backgrounds with plenty of food and some books and art, where the youth is seduced by the prospect of money and status, but even more where he is terrified to jeopardize the only pattern of life he knows.

It is in the schools and from the mass media, rather than at home or from their friends, that the mass of our citizens in all classes learn that life is inevitably routine, depersonalized, venally graded; that it is best to toe the mark and shut up; that there is no place for spontaneity, open sexuality, free spirit. Trained in the schools, they go on to the same quality of jobs, culture, politics. This *is* education, mis-education, socializing to the national norms and regimenting to the national "needs."

John Dewey used to hope, naïvely, that the schools could be a community somewhat better than society and serve as a lever for social change. In fact, our schools reflect our society closely, except that they *emphasize* many of its worst features, as well as having the characteristic defects of academic institutions of all times and places.

v

Let us examine realistically half a dozen aspects of the school that is dropped out *from*.

(a) There is widespread anxiety about the children not learning to read, and hot and defensive argument about the methods of teaching reading. Indeed, reading deficiency is an accumulating scholastic disadvantage that results in painful feeling of inferiority, truancy, and drop-out. Reading is crucial for school success—all subjects depend on it—and therefore for the status-success that the diploma is about. Yet in all the anxiety and argument, there is no longer any mention of the freedom and human cultivation that literacy is supposed to stand for.

In my opinion, there is something phony here. For a change, let us look at this "reading" coldly and ask if it is really such a big deal except precisely in the school that is supposed to teach it and is sometimes failing to do so.

With the movies, TV, and radio that the illiterate also share, there is certainly no lack of "communications." We cannot say that as humanities or science, the reading-matter of the great majority is in any way superior to the content of these other media. And in the present stage of technology and economy, it is probably *less* true than it was in the late nineteenth century—the time of the great push to universal literacy and arithmetic—that the mass-teaching of reading is indispensable to operate the production and clerical system. It is rather our kind of urbanism, politics, and buying and selling that require literarcy. These are not excellent.

Perhaps in the present dispensation we should be as well off if it were socially acceptable for large numbers not to read. It would be harder to regiment people if they were not so well "informed"; as Norbert Wiener used to point out, every repetition of a cliché only increases the noise and *prevents* communication. With less literacy, there would be more folk culture. Much suffering of inferiority would be avoided if youngsters did not have to meet a perhaps unnecessary standard. Serious letters could only benefit if society were less swamped by trash, lies, and bland verbiage. Most important of all, *more* people might become genuinely literate if it were understood that reading is not a matter-of-course but a *special useful art with a proper subject-matter, imagination and truth,* rather than a means of communicating top-down decisions and advertising. (The advertising is a typical instance: when the purpose of advertising was to give information—"New shipment of salt fish arrived, very good, foot of Barclay Street"—it was useful to be able to read; when the point of advertising is to create a synthetic demand, it is better not to be able to read.)

(b) Given their present motives, the schools are not competent to teach authentic literacy, reading as a means of liberation and cultivation. And I doubt that most of us who seriously read and write the English language ever learned it by the route of "Run, Spot, Run" to *Silas Marner*. Rather, having picked up the rudiments either in cultured homes or in the first two grades, we really learned to read by our own will and free exploration, following our bent, generally among books that are considered inappropriate by school librarians!

A great neurologist tells me that the puzzle is not how to teach reading, but why some children fail to learn to read. Given the amount of exposure that any urban child gets, any normal animal should spontaneously catch on to the code. What prevents? It is almost demonstrable that, for many children, it is precisely going to school that prevents—because of the school's alien style, banning of spontaneous interest, extrinsic rewards and punishments. (In many underprivileged schools, the I.Q. steadily falls the longer they go to school.) Many of the backward readers might have had a better chance on the streets.

But let me say something, too, about the "successful" teaching of reading and writing in the schools. Consider, by contrast, the method employed by Sylvia Ashton-Warner in teaching little Maoris. She gets them to ask for their *own* words, the particular gut-word of fear, lust, or despair that is obsessing the child that day; this is written for him on strong cardboard; he learns it instantaneously and never forgets it; and soon he has an exciting, if odd, vocabulary. From the beginning, writing is by demand, practical, magical; and of course it is simply an extension of speech—it is the best and strongest speech, as writing should be. What is read is what somebody is importantly trying to tell. Now what do our schools do? We use tricks of mechanical conditioning. These do positive damage to spontaneous speech, meant expression, earnest understanding. Inevitably, they create *in the majority* the wooden attitude toward "writing," as entirely different from speech, that college-teachers later try to cope with in Freshman Composition. And reading inevitably becomes a manipulation of signs, e.g. for test-passing, that has no relation to experience.

(Until recently, the same discouragement by school-teachers plagued children's musical and plastic expression, but there have been attempts to get back to spontaneity—largely, I think, because of the general revolution in modern art and musical theory. In teaching science, there is just now a strong movement to encourage imagination rather than conditioned "answers." In teaching foreign languages, the emphasis is now strongly on vital engagement and need to speak. Yet in teaching reading and writing, the direction has been the contrary; even progressive education has gone back to teaching spelling. These arts are regarded merely as "tools.")

(c) The young rightly resist animal constraint. But, at least in New York where I have been a school-board Visitor, most teachers—and the principals who supervise their classes—operate as if progressive education had not proved the case for noise and freedom of bodily motion. (Dewey stresses the salutary alternation of boisterousness and tranquility.) The seats are no longer bolted to the floor, but they still face front. Of course, the classes are too large to cope with without "discipline." Then make them smaller, or don't wonder if children escape out of the cage, either into truancy or baffled daydream. Here is a typical case: an architect replacing a Harlem school is forbidden by the Board to spend money on soundproofing the classrooms, even though the principal has called it a necessity for the therapy of pent-up and resentful children. The resentment, pent-up hostility, is a major cause of reactive stupidity; yet there is usually an absolute ban on overt expression of hostility, or even of normal anger and aggression.

Again, one has to be blind not to see that, from the onset of puberty, the dissidence from school is importantly sexual. Theoretically, the junior high school was introduced to fit this change of life; yet astoundingly, it is sexless. My own view, for what it's worth, is that sexuality is lovely, there cannot be too much of it, it is self-limiting if it is satisfactory, and satisfaction diminishes tension and clears the mind for attention and learning. Therefore, sexual expression should be approved in and out of season, also in school, and where necessary made the subject of instruction. But whether or not this view is correct, it certainly is more practical than the apparent attempt of the schools to operate as if sexual drives simply did not exist. When, on so crucial an issue, the schools act a hundred years out of date, they are crucially irrelevant.

But the following *is* something new:

"Trenton, May 24 (AP)—A state health official believes some overanxious New Jersey parents are dosing their children with tranquilizers before sending them to school . . . the Health Department pediatrician assigned to the State Education Department said the parents apparently are trying to protect the children from cracking under pressure for good grades."

(d) (Terrible damage is done to children simply by the size and standardization of the big system. Suppose a class size of 20 is good for average purposes; it does *not* follow that 35 is better than nothing. Rather, it is likely to be positively harmful, because the children have ceased to be persons and the teacher is destroyed as a teacher.) A teacher with a 10-year-old class reading at 7-year level will have to use the content as well as the vocabulary of *Dick and Jane* since that is the textbook bought by the hundred thousands. The experience of a wise principal is that the most essential part of his job is to know every child's name and be an available "good father," so he wants a school for 400. Yet the city will build the school for 2000, because only that is practical, even though the essence is entirely dissipated. The chief part of learning is in the community of scholars, where classwork and social life may cohere; yet social engineers like Dr. Conant will, for putative efficiencies, centralize the high schools—the "enriched" curriculum with equipment is necessary for the national needs.

A program—e.g. to prevent drop-out—will be, by an attentive teacher, exquisitely tailored to the children he works with; he will have a success. Therefore his program must be standardized, watered down, for 75 schools—otherwise it cannot be financed—although now it is worthless. But here is an unbeatable anecdote: An architect is employed to replace a dilapidated school but is forbidden to consult the principal and teachers of the school about their needs, since his building must conform to uniform plans at headquarters, the plans being two generations out of date. As a functionalist, the architect demurs, and it requires an *ad hoc* assembly of all the superintendents to give him special permission.

Presumably all this is administratively necessary, but then it is also necessary for bruised children to quit. Our society makes a persistent error in metaphysics. We are so mesmerized by the operation of a system with the appropriate name, for instance "Education," that we assume that it *must* be working somewhat, though admittedly not perfectly, when perhaps it has ceased to fulfill its function altogether and might even be preventing the function, for instance education.

(e) Especially today, when the hours of work will sharply diminish, the schools are supposed to educate for the satisfaction of life and for the worthwhile use of leisure. Again, let us try to be realistic, as a youngster is. For most people, I think, a candid self-examination will show that their most absorbing, long, and satisfactory hours are spent in activities like friendly competitive sports, gambling, looking for love and love-making, earnest or argumentative conversation, political action with signs and sit-ins, solitary study and reading, contemplation of nature and cosmos, arts and crafts, music, and religion. Now none of these requires much money. Indeed, elaborate equipment takes the heart out of them. Friends use one another as resources. God, nature, and creativity are free. The media of the fine arts are cheap stuff. Health, luck, and affection are the only requirements for good sex. Good food requires taking pains more than spending money.

What is the moral for our purposes? Can it be denied that in some respects the drop-outs make a wiser choice than many who go to school, not to get real goods but to get money? Their choice of the "immediate"—their notorious "inability to tolerate delay"—is not altogether impulsive and neurotic. The bother is that in our present culture, which puts its entire emphasis on the consumption of expensive commodities, they are so nagged by inferiority, exclusion, and despair of the future that they cannot enjoy their leisure with a good conscience. Because they know little, they are deprived of many profound simple satisfactions and they never know what to do with themselves. Being afraid of exposing themselves to awkwardness and ridicule, they just hang around. And our urban social arrangements— e.g. high rent—have made it impossible for anybody to be decently poor on a "low" standard. One is either in the rat-race or has dropped out of society altogether.

(f) As a loyal academic, I must make a further observation. Mainly to provide Ph.D.'s, there is at present an overwhelming pressure to gear the "better" elementary schools to the graduate-universities. This is the great current reform, genre of Rickover. But what if the top of the ladder is corrupt and corrupts the lower grades? On visits to 70 colleges everywhere in the country, I have been appalled at how rarely the subjects are studied in a right academic spirit, for their truth and beauty and as part of humane international culture. The students are given, and seek, a narrow expertise, "mastery," aimed at licenses and salary. They are indoctrinated with a national thoughtlessness that is not even chauvinistic. Administrators sacrifice the community of scholars to aggrandizement and extramurally sponsored research.

Conversely, there is almost never conveyed the sense in which learning is truly practical, to enlighten experience, give courage to initate and change, reform the state, deepen personal and social peace. On the contrary, the entire educational system itself creates professional cynicism or the resigned conviction that Nothing Can Be Done. If this is the University, how can we hope for aspiring scholarship in the elementary schools? On the contrary, everything will be grades and conforming, getting ahead not in the subject of interest but up the ladder. Students "do" Bronx Science in order to "make" M.I.T. and they "do" M.I.T. in order to "make" Westinghouse; some of them have "done" Westinghouse in order to "make" jail.

vi

What then? The compulsory system has become a universal trap, and it is no good. Very many of the youth, both poor and middle class, might be better off if the system simply did not exist, even if they then had no formal schooling at all. (I am extremely curious for a philosophic study of Prince Edward County in Virginia, where for some years schooling did not exist for Negro children.)

But what would become of these children? For very many, both poor and middle class, their homes are worse than the schools, and the city streets are worse in another way. Our urban and suburban environments are precisely not cities or communities where adults naturally attend to the young and educate to a viable life. Also, perhaps especially in the case of the overt drop-outs, the state of their body and soul is such that we must give them refuge and remedy, whether it be called school, settlement house, youth worker, or work camp.

There are thinkable alternatives. Throughout this little book, as occasion arises, I shall offer alternative proposals that I as a single individual have heard of or thought up. Here are half a dozen directly relevant to the subject we have been discussing, the system as compulsory trap. In principle, when a law begins to do more harm than good, the best policy is to alleviate it or try doing without it.

i. Have "no school at all" for a few classes. These children should be selected from tolerable, though not necessarily cultured, homes. They should be neighbors and numerous enough to be a society for one another and so that they do not feel merely "different." Will they learn the rudiments anyway? This experiment cannot do the children any academic harm, since there is good evidence that normal children will make up the first seven years school-work with four to seven months of good teaching.

ii. Dispense with the school building for a few classes; provide teachers and use the city itself as the school—its streets, cafeterias, stores, movies, museums, parks, and factories. Where feasible, it certainly makes more sense to teach using the real subject-matter than to bring an abstraction of the subject-matter into the school-building as "curriculum." Such a class should probably not exceed 10 children for one pedagogue. The idea—it is the model of Athenian education—is not dissimilar to Youth gang work, but not applied to delinquents and not playing to the gang ideology.

iii. Along the same lines, but both outside and inside the school building, use appropriate *unlicensed* adults of the community—the druggist, the storekeeper, the mechanic—as the proper educators of the young into the grown-up world. By this means we can try to overcome the separation of the young from the grown-up world so characteristic in modern urban life, and to diminish the omnivorous authority of the professional school-people. Certainly it would be a useful and animating experience for the adults. (There is the beginning of such a volunteer program in the New York and some other systems.)

iv. Make class attendance not compulsory, in the manner of A. S. Neill's Summerhill. If the teachers are good, absence would tend to be eliminated; if they are bad, let them know it. The compulsory law is useful to get the children away from the parents, but it must not result in trapping the children. A fine modification of this suggestion is the rule used by Frank Brown in Florida: he permits the children to be absent for a week or a month to engage in any worthwhile enterprise or visit any new environment.

v. Decentralize an urban school (or do not build a new big building) into small units, 20 to 50, in available store-fronts or clubhouses. These tiny schools, equipped with record-player and pin-ball machine, could combine play, socializing, discussion, and formal teaching. For special events, the small units can be brought together into a common auditorium or gymnasium, so as to give the sense of the greater community. Correspondingly, I think it would be worthwhile to give the Little Red Schoolhouse a spin under modern urban conditions, and see how it works out: that is, to combine all the ages in a little room for 25 to 30, rather than to grade by age.

vi. Use a pro rata part of the school money to send

children to economically marginal farms for a couple of months of the year, perhaps 6 children from mixed backgrounds to a farmer. The only requirement is that the farmer feed them and not beat them; best, of course, if they take part in the farm-work. This will give the farmer cash, as part of the generally desirable program to redress the urban-rural ratio to something nearer to 70% to 30%. (At present, less than 8% of families are rural.) Conceivably, some of the urban children will take to the other way of life, and we might generate a new kind of rural culture.

I frequently suggest these and similar proposals at teachers colleges, and I am looked at with an eerie look—do I really mean to *diminish* the state-aid grant for each student-day? But mostly the objective is that such proposals entail intolerable administrative difficulties.

Above all, we must apply these or any other proposals to particular individuals and small groups, without the obligation of uniformity. There is a case for uniform standards of achievement, lodged in the Regents, but they *cannot* be reached by uniform techniques. The claim that standardization of procedure is more efficient, less costly, or alone administratively practical, is often false. Particular inventiveness requires thought, but thought does not cost money.

Chapter 2

VISITING A SCHOOL

i

Leading a seminar in the philosophy of Education—
it was at Antioch—I was met by the point-blank question: "What would you say is the chief use of the
elementary schools?" After a moment, I found myself
blurting out, "Why, I suppose it's to undo the damage
done at home, so the child can begin to breathe again
and be curious." At this the student-teachers laughed
and asked what was the purpose of high school. I had
to answer, of course, "To undo the damage done by
the elementary schools." And any one who has had the
misfortune of teaching college freshmen will agree that
the chief aim of at least the freshman year in college
is to try and undo some of the damage done by the
high schools. No doubt, the chief purpose of the
school of hard knocks is to undo the effects of the colleges. But perhaps, in our highly interlocked society,
it's all of a piece.

We can look at it the other way and say that the
chief purpose of the elementary schools is to relieve
the home, to baby-sit. But it is such an expensive kind

of baby-sitting!—it costs annually $650 a child in a New York City grade school, about $1000 in high school.

ii

What kind of alternative environment to the home does the school in fact give? What is its animal and moral tone? Let me describe a school Visit. (West Side of Manhattan, predominantly a Puerto Rican area.)

It was a luckily small class—I counted less than 20 —exceptional in the New York system where the classes run to 35 and more, though the technical "average" is 29. The lesson was on Weather, and what the teacher wanted was to get them to say that temperature varies with altitude, latitude, and season. She intended to write these words on the board, and that's what she was after. She was not a bad gal, but a poor teacher. She did not ask about the weather in Puerto Rico, where several had undoubtedly been.

But the salient condition in that class was that every few moments—during the 40 minutes I sat there, about 10 times—she said, "Now speak louder! I can't hear. Louder!" And she repeated her question on latitude and altitude. It was obvious enough that the foreground object, which in fact demanded pedagogy, was that the children were muffled. They sat in a dejected posture, and they could not, physically could not, throw out their voices. Psychosomatically, they could not then have a very aggressive attitude toward the subject-matter either, toward grasping it, taking it in.

One expedient would have been to go close to the kid and say, "Sit up, young lady, and breathe from the diaphragm. Here, where I'm touching you. You aren't using these muscles. See, if I press your ribs they hurt. Now move your bottom ribs here—that's the diaphragm, and throw *out* your breath and shout . . . What should you shout? Just shout Shout!" If she had done that, the children would very soon have been able to throw their voices; they would have been breathing better; some of them might have gotten a little dizzy. They would also soon have had a more aggressive attitude toward the lesson.

It happened in that school, however, that the principal was a little of a maniac on noise. He had instituted silent passing in the halls. He explained to me that the Puerto Rican children were very wild; if he let them talk to one another between classes, they soon became boisterous, and then ten minutes of the class time was spent in calming them down. They were calmed down only too well, for the 40 minutes of every hour.

While I was talking with him, there was a petty noise in the hall. He jumped out of his skin and rushed with angry shouts, to find who had made that noise. Clearly, if the teacher had had the kids shout, a supervisor would have descended on her, and she would have had something to answer for.

All right, one went into the shop class, where there was some noise. But here was a kid who couldn't hammer a nail; he missed, or he controlled the swing and only tapped. The teacher did nothing about it. But it seemed to me that the way the kid kept his shoulders tense—perhaps against letting out hostility—he *couldn't* hammer, any more than he could throw a punch. The important thing in a seventh grade shop-class is not for the kid to make a box, but for him to do it with force and grace, to become an amateur carpenter, and then he might make fine boxes. Would not a good teacher work on this specifically, on force and grace and the emotional liberation of motor execution?

In the gym they were doing the President's push-ups, ordained by John Kennedy who was eager to have the youth physically fit. Apparently, physical fitness was going to be achieved by the ability to do certain calisthenic exercises; or at least it would be measured by the exercises—the teacher would have something to write down. The children were doing the prescribed number of push-ups, the prescribed number of chin-ups. In fact, three quarters of the class were faking the chin-up outrageously (just as I always did), elbows rigid, holding breath, but making like they had done the exercise. In a few cases, this was probably positively damaging, straining; in most cases, the business was a perfunctory proof performance, meaning "O.K., let me alone." In some cases, it would be part of a distaste and shame for the use of one's body altogether, not giving in to the physical effort.

It seems to me that the authentic methods for elementary physical education—but of course no normal schools are teaching such methods—are eurhythmics and what the psychologists call Character Analysis, the training of emotion, and the liberation of inhibited emotion, by psychosomatic and muscular behavior. The problem of each of these children is that he is unable to express his anger, his grief, his sexuality. Yet nothing is done to unblock the fear of expression, of body contact, of nakedness. There is a kind of music-teaching, but it does not seek to draw on actual feeling and to integrate feeling by rhythm and harmony.

Rather amusingly, this same school happened to have an extra-curricular activity, social dancing, with the children as drummers, initiated by a lively young woman teacher. Dancing their cha-cha, the children were marvelous little acrobats, with plenty of grace and force and intricate rhythms that would have delighted Dalcroze. They had no need of the President's exercises at all. I Calvinistically thought it was a pity that they were not also learning to notate all this and go on to composition—but that no doubt would have spoiled it.

...
iii

What, realistically, was a member of Local Board 6 & 8 to advise, as a result of that Visit? Suppose that the gym teacher, or the shop teacher, or the teacher of meteorology *did* pursue a proper educational course. Without doubt, in some cases there would be a great outburst of dammed up hostility, and plenty of tears. A child might go home and tell off his father. He might even tell off the teacher. The expression of that hostility—and even more, the expression of grief or sexual desire—might lead to the most horrendous consequences. The church would complain. The newspapers, that thrive on pornography and murder, would surely note with alarm. The Mayor would be called on. And the teacher would very soon be fired. Nor— my guess is—would the Teachers Union come to the rescue.

But the children might get over their retroflected rage and shame, relax their reactive stupidity (almost all stupidity is a "defense"), and find themselves again in a *possible* environment.

Chapter 3

THE PRESENT MOMENT IN PROGRESSIVE EDUCATION

i

The program of progressive education always antici-
pates the crucial social problems that everybody will be
concerned with a generation later, when it is too late
for the paradisal solutions of progressive educators.
This is in the nature of the case. Essentially, progressive
education is nothing but the attempt to naturalize, to
humanize, each new social and technical development
that is making traditional education irrelevant. It is not
a reform of education, but a reconstruction in terms of
the new era. If society would *once* adopt this reconstruction, we could at last catch up with ourselves and
grow naturally into the future. But equally in the nature
of the case, society rejects, half-accepts, bastardizes
the necessary changes; and so we are continually stuck
with "unfinished revolutions," as I called them in
Growing Up Absurd. Then occur the vast social problems that *could* have been avoided—that indeed the
older progressive education had specifically addressed—

but it is too late. And progressive educators stoically ask, What is the case *now?*

During the current incredible expansion of increasingly unnatural schooling, and increasing alienation of the young, it is useful to trace the course of progressive education in this century, from John Dewey to the American version of A. S. Neill.

ii

The recent attacks on Deweyan progressive education, by the Rickovers and Max Raffertys, have really been outrageous—one gets impatient. Historically, the intent of Dewey was exactly the opposite of what the critics say. Progressive education appeared in this country in the intellectual, moral, and social crisis of the development of big centralized industrialism after the Civil War. It was the first thoroughgoing analysis of the crucial modern problem of every advanced country in the world: how to cope with high industrialism and scientific technology which are strange to people; how to restore competence to people who are becoming ignorant; how to live in the rapidly growing cities so that they will not be mere urban sprawl; how to have a free society in mass conditions; how to make the high industrial system good for something, rather than a machine running for its own sake.

That is, progressive education was the correct solution of a real problem that Rickover is concerned with, the backwardness of people in a scientific world. To put it more accurately, if progressive education had been generally adopted, we should not be so estranged and ignorant today.

The thought of John Dewey was part of a similar tendency in architecture, the functionalism of Louis Sullivan and Frank Lloyd Wright, that was trying to invent an urbanism and an esthetic suited to machine-production and yet human; and it went with the engineering orientation of the economic and moral theory of Veblen. These thinkers wanted to train, teach—perhaps accustom is the best word— the new generation to the actualities of industrial and technical life, working practically with the machinery, learning by doing. People could then be at home in the modern world, and possibly become free.

At-homeness had also a political aspect. Dewey was distressed by both the robber-baron plutocracy and the bossed mass-democracy; and he was too wise to espouse Veblen's technocracy, engineer's values. Dewey put a good deal of faith in industrial democracy, overestimating the labor movement—he did not foresee the bureaucratization of the unions. As a pragmatist he probably expected that the skilled would become initiators in manangement and production; he did not foresee that labor demands would diminish to wages and working conditions.

But the school, he felt, could combine all the necessary elements: practical learning of science and technology, democratic community, spontaneous feeling liberated by artistic appreciation, freedom to fantasize, and animal expression freed from the parson's morality and the schoolmaster's ruler. This constituted the whole of Deweyan progressive education. There would be spontaneous interest (including animal impulse), harmonized by art-working; this spontaneity would be controlled by the hard pragmatism of doing and making the doing actually work; and thus the young democratic community would learn the modern world and also have the will to change it. Progressive education was a theory of continual scientific experiment and orderly, nonviolent social revolution.

As was inevitable, this theory was entirely perverted when it began to be applied, either in private schools or in the public system. The conservatives and the businessmen cried out, and the program was toned down. The practical training and community democracy, whose purpose was to live scientifically and change society, was changed into "socially useful" subjects and a psychology of "belonging." In our schools, driver-training survives as the type of the "useful." (By now, I suspect, Dewey would have been urging us to curtail the number of cars.) Social-dancing was the type of the "belonging." The Americans had no intention of broadening the scientific base and taking technological expertness and control out of the hands of the top managers and their technicians. And democratic community became astoundingly interpreted as conformity, instead of being the matrix of social experiment and political change.

iii

Curiously, just in the past few years, simultaneous with the attack on "Dewey," his ideas have been getting most prestigious official endorsement (though they are not attributed to Dewey). In the great post-Sputnik cry to increase the scientific and technical pool, the critics of "Dewey" call for strict lessons and draconian grading and weeding-out (plus bribes), to find the élite group. (Dr. Conant says that the "academically talented" are 15% and these, selected by national tests, will be at home *for* us in the modern technical world as its creative spirits.) However, there is an exactly contrary theory, propounded by the teachers of science, e.g. the consensus of the Woods Hole Conference of the National Science Foundation, reported in Professor Bruner's *The Processes of Education*. This theory counsels practical learning by doing, entirely rejects competition and grading, and encourages fantasy and guesswork. There is no point, it claims, in learning the "answers," for very soon there will be different answers. Rather, what must be taught are the underlying ideas of scientific thought, continuous with the substance of the youngster's feelings and experience. In short, the theory is Deweyan progressive education.

To be sure, Professor Bruner and his associates do not go on to espouse democratic community. But I am afraid they will eventually find that also this is essential, for it is impossible to do creative work of any kind when the goals are pre-determined by outsiders and cannot be criticized and altered by the minds that have to do the work, even if they are youngsters. (Dewey's principle is, simply, that good teaching is that which leads the student to want to learn something more.)

The compromise of the National Science Foundation on this point is rather comical. "Physical laws are not asserted; they are, it is hoped, discovered by the student"; "there is a desire to allow each student to experience some of the excitement that scientific pursuits afford"—I am quoting from the NSF's *Science Course Improvement Projects*. That is, the student is to make a leap of discovery to—what is already known, in a course precharted by the Ph.D.'s at M.I.T. Far from being elating, such a process must be profoundly disappointing; my guess is that the "discovery" will be greeted not by a cheer but by a razz. The excitement of discovery is reduced to the animation of puzzle-solving. I doubt that puzzle-solving is what creative thought is about, though it is certainly what many Ph.D.'s are about.

iv

Authentic progressive education, meantime, has moved into new territory altogether, how to cope with the over-centralized organization and Organization Men of our society, including the top-down direction of science by the National Science Foundation. The new progressive theory is "Summerhill."

The American Summerhill movement is modeling itself on A. S. Neill's school in England, but with significant deviations—so that Neill does not want his name associated with some of the offshoots.

Like Dewey, Neill stressed free animal expression, learning by doing, and *very* democratic community processes (one person one vote, enfranchising small children!). But he also asserted a principle that to Dewey did not seem important, the freedom to choose to go to class or stay away altogether. A child at Summerhill can just hang around; he'll go to class when he damned well feels like it—and some children, coming from compulsory schools, don't damned well feel like it for eight or nine months. But after a while, as the curiosity in the soul revives—and since their friends go—they give it a try.

It is no accident, as I am trying to show in this book, that it is just *this* departure in progressive education that is catching on in America, whereas most of the surviving Deweyan schools are little better than the good suburban schools that imitated them. The advance-guard problem is that the compulsory school system, like the whole of our economy, politics, and standard of living, has become a lockstep. It is no longer designed for the maximum growth and future practical utility of the children into a changing world, but is inept social engineering for extrinsic goals, pitifully short-range. Even when it is benevolent, it is in the bureacratic death-grip of a uniformity of conception, from the universities down, that cannot possibly suit the multitude of dispositions and conditions. Yet 100% of the children are supposed to remain for at least 12 years in one kind of box; and of course those who attend private Deweyan schools are being aimed for 4 to 8 years more. Thus, if we are going to experiment with real universal education that educates, we have to start by getting rid of compulsory schooling altogether.

v

One American variant of Summerhill has developed in a couple of years in an unforseen direction. Like Summerhill this school is not urban, but, unlike Summerhill, it is not residential. Many of the children come from a nearby colony of artists, some of them of international fame. The artist parents, and other parents, come into the school as part-time teachers, of music, painting, building, dancing.

Being strong-minded, they, and the regular teachers, soon fell out with the headmaster, the founder, who had been a Summerhill teacher; they stripped him of important perogatives and he resigned. Inevitably other parents had to join the discussions and decisions, on real and difficult issues. The result seems to have been the formation of a peculiar kind of extended family, unified by educating the children, and incorporating a few professional teachers. But meantime, imitated from Neill, there is the democratic council, in which the children have a very loud voice and an equal vote, and this gives them an institutional means to communicate with, and get back at, their parents. It is stormy and factional. Some parents have pulled out and teachers have quit. Yet, inadvertently, there is developing a brilliant solution to crucial problems of American life: how can children grow up in live contact with many adults; how can those who do the work run the show; how to transcend a rigid professionalism that is wasteful of human resources.

At present one of the teachers at this school is preparing to try out a little Summerhill school in a slum area in New York.

Another Summerhill variant has taken a different course: to use the school almost directly as social action. To overcome the artificial stratification of modern society, it brings together not only Negroes and whites but delinquents and the well-behaved. Naturally this gets the school into trouble with its surroundings. It has had to flee from the South to the North, and it is in trouble again in the North.

Such a combination of education and direct social action is springing up on all sides. The so-called Northern Student Movement is a group of college-students who take a year off from college to tutor urban underprivileged kids referred by the public schools; but the NSM has now declared as its policy *not* to restrict itself to the curriculum and aims of the school system. The Student Non-Violent Coordinating Committee is about —I am writing in June 1964—to go down to the deep South, primarily to help in the voter-registration of disenfranchised Negroes, but also to try out little colleges for adolescents, with 5 graduate-students teaching 25 teenagers a curriculum relevant to their economic and political advancement. Accompanying the numerous school-boycotts there have sprung up "Freedom" schools that started as one-day propaganda demonstrations but have been lively enough to warrant continuing.

In my opinion, the highly official Peace Corps has the same underlying educational significance. At present it is rigidly selective and super-collegiate; indeed it is, by and large, an operation for upper-middle-class youth and well-paid professors and administrators: it costs $15,000 to get one youngster in the field for a year. Nevertheless, the whole conception is unthinkable except as dissatisfaction with orthodox schooling and with the status-careers that that schooling leads to.

vi

The future—if we survive and have a future, which is touch and go—will certainly be more leisurely. If that leisure is not to be completely inane and piggishly affluent, there must be a community and civic culture. There must be more employment in human services and less in the production of hardware gadgets; more citizenly initiative and less regimentation; and in many spheres, decentralization of control and administration. For these purposes, the top-down dictated national plans and educational methods that are now the fad are quite irrelevant. And on the contrary, it is precisely the society of free choice, lively engagement, and social action of Summerhill and American Summerhill that are relevant and practical.

Thus, just as with Dewey, the new advance of progressive education is a good index of what the real situation is. And no doubt society will again seek to abuse this program which it needs but is afraid of.

PART TWO

High School

Chapter 4

A PROPOSAL
TO EXTEND
COMPULSORY
SCHOOLING

i

In an address to the American Bankers Association on February 24, 1964, the Secretary of Labor proposed to *extend* compulsory schooling to the age of 18. This at a time when in New York a Kings County Grand Jury proposed *reducing* it to 15 and giving the superintendent of schools leeway to kick out the unruly. In many schools in the country policemen are stationed to keep guard over youngsters who do not want to be there. And the majority of drop-outs who were cajoled into returning to school in 1963 soon dropped out again, since nothing essential had been changed in purpose, method, or curriculum; they only suffered a new humiliation by being conned. And—*verb. sat. sap.*—older lads tend to be heavier and to carry more powerful armament. Did the Secretary of Labor think it through?

In some places, e.g. Milwaukee, the compulsory age

is at present 18, on the following arrangement: if, after 16, a youngster has a job, he goes to Continuation School (Milwaukee Vocational) one day a week; if he has no job, he attends full time, till 18. How does this work out? An administrator of the school tells me, "We don't teach them anything, neither academic subjects nor a trade. They're ineducable, and there aren't any jobs for them to train for anyway. But we do try to improve their attitude. Of course, we usually only have them for about 7 months."

"Why? What happens to them?"

"Oh, they join the Army or end up in Wales"—Wales is the reform school.

Naturally I become indignant and say, "What would become of *your* attitude if I caged you in a schoolroom and didn't even attempt to teach you anything? Wouldn't it be better to go to an honest jail?" But these angry questions do not seem to flurry him at all. Obviously I am not in touch with the concrete realities of his situation.

ii

In his address, Secretary Wirtz makes the usual correlation between employment and years of schooling: "The unemployment rate for individuals today with less than 5 years of school is 10.4 percent. For those with 9 to 11 years of school, it is 7.8 percent; for those with 13 to 15 years of school, 4 percent; but for those with 6 or more years of school, the unemployment rate drops to 1.4 percent."

But these figures are unimpressive. As he himself implies in another context, the *prima facie* explanation of the correlation is the parents' income: By connections, manners and aspirations, middle-class children get middle-class jobs; schooling is an incidental part of it.

Lower-class children used to get lower-class jobs, but just these jobs have petered out; in the present *structure* of the economy, the money and jobs do not filter down. Similarly, the docility, neatness of appearance, etc. that are useful for getting petty jobs, are not created by years of schooling but they are accurately measured by them. In my opinion, the same line of criticism strongly applies to the spectacular correlations between life-time income and years of schooling. Looking for his first job, a middle-class youth decides he wants $80 to start, and he can afford to shop around till he gets it; a poor boy must take anything and starts at $35. For obvious reasons, this initial difference will usually predetermine the whole career. Conversely, a sharp poor boy, seeing that this is the score, might choose not to bestir himself and prefer to look for a racket.

Again, Negro college graduates average in a lifetime the same salary as white high school graduates. It seems to be *not* the years of schooling but the whole context that makes the difference. Consider. If after seven or eight years, the salary increase of Negro or Puerto Rican high school graduates over those who have dropped out is perhaps $5 a week, is this worth the painful effort of years of schooling that is intrinsically worthless and spirit-breaking?

In these circumstances, it is wiser to think exactly the opposite way. It would probably help to improve the educational aspiration and educability of poor youngsters to give the money to poor families *directly,* rather than to channel it through school systems or other social agencies that drain off most of it for the same middle class. If we pension the poor as consumers in a consumption-oriented society, they will also send their children to school, a form of consumption. I take it that this is what Galbraith and Theobald are essentially saying. And the proposals of Myrdal and Keyserling are meant to accomplish the same purpose: public works to provide *unskilled* jobs.

iii

It is claimed that society needs more people who are technically trained. But informed labor people tell me that, for a job requiring skill but no great genius, a worker can be found at once, or quickly trained, to fill it. For instance, the average job in General Motors' most automated plant requires three weeks of training for those who have no education whatever. It used to require six weeks; for such jobs, automation has diminished rather than increased the need for training. In the Army and Navy, fairly complicated skills, e.g. radar operation and repair, are taught in a year *on the job,* often to practical illiterates.

Naturally, if diplomas are pre-requisite to hiring a youngster, the correlation of schooling and employment is self-proving. Because of this fad, there is a fantastic amount of mis-hiring, hiring young people far too school-trained for the routine jobs they get. I was struck by a recent report in the *Wall Street Journal* of firms philanthropically deciding to hire *only* drop-outs for certain categories of jobs, since the diploma made no difference in performance.

Twist it and turn it how you will, there is no logic to the proposal to extend compulsory schooling *except* as a device to keep the unemployed off the streets by putting them into concentration camps called schools. The Continuation branch of Milwaukee Vocational is, then, typical of what we can expect. (By the way, Milwaukee Vocational is otherwise a justly famous school, a fine product of Populism and right-wing Socialism.)

As an academic, I am appalled by this motivation for schooling. As a citizen and human being, I am appalled by this waste of youthful vitality. It is time that we stopped using the word "education" honorifically. We must ask, education how? where? for what? and under whose administration? Certainly every youth should get the best possible education, but, in my opinion, the present kind of compulsory schooling under the present administrators, far from being extended, should be sharply curtailed.

iv

As I have been saying, by and large primary schooling is, and should be, mainly baby-sitting. It has the great mission of democratic socialization—it certainly must not be segregated by race and income; apart from this, it should be happy, interesting, not damaging. The noise about stepping-up the primary curriculum is quite uncalled for; I have seen no convincing evidence—not by progressive educators either—that early schooling makes much academic difference in the long run. But in the secondary schools, after puberty, the tone of the baby-sitting must necessarily turn to regimentation and policing, and it is at peril that we require schooling; it fits some, it hurts others. A recent study by Edgar Friedenberg concludes that spirit-breaking is the *principal* function of typical lower-middle-class schools.

I wonder whether the Secretary of Labor thought through the constitutionality, not to speak of the morals, of his compulsory proposal. The legal justifications for compulsory schooling have been to protect children from exploitation by parents and employers, and to ensure the basic literacy and civics necessary for a democratic electorate. It is quite a different matter to deprive adolescents of their freedom in order to alleviate the difficulties of a faulty economic and political system. Is this constitutional?

We are back, in another context, to Dr. Conant's intolerable distinction between "individual development" and "national needs"; Dr. Conant was talking about the post-Sputnik putative need for scientists, Secretary Wirtz was talking about unemployment. So let us go over the ground again and look at the picture squarely. At present, in most states, for 10 to 13 years every young person is obliged to sit the better part of his day in a room almost always too crowded, facing front, doing lessons predetermined by a distant administration at the state capital and that have no relation to his own intellectual, social, or animal interests, and not much relation even to his economic interests. The overcrowding precludes individuality or spontaneity, reduces the young to ciphers, and the teacher to a martinet. If a youth tries to follow his own bent, he is interrupted and even jailed. If he does not perform, he is humiliated and threatened, but he is *not allowed to fail and get out.* Middle-class youth go through this for at least four more years—at the college level, the overcrowding has become an academic scandal—but they are steeled to it and supported by their middle-class anxiety and middle-class perquisites, including money to spend. Secretary Wirtz now wants poor youth, not thus steeled and supported, to get two more years of it. What will this 17-year-old do for spending money?

In his speech the Secretary referred to the admirable extension of free education from 1850 to, say, 1930. But this is again entirely misleading with regard to our present situation. To repeat, that opening of opportunity took place in an open economy, with an expanding market for skills and cultural learning. Young people took advantage of it *of their own volition;* therefore there were no blackboard jungles and endemic problems of discipline. Teachers taught those who wanted to learn; therefore there was no especial emphasis on grading. What is the present situation? The frantic competitive testing and grading means that the market for skills and learning is *not* open, it is tight. There are relatively few employers for those who score high; and almost none of the high-scorers become independent enterprisers. This means, in effect, that a few great corporations are getting the benefit of an enormous weeding-out and selective process—all children are fed into the mill and everybody pays for it.

If our present high schools, junior colleges, and colleges reflected the desire, freedom, and future of opportunity of the young, there would be no grading, no testing except as a teaching method, and no blackboard jungles. In fact, we are getting lockstep scheduling and grading to the point of torture. The senior year of high school is sacrificed to batteries of national tests, and policemen are going to stand in the corridors. Even an élite school such as Bronx Science—singled out by Dr. Conant as the best school in the country—is run as if for delinquents, with corridor passes and a ban on leaving the building. The conclusion is inevitable(The scholastically bright are not following their aspirations but are being pressured and bribed; the majority—those who are bright but not scholastic, and those who are not especially bright but have other kinds of vitality—are being subdued)

v

This is the schooling that Secretary Wirtz says we "ought to make the biggest industry in the country." I thought it already was! As one observes the sprawling expansion of the universities and colleges, eating up their neighborhoods, dislocating the poor, dictating to the lower schools, battening on Federal billions for research and development, and billions for buildings, and billions through the National Defense Education Act, and billions from foundations and endowments—one suddenly realizes that here again is the Dead Hand of the medieval church, that inherits and inherits and never dies. The University, which should be dissident and poor, has become the Establishment. The streets are full of its monks.

What a bad scene! Its spirit pervades all of society. Let me quote from a man in Secretary Wirtz's own department, in charge of retraining: "We retrain him, but before the course is finished, that job too has vanished. So we begin again. But after the fourth or fifth retraining, he has a job that doesn't vanish: he becomes a Teacher of Retraining." We must remember that, whatever the motive, *pouring money into the school-and-college system and into the academic social-work way of coping with problems, is strictly class legislation that confirms the inequitable structure of the economy.* I have mentioned how the professor-ridden Peace Corps needs $15,000 to get a single youngster in the field for a year, whereas the dedicated Quakers achieve almost the same end for $3,500. Again, when $13 millions are allotted for a local Mobilization for Youth program, it is soon found that nearly $12 millions have gone for sociologists doing "research," diplomated social workers, the N.Y. school system, and administrators, but only one million to field workers and the youths themselves.

vi

In my opinion, the public buys this unexamined "education" because of the following contradiction: The Americans are guilty because these youth *are* useless in the present set-up, so they spend money on them (though they get oddly stingy at crucial moments); on the other hand, they insist that the youth work hard at something "useful"—namely useless training. One can't just let them play ball; they must compete and suffer.

I agree that we ought to spend more public money on education. And where jobs exist and there is need for technical training, the corporations ought to spend more money on apprenticeships. We are an affluent society and can afford it. And the conditions of modern life are far too complicated for independent young spirits to get going on their own. They need some preparation, though probably not as much as is supposed; but more important, they need various institutional frameworks in which they can try out and learn the ropes.

Nevertheless, I would not give a penny more to the present school administrators. The situation is this: to make the present school set-up even *tolerable,* not positively damaging—e.g. to cut the elementary class size to 20 or to provide colleges enough to diminish the frantic competition for places—will require at least *doubling* the present school budgets. I submit that this kind of money should be spent in other ways.

vii

What, then, ought the education of these youth to be? We are back to our fundamental question: what are the alternatives?

Fundamentally, there is no right education except growing up into a worthwhile world. Indeed, our excessive concern with problems of education at present simply means that the grown-ups do not have such a world. The poor youth of America will *not* become equal by rising through the middle class, going to middle-class schools. By plain social justice, the Negroes and other minorities have the right to, and must get, equal opportunity for schooling with the rest, but the exaggerated expectation from the schooling is a chimera—and, I fear, will be shockingly disappointing. But also the middle-class youth will not escape their increasing exploitation and *anomie* in such schools. (A decent education aims at, prepares for, a more worthwhile future, with a different community spirit, different occupations, and more real utility than attaining status and salary.)

We are suffering from a bad style, perhaps a wrong religion. Although it is pretty certain, as I have said, that the automated future will see less employment in the manufacture of hardware and more employment in service occupations, as well as more leisure, yet astoundingly the mass-production and cash-accounting attitude toward the hardware is carried over unchanged. into the thinking about the services and leisure! The lockstep regimentation and the petty-bourgeois credits and competitive grading in the schooling are typical of all the rest. (For a charming, and grim, study of the spread of "business methods" to schooling, from 1900 to 1930, let me refer the reader to Callahan's *The Cult of Efficiency in American Education.*)

My bias is that we should maximize automation as quickly as possible, *where it is relevant*—taking care to cushion job dislocation and to provide adequate social insurance. But the spirit and method of automation, logistics, chain of command, and clerical work are *entirely irrelevant* to humane services, community service, communications, community culture, high culture, citizenly initiative, education, and recreation. To give a rather special but not trivial example of what I mean, TV sets should be maximum-mass-produced with maximum automation, in a good standard model, as cheaply as possible; but TV programming should, except for a few national services, be as much decentralized, tailor-made, and reliant on popular and free-artist initiative as possible.

The dangers of the highly technological and automated future are obvious: We might become a brainwashed society of idle and frivolous consumers. We might continue in a rat race of highly competitive, unnecessary busy-work with a meaninglessly expanding Gross National Product. In either case, there might still be an out-cast group that must be suppressed. To countervail these dangers and make active, competent, and initiating citizens who can produce a community culture and a noble recreation, we need a very different education than the schooling that we have been getting.

Large parts of it must be directly useful, rather than useless and merely aiming at status. Here we think of the spending in the public sector, advocated by Myrdal, Keyserling, Galbraith, and many others. E.g. the money spent on town improvement, community service, or rural rehabilitation can also provide educational occasions. (When these economists invariably list schooling as high—and often first—in the list of public expenditures, they fail to realize that such expense is probably wasted and perhaps even further dislocates the economy. I would say the same about Galbraith's pitch for new highways.)

On the whole, the education must be voluntary rather than compulsory, for no growth to freedom occurs except by intrinsic motivation. Therefore the educational opportunities must be various and variously administered. We must diminish rather than expand the present monolithic school system. I would suggest that, on the model of the GI-Bill, we experiment, giving the school money directly to the high-school age adolescents, for any plausible self-chosen educational proposals, such as purposeful travel or individual enterprise. This would also, of course, lead to the proliferation of experimental schools.

Unlike the present inflexible lockstep, our educational policy must allow for periodic quitting and easy return to the scholastic ladder, so that the young have time to find themselves and to study when they are themselves ready. This is Eric Erickson's valuable notion of the need for *moratoria* in the life-career; and the anthropological insistence of Stanley Diamond and others, that our society neglects the crises of growing up. (Education must foster independent thought and expression, rather than conformity.) For example, to countervail the mass communications, we have an imperative social need, indeed a constitutional need to protect liberty, for many thousands of independent media: local newspapers, independent broadcasters, little magazines, little theaters; and these, under professional guidance, could provide remarkable occasions for the employment and education of adolescents of brains and talent. (I have elsewhere proposed a graduated tax on the audience-size of mass-media, to provide a Fund to underwrite such new independent ventures for a period, so that they can try to make their way.)

Finally, contemporary education must inevitably be heavily weighted toward the sciences. But this does not necessarily call for school-training of a relatively few technicians, or rare creative scientists (if such can indeed be trained in schools). Our aim must be to make a great number of citizens at home in a technological environment, not alienated from the machines we use, not ignorant as consumers, who can somewhat judge governmental scientific policy, who can enjoy the humanistic beauty of the sciences, and, above all, who can understand the morality of a scientific way of life. I try to spell out the meaning of this below. (See Chapter 7.)

When Secretary Wirtz means by education something like this, and not compulsory junior college for delinquents, we can think of extending education as a device for diminishing youth unemployment. Because it will then be more useful employment than most of the available, or non-available, jobs. It will be relevant to a good future rather than a morally-bankrupt past.

Chapter 5

THE UNIVERSE
OF DISCOURSE
IN WHICH
THEY GROW UP

i

Let us now consider the interaction of school and the general culture as a climate of communication and ask:

What happens to the language and thought of young Americans as they grow up toward and through adolescence?

In the institutional speech, a child hears only one world-view. In the nature of the case, every mass-medium caters to a big common-denominator of opinion and taste, but even more influential is that the mass-media interlock. "News," for instance, is what is selected as newsworthy by two or three news-services; three almost identical broadcasting networks abstract from the same; and the same is again abridged for the *Junior*

Scholastic. Even for this news, only 60 towns in America now have competing newspapers (in 1900 there were 600). Similarly, the "standard of living," the way to live respectably and decently, is what is shown in the ads in a few mass-circulation magazines and identically in the TV commercials. Movie-sets of respectable life come from the same kind of engineers. Similarly, "political thought" is the platforms of two major parties that agree on all crucial issues, like the Cold War and the Expanding Economy, and that get practically all of the coverage by the same newspapers and broadcasters.

Much of this public speech is quite meaningless. The ads compete with high rhetoric but the commodities are nearly the same, and a child can see that our lives are not *quite* so vastly occupied by soap, cigarettes, and beer. Politicians are very polemical, but they avoid any concrete issues that might differentiate the candidates and lose votes. The real meaning of the speeches, the goal of profits and power, is never stated. By age 11 or 12, bright children, perhaps readers of *Mad* magazine, recognize that most of the speech is mere words.

The interlocking of the schools into the system is more serious, for here the children have to work at it and cooperate. The story is the same. The galloping increase of national tests guarantee that the class-work will become nothing but preparation for these same tests. Corporation talent-scouts hover in the high schools, and even the primary schools are flooded with corporation brochures. Excellent scientists in Washington who chart courses in science and mathematics understand that there must be leeway for individuality and guesswork; but in the hands of incompetent teachers, the national standard naturally becomes an inflexible ruler. And TV and machine-teaching are formal state-

ments that *everybody apperceives in the same way, with
no need for dialogue.*

Apart from family, children have little speech with
any adults except schoolteachers. But the crowding and
scheduling in school allow little chance or time for personal contact. Also, increasingly in grade schools as well
as in colleges, the teachers have abdicated their personal
role to specialist counsellors and administrators, so that
confiding and guidance tend to occur only in extreme
situations. One must be "deviant" to be attended to as
a human being.

This public speech cannot easily be tested against
direct observation or experience. Urban and suburban
children do not see crafts and industries. Playthings are
prefabricated toys; there is little practical carpentry,
plumbing, or mechanics; but there are do-it-yourself
kits. The contrast of city and country vanishes in endless conurbation. Few children know animals. Even
basic foods are packaged and distributed, and increasingly precooked, in the official style.

And a child hears less of any rival style or thought.
The rival world-view of (even hypocritical) religion is
no longer influential. Children do not know the Bible.
Eccentric classical children's literature is discouraged by
librarians because it does not fit educators' word-lists
and is probably unhygienic. The approved books are
concocted according to the official world-view. Other
more exciting reading, like comic books, does not contrast to life but withdraws from it, is without reality or
feeling. The movies are the same more insidiously, because they are apparently adult and real. Finally, the
ideal models of careers with their characters and philosophies—scientist, explorer, nurse, writer—have been
normalized to TV stereotypes: they are all the same
Organization Man, though they wear various costumes.

ii

[Nevertheless, this one system of meaning, although homogeneous and bland, is by no means sparse or quiet. On the contrary, the quantity of public speech, plays, information, cartoons is swamping. The tone is jumpy and distracting. In the schools, exposure occurs with intense pressure of tests for retention and punishment for failure to retain.

No one can critically appreciate so many images and ideas; and there is very little solitude or moratorium to figure them out. A child is confused. And he is also anxious, because if the information is not correctly parroted, he will fall off the school ladder and be a drop-out; or he will not be hep among his little friends.

At a childish level, all this adds up to brainwashing. The components are (a) a uniform world-view, (b) the absence of any viable alternative, (c) confusion about the relevance of one's own experience and feelings, and (d) a chronic anxiety, so that one clings to the one world-view as the only security. This *is* brainwashing.

Of course, in all societies and periods of history small children are subject to brainwashing, for they are weak, ignorant, economically dependent, and subject to bullying. In some ways in our society the brainwashing of children is not so pernicious as it has been at other times, for there is less corporal punishment, less extreme poverty, less fear of death, and less brutal toilet-training and sexual disciplining. On the other hand, the ideological exposure is unusually swamping, systematic, and thorough. Profit societies, like garrison states, invade every detail of life. But worst of all is that parents are as baffled as the children; since the areas of choice and initiative are so severely limited, they too lose touch with personal and practical information.

Thus, despite our technology of surplus, our civil peace(?), and so much educational and cultural opportunity, it is hard for an American child to grow toward independence, to find his identity, to retain his curiosity and initiative, and to acquire a scientific attitude, scholarly habits, productive enterprise, poetic speech.

...
iii

Unfortunately, the pervasive philosophy to which children are habituated as they grow up is the orthodoxy of a social machine not interested in persons, except to man and aggrandize itself. Especially not young persons.

Then what happens when, with this background of impersonal and stereotyped language, the child becomes adolescent: awkward and self-conscious, sexually hungry and falling in love, searching for identity, metaphysical, shaken in religious faith or undergoing religious conversion, his Oedipus-complex reviving, making a bid for freedom from home, grandiosely ambitious, looking for a vocation, eager to be serviceable as a human being? At best, in organic communities, rational communication breaks down and the community has recourse to rites of passage.

The American world-view is worse than inadequate; it is irrelevant and uninterested, and adolescents are spiritually abandoned. They are insulated by not being taken seriously. The social machine does not require or desire its youth to find identity or vocation; it is interested only in aptitude. It does not want new initiative, but conformity. Our orthodoxy does not bear metaphysics. Religious troubles are likely to be treated as psychotic; they are certainly disruptive of urban order and scholastic scheduling. Many, maybe most, of the careers that are open are not services to humanity; that is not why businesses

are run, nor why bombs are stockpiled. Idealism is aston-
ishingly without prestige.

The adolescent sexual situation is peculiarly ambiguous. We are in a transitional phase of the sexual revolution and there is a breakdown of repression (keeping
out of mind) and also less inhibition of sexual behavior.
Yet neither in the economy, the housing, nor the family
pattern is there any provision for the changed mores.
Quite the contrary, the years of tutelage even tend to
lengthen, especially for middle-class youth in colleges
whose administrations regard themselves as *in loco
parentis*. The official mental-hygienic ideology bears
little relation to the stormy images and imperative demands of adolescent love. In the elementary and junior
high schools, sexual facts do not officially exist. But an
adolescent is supposed to be sexual or there is alarm.
' Embarrassment—the inability to express or reveal
one's needs and feelings to the others—is universal
among adolescents. But in our society it is especially
problematic.' The embarrassment contains or will contain hostility to those who will not pay attention or will
put one down; and also despair at the futility of trying
to make oneself clear. For there is not even a common
language relevant to one's burning private facts—how
pathetic it is to hear adolescents using the language of
TV marriage-counsellors, or of movies! Inevitably,
silent hostility is retroflected as self-denigration. ' An
adolescent ceases to believe in the rightness of his own
wants, and soon he even doubts their existence. His rebellious claims seem even to himself to be groundless,
immature, ridiculous. '

Broadly speaking, the difficulties of adolescent communication, both in speaking and listening, are kinds of
embarrassment.' Let us here discuss adolescent speech-
lessness, in-group language and sub-culture, and how

adolescents finally give up their own meaning and swallow the official adult philosophy hook, line, and sinker.

iv

Embarrassment may be grounded in too strong desire and confusion, or in hostility and fear.

Paling and blushing embarrassment in expressing lust or aspiration is largely due to confusion caused by powerful feelings that have been untried, or vague new ideas that seem presumptuous. It is akin to ingenuous shame, which is exhibition suddenly inhibited because it is (or might be) unacceptable. With courage and encouragement, such speechless embarrassment can falter into sweet or ringing poetic speech, by which the youth explains himself, also to himself. More common with use, however, is for the youth to inhibit his stammering and to brazen out the situation with a line imitated from the mass-media or salesmanship. For example, the strategy is to "snow" the girl rather than talk to her. Thereby he proves that he is grownup, has an erection, etc., but he sacrifices feeling, originality, the possibility of growth, and the possibility of love.

The speechless embarrassment of hostility is fear of retaliation if one reveals oneself. Suppose a youth is reprimanded, advised, or perhaps merely accosted by an authoritative adult, e.g. a guidance counsellor; he will maintain a sullen silence and not give the adult the time of day. His presumption is that the adult is setting a trap, could not understand, does not care anyway. The youth cannot adopt a breezy line, as with a peer, for the adult has more words. He will be taken as fresh, hostile, or in bad taste. Therefore it is best to say nothing, expressing (perhaps unconsciously) a blazing contempt. In this situation, the youth's interpretation is not too erroneous, except that the authority is usually not malevolent but busy and perhaps insensitive.

Suppose, however, the adult is a good teacher who does care for the young persons and would like to reach them in meaningful terms, not the orthodoxy. Then, as Frank Pinner has pointed out, it likely that the teacher's dissenting ideas will be met by a wall of silence that makes communication impossible. The young are so unsure, and their distrust is such, that in the crisis of possible contact they prefer to cling to safe conformity, even though among themselves they may bitterly attack these same conformist ideas.

Even worse, there is an hermetic silence about anything deeply felt or threatening; such things are unspeakable even to one's peers, no less to adults! One may boast to a friend about a sexual conquest or fret about poor grades, but one may not reveal that one is in love or has a lofty aspiration. Or to give a tragic example: Puerto Rican boys will chatter endless small talk and one-up one another, but nobody will mention that one of their number has just been sent to jail or that one has just died of an overdose of heroin. If the forbidden subject is mentioned, they do not hear it. They cannot psychologically afford to relate themselves, their verbal personalities, to the terrible realities of life. (Incidentally, I have heard from teachers in the New York schools that there is a similar cleavage in many young Puerto Rican's knowledge of the English language. They seem to talk English fluently as long as the subject is superficial and "grown-up"; but they are blank in many elementary words and phrases, and are quite unable to say, in English, anything that they really want or need.)

v

To diminish embarrassment, since communication with the adults is cut off, there is developed an increasingly exaggerated adolescent "sub-culture," with its jargon, models, authors, and ideology. Let us first distinguish between a "sub-culture" and a "sub-society."

An intense youth sub-society is common in most cultures. In our culture, the interest in sexual exploration, dancing, simple exciting music, athletics, cars and races, clubs and jackets, one-upping conversation, seems to be natural to youth—just as many adult interests are naturally irrelevant and boring to them. Also, the sharing of secrets, often mysterious even to themselves, is everywhere a powerful bond of union among adolescents; and certainly their business is nobody else's business. The Youth Houses of some primitive communities institutionalize all this rather better than our own boarding-schools and colleges, which are too ridden with *in loco parentis* regulations.

The development of such a sub-society into a full-blown sub-culture, however, is not normal, but reactive. It signifies that the adult culture is hostile to adolescent interests, or is not to be trusted; that parents are not people and do not regard their children as people; that the young are excluded from adult activities that might be interesting and, on the other hand, that most adult activities are *not* worth growing up into as one becomes ready for them. Rather, on the contrary, the adults are about to exploit the young, to pressure them into intrinsically boring careers, regardless of proper time or individual choice.

Normally there is not a "youth culture" and an "adult culture," but youth is the period of growing up in the one culture. With us, however, youth feels itself to be almost out-caste, or at least manipulated. It therefore has secrets, jargon, and a lore of sabotage and defense *against* the adult culture.

But then, since the intellectual life of callow boys and girls in isolation from the grown-up economy and culture is thin gruel, youth interests are vastly puffed up into fads, disk-jockeys, politically organized gangs and wars, coterie literature, drugs and liquor, all frantically energized by youthful animal spirits—and cleverly managed by adult promoters. The teen-age market is more than $10 billions a year, in jackets, portable radios, sporting goods, hair-dos, bikes, and additional family cars. Needless to say, this secondary development is simply a drag on the youthful spirit. It is largely frivolous and arbitrary, yet it is desperately conservative and exerts a tremendous pressure of blackmail against nonconformers or those ignorant of the latest, who will be unpopular. It makes it hard to talk sense to them, or for them to talk sense, whether adolescent or adult. And of course there is no chance for intelligent dissent from the official philosophy and standard of life. Naturally, too, especially in the middle class, the regressed adults play at and sponsor every teen-age idiocy.

Inevitably, the high school—with its teen-age majority and adult regime—becomes a prime area for sabotage and other fun and games. I have heard James Coleman, who has most studied these phenomena, express the opinion that the average adolescent is really *in* school, academically, for about ten minutes a day! Not a very efficient enterprise.

A certain number of the young gang up and commit defiant delinquencies. These are partly the revolt of nature—for there is much in our society that is insulting and intolerably frustrating. They are partly reactive against *whatever* happens to constitute "correct" behavior. And they are partly a pathetic bid for attention, as it is said, "We're so bad they give us a Youth Worker."

A pathetic characteristic of recent middle-class adolescent sub-culture is taking on the language and culture of marginal groups, Negroes and Latin Americans, addicts, Beat drop-outs from the colleges and the Organized System. This is appropriate, for these others too are abused and disregarded; they are in the same case as the adolescents. But such a culture is hardly articulate. Also there is something exploiting about imitating authentic out-caste people, who live as they do not by choice but by necessity.

Nevertheless, for many of the woefully embarrassed, this semi-articulate speech—saying "man" and "cat" and "like, man"—makes conversation possible. The adolescent culture is something to talk about and this is a style to talk in. The words of one syllable of jive, the thoughts of one syllable of Beat, the content of kicks, movies, and high school dances, are not a wide discourse, but they foster being together, and everybody can democratically participate.

Unfortunately, the small talk drives out real talk. It is incredibly snobbish and exclusive of sincerity and originality. Embattled against the adult world that must inexorably triumph, adolescent society jealously protects itself against meaning.

vi

To adolescents of sixteen, the adult world must seem like a prison door slamming shut. Some must get jobs which are sure not to fit them and in which they will exercise no initiative whatever. Others must engage in the factitious competition for college-entrance. Either process is formidable with forms and tests. The kids are ignorant of the ropes and ignorant of what they want. Disregarded by the adults, they have in turn excluded adult guidance or ideas looking toward the future. But their adolescent bravado is now seen to be unrealistic and even ridiculous. Having learned nothing, nor fought any battles, they are without morale.

Their weakness can be observed vividly on college campuses. Students gripe about the moral rules by which they are still absurdly harassed at 18 and 19 years of age. It's ironical; if they had quit school and were assembly-line workers, they would be considered responsible enough to come and go, have sex, and drink.— Yet it comes to nothing but griping; they do not feel justified to enforce their demands, for they have never had this issue, or any issue, out with their parents. Similarly, they are unhappy about the overcrowded classes, the credits, the grading; they know they are disappointed in the education they are getting; yet they are so confused about what they do want that they are speechless.

And just in the colleges, which are supposed to be communities of scholars, face-to-face communication is diminished. The adolescent sub-culture that persists is irrelevant to the business going on, except to sabotage it, but the adolescent community is *not* replaced by close acquaintance with learned adults. The teachers hold the students off and, as I argued in *The Community of Scholars,* it is a chief function of orderly administration to keep the students out of contact with the teachers and the teachers out of contact with one another. Naturally, as long as the students are isolated with one another, they can be treated as immature, which they are.

The dialogue with the subject-matter, with Nature and History, is as skimpy as with the teacher. Colleges are not interested in such things any more—it has little

Ph.D. value. The student is told the current doctrine and is trained to give it back accurately. And still proving his masculinity and doing a snow-job, the student thinks that the purpose of a course is to "master the subject." Necessarily, in the conflict with the adult world, the young suffer a crushing defeat. There are various ways of surviving it. Some give up on themselves and conform completely—a few indeed become more royalist than the king (but these are often psychopathic, middle-class delinquents). Others make rationalizations: they will return to the fray later when they are "better prepared." Or, "The most important thing is to get married and raise a normal family," they will hold onto feeling and meaning for their family life, or perhaps for their "personal" behavior. A surprising number tell you that the goal of life is $50,000 a year.

The psychology of the introjection is evident: defeated, they identify with what has conquered them, in order to fill the gap with some meaning or other. Once they have made the new identification, they feel strong in it, they defend it by every rationalization.

An alternative philosophy that has recommended itself to some older adolescents is hipsterism. A hipster cushions the crushing defeat by society by *deliberately* assuming convenient roles in the dominant system, including its underworld, to manipulate it for his own power or at least safety. The bother with this idea—it is the argument of Thrasymachus in Plato's *Republic*—is that the hipster cannot afford to lose himself, or even to become un-selfconscious. He must be ahead of every game. Then he cannot grow by loving or believing anything worthwhile, and he exhausts himself in business with what he holds in contempt, deepening his own cynicism and self-contempt. But hipsterism does provide a satisfaction of mastery and victory which ward off his panic of powerlessness, passivity, and emasculation. It is a philosophy for chronic emergency, during which communication consists inevitably of camouflage and secrecy, "playing it cool," or of gambits of attack to get the upper hand.

vii

The conditions that I have been describing, and the youthful responses to them, sadly limit human communication and even the concept of it. "Communication" comes to be interpreted as the transfer of a processed meaning from one head to another which will privately put it in a niche in its own system of meanings. This system is presumably shared with the others—one can never know. And in this presumptive consensus, the exchanged information adds a detail or a specification, but it does not disturb personality or alter characteristic behavior, for the self has not been touched. At most, the information serves as a signal for action from the usual repertory.

Among Americans, this sentiment of consensus, "understanding," is so important that much speech and reading does not even give new information, but is a ritual touching of familiar bases. (This is evident in much newspaper reading, in after-dinner speeches, and so forth.) But the case is not much different with active speech that is supposed to affect choice, e.g. in politics, for no disturbing issues are broached, nor anything that one would have to think new thoughts about. The underlying consensus is assumed—is signalled by the usual words—and no important alternative is offered.

The consensus is *presumably* shared, but any dialectic to test this assumption is in bad form, just as it is impolite to question a loose generalization made in small talk, and say "Prove it." In ideal cybernetic theory, the exchange of information is supposed to alter the organisms conversing, since they must make internal readjustments to it; but my observation is that no such alteration occurs. The chief meaning of conversation is its own smooth going on.

By contrast, the active speech of salesmanship is more lively, because it is meant importantly to change behavior, toward buying something; it is not meant merely to soothe. Thus, strikingly, TV commercials are the only part of TV that makes novel use of the medium itself, employing montage and inventive music, playing with the words, images and ideas. The pitch of a salesman is likely to be *ad hominem,* in bad form, both flattering and and threatening. (Needless to say, there is no dialogue; the hearer is passive or dumbly resistant.) But of course, in salesmanship, apart from the one pre-thought transaction, the consensus is powerfully protected; the TV ad and the program that it sponsors avoid anything that might surprise, provoke, or offend any single person in an audience of millions.

Consider what is lost by this narrow concept of communication as the exchange of processed information with which each communicant copes internally. (a) The function of speech as the shaping expression of preverbal needs and experiences, by which a speaker first discovers *what* he is thinking. Such speech cannot be entirely pre-thought and controlled; it is spontaneous. (b) The function of speech as personally initiating something by launching into an environment that is *unlike* oneself. Initiating, one presumes there is no consensus; otherwise why bother speaking? (c) Most important of all, the function of speech as dialogue between persons *committed to the conversation*—or between a person and a subject-matter in which he is absorbed. This results in change of the persons because of the very act of speaking; they are not fixed roles playing a game with rules.

Speaking is a way of making one's identity, of losing oneself with others in order to grow. It depends not on prior consensus with the others, but on trust of them. But, in my opinion, the speech defined in most contemporary communication theory is very like the speech of the defeated adolescents I have been describing. It is not pragmatic, communal, poetic, or heuristic. Its function is largely to report in a processed *lingua franca*.

Speech cannot be personal and poetic when there is embarrassment of self-revelation, including revelation to oneself, nor when there is animal diffidence and communal suspicion, shame of exhibition and eccentricity, clinging to social norms. Speech cannot be initiating when the chief social institutions are bureaucratized and pre-determine all procedures and decisions, so that in fact individuals have no power anyway that is useful to express. Speech cannot be exploratory and heuristic when pervasive chronic anxiety keeps people from risking losing themselves in temporary confusion and from relying for help precisely *on* communicating, even if the communication is Babel.

As it is, people have to "think" before they speak, rather than risking speaking and finding out what they mean by trying to make sense to others and themselves. In fact, they finally speak English as though they were in school.

Chapter 6

PROGRAMMED

i

Programmed teaching adapted for machine use goes a further step than conforming students to the consensus which is a principal effect of schooling interlocked with the mass media. In this pedagogic method it is *only* the programmer—the administrative decision-maker—who is to do any "thinking" at all; the students are systematically conditioned to follow the train of the *other's* thoughts. "Learning" means to give some final response that the programmer considers advantageous (to the students). There is no criterion of *knowing* it, of having learned it, of Gestalt-forming or simplification. That is, the student has no active self at all; his self, at least as student, is a construct of the programmer.

What does this imply? Let me analyze a very high-level argument for such teaching by Lauren Resnick, "Programmed Instruction of Complex Skills," in *The Harvard Educational Review* of Fall 1963.

In the conclusion of this perspicuous article, Dr. Resnick tells us:

"By explicit instruction I mean the deliberate modification of the behavior of other human beings. Programmed instruction is not interested in the teacher as stimulator of interest, role model, or evaluator of progress. It is interested in him as instructor, or controller of behavior. This means that programmed instruction is applicable only where we do in fact want to change behavior in a given direction. There are cases where for political or ethical reasons we do not want to. We do not, for example, want to train all students to be active partisans of a given political or religious viewpoint, or make everyone like the same kind of literature or music. In such cases . . . 'exposure' is the most we should attempt." (p. 467)

Let me put this dramatic statement in juxtaposition with an earlier statement in her essay:

"In the context of behavorial analysis, knowledge, skill, and ability can be dealt with only insofar as they can be described in terms of performance. This description is not a matter of listing 'correlates' of ability or knowledge, but of deciding what observable behaviors will be accepted as evidence of their existence. The behaviorist simply eschews the question of whether knowledge, for instance, exists apart from observable behaviors. While, in so doing, he may fail to answer to the philosopher's satisfaction the question, 'What is knowledge?', he very effectively provides himself with a set of usable goals for instruction." (p. 448)

I do not much want to discuss the pedagogic relevance of these ideas. The only evidence of "performance" that school people ever draw on for their experiments is scoring on academic tests, and it seems to be impossible to disabuse school people of the notion that test-passers have necessarily learned anything relevant to their further progress or careers; or of advantage to the body politic; or indeed anything whatever that will not vanish in a short time, when the *real* life-incentive, of passing the test, has passed away. But I want to ask if this kind of *formulation* of teaching does not involve serious legal difficulties, in terms of civil liberties, especially where schooling is compulsory, when the child *must* go to school and submit to having his behavior shaped.

It may seem odd that I keep referring to the constitutional question; but it is a way of asking what kind of democracy we envisage in our curriculum and methods of schooling. Besides, since the young have become so clearly both an exploited and an outcast class, we must begin to think of legal rights.

ii

Our Bill of Rights guarantees were grounded in a very different epistemological theory from operant-conditioning, the method that Dr. Resnick has learned from B. F. Skinner. Roughly, the Enlightenment conception was that intellect, like conscience, was something "inward," and the aim of teaching was to nurture its "growth" by "knowledge." Even more important, behavior was the "external" effect of an initiating or self-moving of the "soul"; therefore the student was or became "responsible." In my opinion, the inner-outer metaphor of this conception is quite useless; there is not much use in a psychological theory for entities that are not observable as behavior. But the Aristotelian emphasis on the self-moving organism is solid gold.

Now compulsory schooling, as I have pointed out,

was justified in this theory, e.g. by Jefferson, as necessary to bring children to the point of self-government, of exercising citizenly initiative, as well as the animal and social initiative that they had by "nature" and the moral initiative that they had by "conscience." Democracy required an educated electorate. To this was later added the justification that only by compulsory education could the poor get an equal democratic opportunity with the rich; poor parents were likely to put their children to work too early, and not give them a chance to develop to their full powers.

In turn, any course of the curriculum or detail of method was justified by showing that it nurtured the growth of the inward intellect, encouraged initiative, and fitted the young to take a free part in political society. On this view, school teaching was precisely not "training," though parents were allowed to train minor children and the masters of apprentices were allowed to train their bonded apprentices. School subjects either had to contain values ideal in themselves, as good, true, or beautiful, which were "liberal" by definition; or they strengthened the "logical faculty," which the young citizen would then apply to all kinds of matters (this was the traditional notion of "transfer"); or they gave him orientation in space and time—as I have mentioned, especially History was prized, because its horrible and noble examples inspired youth to preserve freedom.

Of course, the late nineteenth century compulsory education in the mechanical arts, to the degree that they were merely utilitarian, could not so easily be justified in these "inward" ways—it tended to seem like apprentice-training at the public expense. But in an expanding economy with high social mobility, and where there was considerable self-employment and much new enterprise, there was no occasion to cavil; a free soul would want such advantageous skills of its own volition. Few adolescents went to school anyway, and children never did have many rights, though plenty of privileges.

iii

Dr. Resnick's system explicitly excludes all notions of "inward" meaning. And she is also unhappy about the sneaking in of any factor of initiative. For example, in discussing Shaping—the approximation of the responses to the final response—she sharply disagrees with those experimenters who wait for the organism to make a small move in the right direction, to reinforce it. "Programmed instruction," she says, "cannot afford to proceed in this way." (But she never does make clear, at least to me, how she gets the beast to move *ab extra*, in order to have something to shape.)

Also, unlike the liberal or "faculty-developing" curriculum of the Enlightenment theory, no particular subject of learning is chosen because of its characteristic appeal to or stimulation of the powers, liberation, or needs of the learner. Operant-conditioning theory, she says, is essentially "contentless"; it is a pure technique that can teach anything to almost anybody. This might be Dr. Conant's "national needs"; it might be the "improved attitudes" of the Continuation branch of Milwaukee Vocational; it might be the vagaries of Big Brother.

In sum, on this view, compulsory schooling, so far as it is programmed, is identical with compulsory training to the goals of the controllers of behavior, and such goals are set by the "we want" of the first paragraph I have cited Then I am curious to hear from Dr. Resnick the constitutional justification for compulsory schooling in terms of the "we want" and "we do not want" of that paragraph. Who, we? and what limitation is there to "want" or happen to want? The title of her essay, let us remember, is "Instruction of Complex Skills"; she is not restricting behavior-control to rote and drill subjects, but extending it to the higher branches, to criticism, problem-solving, appreciation, except where "we do not want to."

Needless to say, curriculum, methods, and the school-system itself have *always* been determined by social goals and National Goals, parental ambitions, and the need to baby-sit and police the young. But it is one thing to believe—or pretend—that these educate the children, and quite another thing to *say* that they are behavior-controllers.

iv

Our author's indifference to this kind of consideration appears strongly in an otherwise excellent analysis of the "Discovery Method" as contrasted with step-by-step programmed instruction. One advantage claimed for the Discovery Method—for which, we saw, Dr. Zacharias and the National Science Foundation have manifested enthusiasm—is that the leap over the gap is itself exciting and reinforcing, providing stronger motivation. Dr. Resnick agrees that this might be true for bright students; but she wisely points out that culturally-deprived, poorly achieving youngsters get more satisfaction from steady success, without risk of new failure. A second advantage claimed is that the trial and error in the Discovery process fits the student for the kind of learning that he will have to do outside the classroom; but here Dr. Resnick doubts that the student learns from his errors unless he is trained in what to ask about them, that is, to notice them. (She is right. For example, a good piano teacher will have the student deliberately play the wrong note that he repeats inadvertently.) Finally, it is claimed, the quality of what is learned by Discovery—the synoptic, the law, the solution of the problem—is superior. This, says Dr. Resnick, is because programmed instruction has so far concentrated almost exclusively on teaching mere concepts and information, rather than complex wholes of learning.

What is astonishing in this thoughtful analysis, however, is that she entirely omits the *salient* virtue that most teachers, classical or progressive, have always hoped for in letting the student discover for himself, namely the development of his confidence that he *can,* that he is adequate to the nature of things, can proceed on his own initiative, and ultimately strike out on an unknown path, where there is no program, and assign his own tasks to himself. The classical maxim of teaching is: to bring the student to where he casts off the teacher. Dewey's model for curriculum and method was: any study so pursued that it ends up with the student wanting to find out something further.

Apparently Dr. Resnick cannot even conceive of this virtue, because it is contradictory to the essence of controlled behavior toward a predetermined goal. It is open. From her point of view, it is not instruction at all. In terms of social theory, it posits an open society of independent citizens—but she and Dr. Skinner think there is a special "we" who "want." Also, scientifically, it posits a more open intellectual future than the complex-skill which programming seems to envisage. Is it indeed the case that so much *is* known—so definitely—that we can tightly program methods and fundamental ideas? Much of the program is bound to be out-of-date before the class graduates.

v

This is a fundamental issue. Intellectually, humanly, and politically, our present universal high-schooling and vastly increasing college-going are a disaster. I will go over the *crude* facts still again! A youngster is compelled for twelve *continuous* years—if middle class, for sixteen years—to work on assigned lessons, during a lively period of life when one hopes he might invent enterprises of his own. Because of the school work, he cannot follow his nose in reading and browsing in the library, or concentrate on a hobby that fires him, or get a job, or carry on a responsible love-affair, or travel, or become involved in political action. The school system as a whole, with its increasingly set curriculum, stricter grading, incredible amounts of testing, is already a vast machine to shape acceptable responses. Programmed instruction closes the windows a little tighter and it rigidifies the present departmentalization and dogma. But worst of all, it tends to nullify the one lively virtue that any school does have, that it is a community of youth and of youth and adults.

Dr. Resnick can assert that there are areas where "we do not want" to control behavior—political, religious, esthetic, perhaps social. But the case is that for sixteen years it is precisely docility to training and boredom that is heavily rewarded with approval, legitimacy, and money; whereas spontaneous initiation is punished by interruption, by being considered irrelevant, by anxiety of failing in the "important" work, and even by humiliation and jail. Yet somehow, after this hectic course of conditioning, young men and women are supposed, on commencement, suddenly to exercise initiative in the most extreme matters: to find jobs for themselves in a competitive market, to make long career plans, to undertake original artistic and scientific projects, to marry and become parents, to vote for public officers. But their behavior has been shaped only too well. Inevitably most of them will go on with the pattern of assigned lessons, as Organization Men or on the assembly-line; they will vote Democratic-Republican and buy right brands.

I am rather miffed at the vulgarity of the implication that, in teaching the humanities, we should at most attempt "exposure"—as if appreciation were entirely a private matter, or a matter of unstructured "emotion." (There is no such thing, by the way, as unstructured emotion.) When Dr. Resnick speaks of the unshaped response to the kind of literature or music "they like," she condemns their esthetic life to being a frill, without meaning for character, valuation, recreation, or how one is in the world. Frankly, as a man of letters I would even prefer literature to be programmed, as in Russia.

That is, *even if behavioral analysis and programmed instruction were the adequate analysis of learning and method of teaching, it would still be questionable, for overriding political reasons, whether they are generally appropriate for the education of free citizens.*

vi

To be candid, I think operant-conditioning is vastly overrated. It teaches us the not newsy proposition that if an animal is deprived of its natural environment and society, sensorily deprived, made mildly anxious, and restricted to the narrowest possible spontaneous motion, it will emotionally identify with its oppressor and respond—with low-grade grace, energy, and intelligence —in the only way allowed to it. The poor beast must do something, just to live on a little. There is no doubt that a beagle can be trained to walk on its hind legs and balance a ball on the tip of its nose. But the dog will show much more intelligence, force, and speedy feedback when chasing a rabbit in the field. It is an odd thought that we can increase the efficiency of learning by nullifying *a priori* most of an animal's powers to learn and taking it out of its best field.

It has been a persistent error of behaviorist psychologies to overlook that there are overt criteria that are organically part of *meaningful* acts of an organism in its environment; we can observe grace, ease, force, style, sudden simplification—and some such characteristics are at least roughly measurable. It is not necessary, in describing insight, knowledge, the kind of assimilated learning that Aristotle called "second nature," to have recourse to mental entities. It is not difficult to *see* when a child *knows* how to ride a bicycle; and he never forgets it, which would not be the case if the learning were by conditioning with reinforcement, because that can easily be wiped away by a negative reinforcement. (Kurt Goldstein has gone over this ground demonstratively.)

On the other hand, it is extremely dubious that by controlled conditioning one *can* teach organically meaningful behavior. Rather, the attempt to control *prevents* learning. This is obvious to anyone who has ever tried to teach a child to ride a bicycle; the more you try, the more he falls. The best one can do is to provide him a bicycle, allay his anxiety, tell him to keep going, and *not* to try to balance. I am convinced that the same is true in teaching reading.

vii

As is common in many (sometimes excellent) modern scientific papers—whether in linguistics or studies of citizen participation or the theory of delinquency—Dr. Resnick asks for more money; and of course, for purposes of pure research, the higher investigations that she asks for should be pursued as long as her enthusiasm lasts and should be supported. Any definite hypothesis that is believed in by a brilliant worker is likely to yield useful by-products that can then be reinterpreted; nor is there any other guide for the advancement of science except the conviction and competence of the researchers.

But I am puzzled at what widespread social benefits she has in mind that warrant a *lot* of expense in brains and machinery. She seems to agree that bright children do not learn most efficiently by these extrinsic methods; and for the average the picture is as I have described it: average employment in a highly automated technology requires a few weeks' training on the job and no schooling at all, and for the kind of humane employment and humane leisure that we hopefully look toward, we require a kind of education and habit entirely different from programmed instruction.

But I am more impressed by what is perhaps Dr. Resnick's deepest concern, the possible *psychotherapeutic* use of more complex programming for the remedial instruction of kids who have developed severe blocks to learning and are far behind. For youngsters who have lost all confidence in themselves, there is a security in being able to take small steps entirely at their own pace and entirely by their own control of the machine. Also, though the chief use of schools is their functioning as a community, under present competitive and stratified conditions it is often less wounding for a kid who has fallen behind to be allowed to withdraw from the group and recover. And this time can usefully and curatively be spent in learning the standard "answers" that can put him in the game again.

There is a pathos in our technological advancement, well exemplified by programmed instruction. A large part of its consists in erroneously reducing the concept of animals and human beings in order to make them machine-operable. The social background in which this occurs, meanwhile, makes many people out-caste and in fact tends to reduce them as persons and make them irresponsible. The refined technique has little valid use for the dominant social group for which it has been devised, e.g. in teaching science; but it does prove to have a use for the reduced out-castes, in teaching remedial arithmetic.

Chapter 7

TEACHING SCIENCE

i

A century ago, Matthew Arnold and Thomas Huxley debated whether Science, rapidly growing in importance, should become preponderant over the humanities in the popular curriculum. Arnold opted for the humanities because they give us "criticism of life" and teach us "conduct," the main business of most men. He conceded that for the unusual persons who are scientifically gifted, the philosophy and practice of science itself provide a guide to life. But Huxley's view—in the line leading from the Encyclopedists and Comte to the naturalistic novelists and Veblen—was basically that there is a scientific way of life, a new and better ethic, possible for the majority.

We have seen that the progressive education of the early twentieth century shared this belief in the scientific ethic and added to it the great modern issue: how to be at home in the modern environment which has, willy nilly, become overwhelmingly industrial and technological. In this country, Dewey was a leader in the struggle to secure for science a big place in education.

Yet by 1916, Dewey spoke of his "painful" disappointment in the fruits of the scientific curriculum; it had *not* paid off in life-values, but had become scholastic and arid. And we know that in his last period, he estimated more and more highly the experience and structured emotion of art.

By the time we come to C. P. Snow in the fifties, the debate between the humanities and science, like most other serious topics, has become pretty vulgarized. As Snow speaks of them, the humanities are little better than frills and snobbery; but science, correspondingly, is mainly praised as if it were identical with technology and must be universally studied to improve the standard of living of the Africans (though he offers no evidence that, with modern methods of production, we need quite so many technicians to achieve this unexamined purpose). But the nadir of this kind of pitch for science has been, I suppose, the calamitous sentence in the late President Kennedy's message on Education of 1963: "Vast areas of the unknown are daily being explored for economic, military, medical, and other reasons." (The "other reasons" include those of Galileo and Darwin.) Neither the scientific conduct of life, nor any conduct, is thought of as a purpose of education, or thought of at all.

ii

The intervention of the National Science Foundation in improving the science and mathematics courses in the elementary and high schools is on a much higher plane; its avowed aims are reasonable and not base. (It began a few years before the panic about Sputnik, though all the public enthusiasm has been since.) "Literacy in science is becoming essential for all citizens who wish to comprehend the world they live and work in, and to participate in the increasing number of decisions, some of the gravest import, that require an understanding of science. Further, more and more students must be attracted to scientific and technical pursuits, and these students must be prepared to work with increasingly sophisticated ideas and techniques. . . . And there is another aspect . . . more emphasis should be given to disciplined, creative, intellectual activity as an end in itself . . . for each student to experience some of the excitement, beauty, and intellectual satisfaction that scientific pursuit affords." (From the Foreword to *Science Course Improvement Projects*.)

This is a well-rounded educational prospectus, including the citizenly, the vocational, and the humanistic. It is a far cry from "other reasons."

But now another danger has arisen, intrinsic in the composition of the NSF: the kind of people they consult, the kind of people they do not consult. Looking at some of the improved projects and methods reported and the TV films sponsored, one cannot avoid the impression that the curriculum-improvers are professors in graduate schools and cannot finally think of education in science otherwise than as the producing of Ph.D.'s. "Society," says the Foreword a little petulantly, "can no longer afford to wait a generation or more for new knowledge to make its way gradually into school and college programs." By Society we may understand M.I.T. etc.

Of course, the Foreword contains the sanitizing disclaimer: "Decisions on what to teach remain, in the healthy American tradition, the exclusive responsibility of individual schools and teachers. The National Science Foundation does *not* recommend any specific book, film, etc. It is hopeful, however, that the products of these projects will prove to merit serious consideration by every school and college." This is disingenuous. With the incredible amounts of national testing, and with actual courses tailored just for the tests, and with "making the prestige universities" as the grand goal of all middle-class parents, college-guidance counsellors, and superintendents of schools, the humble proposals of the NSF have pretty nearly the force of statutes. . . . The snag is that there aren't enough competent teachers of the new programs. Bright young graduates in science are more likely to stay in the universities or go to the corporations than to teach children and adolescents.

(The science-course-improvement studies by the National Science Foundation cost $50 million. When I raised my eyebrows at this sum, a representative of the NSF pointed out to me that this was only 35¢ a person in the United States. "Naw," said a chap from the United Automobile Workers, "it's fifty million dollars.")

What ought science teaching to be about for the great majority who are *not* going to be graduate students in science?

iii

On reflection, there seem to be more than half a dozen plausible reasons for teaching science as a major part of popular education. Let us spell them out and ask their relevance at present:

(1) The pre-training of technicians is not a good reason. The fact that such apprentices must be prepared to work with "increasingly sophisticated ideas and techniques" is rather a reason *not* to emphasize their preparation by general schooling, for obviously the great majority are not going to become such technicians, and the more intense the specialized instruction necessary for some, the less useful for the future of most. Indeed, with the maturing of automation, this objection will be even stronger: many of the middle technical skills will

surely vanish; semi-skilled "technicians" will require *less* pretraining, not more; whereas the high technical skills required will be so far beyond average aptitude that general schools are hardly the place to pre-train them. Like most apprenticeships, this kind can be taught more practically, more specifically, and more quickly by the ultimate employer, without wasting the time of the majority of youngsters on a kind of mathematics and science that they will promptly forget. And it is hard to see why the public should bear the expense for the pre-selection of lively algebrists for General Electric.

(2) On the other hand, the NSF intention of producing original creative scientists seems to me both pretentious and naïve. We simply do not know how to breed these, nor whether "schools" are the best place, nor even whether they thrive better by exposure to up-to-date teaching or reaction to out-dated teaching. With a good deal of fanfare, the Woods Hole Conference on science-teaching, on which the NSF relies heavily, arrived at the excellent insights that Dewey had prescribed for teaching any subject whatever: encouraging spontaneity, imagination, courage to guess; avoiding "correct" answers and rejecting all grading and competition; maintaining continuity with emotional and day-to-day experience and having each youngster follow his own path. But are the Woods Hole scientists serious about these insights? I have not heard either Dr. Bruner or the NSF lambasting the achievement tests and the National Merit examination; and what plan do they have to make genuine progressive education acceptable in the school systems where it is now *less* acceptable year by year?

Even more important, Dewey would never have claimed that these methods have anything to do with high creative invention, any more than finger-painting and teaching art on sound psychological principles will produce masters. Studying the "sources and conditions that stimulate creativity," the late Harold Rugg came to ideas like "preparatory period of baffled struggle," "interlude in which the scientist apparently gives up, pushes the problem 'out of mind' and leaves it for the non-conscious to work upon," "blinding and unexpected flash of insight." Does the NSF have a clear and distinct idea of such processes in the school-system? We have seen that Dr. Zacharias' cautious reliance on the Discovery Method is not for keeps; it is pre-structured to the already known answers of the Ph.D. If the kind of bafflement and resignation necessary for creativity were seriously meant, the appropriate response of a youngster to such hoaxing would be not insight but disgust or rage, as in Zen teaching.

(3) The NSF intention to teach science for its own "excitement, beauty, and intellectual satisfaction" is entirely acceptable; this is science as one of the humanities. The intention is reinforced by the Woods Hole prescription to teach the "fundamental ideas and methods" rather than the current theories which may soon be outmoded anyway. (A sample list of fundamental concepts is Interaction, Physical System, Relativity of Motion, Equilibrium, Energy, Force, Entropy, Organic Evolution.)

Yet once we push these fundamental concepts beyond the stage of philosophical discussion, there arises a dilemma in the nature of the present state of science. It used to be that the chief excitement of science, which is the exploration and discovery of the nature of things, was easy to keep in the foreground; systematic theory was not too far from observation and experiment. Now, however, observation and experiment occur in a vast framework of systematic explanation, and (I would guess) it must be hard to convey the excitement of discovering the truth without what almost amounts to a

specialist training. To get to this excitement of actual
exploration requires spelling out the fundamental concepts very far; yet without this excitement, the unique
contribution of science to the humanities is lost.

Thus, it might still be best, in order to convey to the
majority the wonders of exploring and explaining nature, to have recourse to the history of classical experiments, as at St. John's of Annapolis—on the theory
that these demonstrate the scientific spirit of man in
action; or to stick to the spectacular popular demonstrations that Helmholtz or Huxley used to go in for;
or perhaps just to explore the solar system with a 6-inch
telescope, plate spoons with silver, cut up dead cats,
plant hybrid squash, or time the traffic lights and count
the cars, in order to show children and adolescents that
there *is* an observable world that can be made intelligi-
ble by explanations (what Plato in the *Timaeus* calls
"likely stories.")

(4) An even stronger reason for teaching science,
which the NSF does not talk about, is its austere morality, accuracy, scrupulous respect for what occurs. (I
myself never learned this and have always regretted it.)
This, I think, is the heart of what Huxley, Veblen, and
Dewey meant by the scientific ethic. But for the majority, unfortunately, this virtue is almost incompatible
with picking up much "content," or in preparing to
become a graduate-student. Simply, the average youngster's chemistry experiment usually does *not* balance out;
and moral science-teaching would then have him spend
the entire semester in explaining the "failure" and
cleaning his test-tubes better. We all know how the
student's drawing of what is seen through the micro-
scope looks remarkably like the picture in the textbook; this is necessarily blinked at by the instructor
who wants to proceed and get to the "subject," but
of course to condone it destroys science. The defect is

glaringly exaggerated in the TV lessons, which not only occur as a sleight-of-hand by experts, but—in every show I have seen—occur entirely too fast and cover too much ground. Undoubtedly the live instructor is supposed to retrace the path more thoroughly, but for the average youngster the effect must be to acquire a system of ideas and explanations, rather than science. The best students who continue in science will eventually learn, as real apprentices, the scientific attitude that has been by-passed; yet even graduate students, like medical students, are often mainly interested merely in going through the paces and adding to the "system of science," with appropriate status and rewards.

(5) The NSF purpose "to comprehend the world one lives and works in" is excellent. But for this purpose, I wonder whether the NSF projects are not too fancy. The underlying fact is that the average person uses ever more, and more complicated, scientific appliances, yet fewer and fewer of us practically understand or can repair the pump, the electric motor, the automobile that we use. Inevitably, people become slaves to repairmen, and as purchasers and consumers our ignorance is colossal. Correspondingly, the design of scientific appliances is increasingly less transparent, and the manufacturers take no account of their comprehensibility and repairability except by experts. Nor have I heard that industrialists make efforts to instruct their workmen in the overall rationale of the jobs they work at; nor that the labor unions demand it. When the NSF speaks of the need to comprehend in order to overcome the dangerous alienation of modern urban people and workmen, they ought to mean something akin to what progressive educators called "learning by doing"; philosophic concepts and their structuring are *not* sufficient.

(6) The purpose "to participate in grave political decisions on scientific matters" is also extremely valid.

If I do not mistake the tone, it is seriously meant by the gentlemen in the NSF, who appreciate the necessity and the dilemma. Decisions involving billions of dollars not only for incomprehensible hardware but in sponsoring research where only a band of experts can even guess the value, and also how to detect phony cover-ups from honorable failures—all these pose an absolutely new problem for democracies. The hope is that by overcoming superstition, including the superstition of "science," by making people more technically at home, and by teaching the relevant economics and sociology of science-expenditures and scientific castes, the dilemma can be alleviated. (I do not see how it can be solved.) Perhaps we can learn to ask the right questions and judge the authenticity, if not the content, of the answers. And at least on some issues like transportation-policy or the export of technologies in foreign aid, intelligent people would be able to decide better if they dared to criticize the experts at all.

(7) Finally, there is a kind of active participation, more and more incumbent on citizens, that requires a new scientific understanding and judgment. These are the matters of ecology, urbanism, and mental health, where physical, biological, and social sciences interact, that so directly determine everybody's everyday life that we simply cannot afford to leave them to experts. This kind of inquiry—in the line of Patrick Geddes, Lewis Mumford, the decentralists and regionalists—is of course partly political and aesthetic; it over-rides the distinction that we began with, between the sciences and the humanities.

iv

The kind of science teaching that emerges from this critique of the improved curricula does not fit easily into the up-the-ladder academic system culminating in graduate-schools and the production of Ph.D.'s. A good deal of training is best done in real apprenticeships; learning to be at home with our technology is best done in workshops, and even requires the cooperation of designers and manufacturers; the humanity of science is perhaps best taught to somewhat older students, 18 to 21, and it looks like an excellent subject for Folk Schools like those in Denmark; ecology and urbanism are surely best learned actively in the field, as in the remarkable work of Karl Linn among the underprivileged adolescents of Philadelphia.

Thus we again come to the same conclusion. We ought to spend more of our wealth on education; perhaps especially we need more understanding and practice of science; but it does not follow that the present system of schools is the appropriate institution for the job.

PART THREE

College

Chapter 8

"I DON'T WANT TO WORK— WHY SHOULD I?"

i

At 17 and 18, nearly half go off to something called college, and the others go to work, if there are jobs. We shall see that college is not a very educative environment, but by and large the world of work is even less so.

For most poor urban youth, the strongest present reason to go to work is family pressure; to bring in some money and not be a drag on the hard-working parents who are supporting them. Needless to say, such a reason springs from a complex of problematic emotions: resentment, spite, need for dependency and independence; and from conditions of poverty often at a crisis just at this juncture. As an incentive for finding a job, finding the right job, or preparing oneself for a job, these are unhappy auspices, and they often operate in reverse, toward balkiness and truancy.

But the more objective social form of this reason—

"You ought to pull your oar as a member of society; by the sweat of thy brow shalt thou eat bread"—is nowadays much less telling. We do not have, in America, an economy of scarcity, only an enormous number of poor people. To expand the economy still further might well be politically expedient, to diminish unemployment and keep up the rate of profit, but the facts are pretty plain that there is a synthetic demand and an absurd standard of living. Every kid jeers at the ads. And the prestigious flashy desirable goods are not such as poor youth beginning in jobs are going to get. In poor neighborhoods the men who do get them—on credit—are not usually models for modest labor.

Nor do the idle actually starve. For political and humanitarian reasons the affluent society doles out a subsistence, although stingy in this as in other public goods such as education, neighborhood beauty, and care for the delinquent and insane. And we can hardly expect a youth to have a sense of responsibility to his community when every force in modern urban life tends to destroy community sentiment and community functioning.

Perhaps most important of all is that the moral ideology and the dominant economic behavior are entirely inconsistent. Managers adopt as many labor-saving machines as possible, but the saving of labor is *not* passed on to society as a whole in shorter work hours, or even cheaper prices. And even in service-operations where there is no automation, such as restaurants, there is a cutback of employment: bigger crowds, and fewer people to serve them. Yet there is political excitement about unemployment.

Add, finally, that at least 25% of the gross national product is rather directly devoted to the 1,000 overkill.

It is hard to know how much these philosophical

considerations weigh with simple folk and children. In a profound sense, people are not fools, and they sniff the atmosphere correctly. In any case, the argument, "If you work, you can hold your head up with self-respect" does not have the overpowering force among our poor youth that it once did. Hipster notions of finding a racket seem also to satisfy the community ethic. And there is even the ethic that to work for a mere living is to be a fool.

ii

There is an evident and sickening disproportion between the money that people work hard for, whether as dish-washer, hospital orderly, stenographer, school-teacher, or artist, and the "soft" money that comes from expense accounts, tax-dodge foundations, having "made it" as a personality. I have referred to the disproportionate cut of the pie that falls to the academic monks in any welfare operation. Then why should those who are not going to be in the Establishment *work* for money, rather than look for an angle or wait for luck? And it does not help when kids see an immense part of their parents' hard-earned money go on usurious installment payments for high-priced hardware, and rent swallowing up more than a quarter of income.

My guess is that many poor kids are in the cruel dilemma of feeling guilty about not working, and yet uneasy among their peers and even in their own better judgment if they do try to get jobs—especially when trying to get a job has its own degrading humiliations, of confronting prejudice, bureaucratic callousness, and gouging agencies, and often when the young are frustrated by sheer ignorance of how to look for a job at all.

iii

And there is another philosophical aspect, usually over-looked, that is obviously important for these young. I have mentioned it before. So far as they can see—and they see clearly—the absorbing satisfactions of life do *not* require all this work and rat-race. In societies where it is possible to be decently poor, persons of superior education and talent often choose to be poor rather than hustle for money.

In the inflationary American economy, however, decent poverty is almost impossible. To be secure at all, one has to engage in the competition and try to rise; and the so-called "education" is geared to economic advancement. Thus, a common-sensible youth—and especially a poor one whose opportunities for advancement are limited and whose cultural background is unacademic—might reasonably judge that games, sex, and the gang are *preferable* to school and work, but he will then get not independence but misery. He will be so out of things that he will have nothing to occupy his mind. He is disqualified for marriage. He is inferior, out-caste.

As it is, the only ones who can afford the absorbing and simple satisfactions that do not cost much money are those who have succeeded economically and are by then likely unfit to enjoy anything. From this point of view, the chief blessing that our copious society could bestow on us would be a kind of subsistence work that allowed spirited people to be decently poor without frantic insecurity and long drudgery.

iv

If we turn to the deeper human and religious answers to the question "Why should I work?"—for example, work as fulfillment of one's potentialities, work as the vocation that gives justification—our present economy has little to offer to poor youth.

Unskilled and semi-skilled jobs are parts of elaborate enterprises rationalized for their own operation and not to fulfill the lives of workmen. Work processes are rarely interesting. Workmen are not taught the rationale of the whole. The products are often humanly pretty worthless, so there is no pride of achievement or utility. Craft and style are built into the machines, lost to the workmen. Labor unions have improved the conditions and dignity of the job, but they have also become bureaucratized and do not give the sense of solidarity.

It is only in the higher job brackets, beyond most poor youth, that there begins to be a place for inventiveness and art; and independent initiative belongs only to top management and expert advisors. There are fewer small shops. Neighborhood stores give way to centralized supermarkets where the employees have no say. There is a great increase in social services, but these require official licenses and are not open to those otherwise qualified who wish to work in them.

The total background of poor youth, including the inadequacies of the schools, conduces to dropping out; but the simplest worthwhile jobs require diplomas.

Here again, it may be asked if these considerations, of vocation, job-interest, job-worthiness, weigh with poor youth. They weigh with everybody. Indeed, the hard task of a youth worker is to find some objective activity that a youth might be interested in, and proud of achieving, that will save him from recessive narcissism and reactive hostility or withdrawal, and give him something to grow on. Further, as I argued in *Growing Up Absurd,* the high premium that workmen put on "Security" is largely a substitute for the feeling of being needed, fully used, indispensable.

v

Some of the human deficiencies in the jobs can be ameliorated—at least until automation makes the whole matter nugatory by vanishing the jobs. For example, with elementary thoughtfulness, a big plant that has many positions can allow a prospective employee to visit and try out various stations, rather than making an arbitrary assignment. Work processes can be efficiently designed on psychological grounds; for instance, a small group assembling a big lathe from beginning to end, so they have something to show for their day, as the crane carries the product away. In a form of "collective contract" or gang-system used in Coventry, England, fifty workers contract with the firm on a piece-work basis, and then settle among themselves the particular assignments, personnel, schedule, and many of the processes; there must be many industries where this humanizing procedure is feasible. With technical education paid for by industry in cooperation with the schools, we could have more understanding workmen.

The important point is that job-worthiness, the educative value of the job, must be recognized by managers and labor-unions as a specific good.

But of course this is part of the much larger need, to make our whole environment more educative, rather than rigidly restricting the concept of education to what happens in schools.

Socially useful work is probably an indispensable element in the education of most adolescents. It provides an objective structure, a bridge of norms and values, in the transition from being in the family to being oneself. This is the rationale of a good Youth Work Camp, as I described it in *Utopian Essays*; a community of youth democratically directing itself, and controlling itself, to do a job. Many colleges have adopted the

Antioch plan of alternating academic periods with periods of work in the economy, which are then made the subject of further academic criticism. But what a pity that precisely the poor youth, who *have* to go to work, get no value from the jobs they work at!

Finally, let me say a word about the miserable job induction at present. I have already mentioned the degrading and humiliating conditions that accompany looking for scarce jobs. Again, we do not appreciate the terrors and hang-ups for the semi-literate and socially paranoiac in filling out personnel forms. Often young human beings are tormented and talent is lost simply for the convenience of business machines. And naturally, for those disposed to feel rejected and inferior, each further frustration rapidly accumulates into an impassable block. A lad soon turns in the form not filled out, or even turns back outside the door. Or, pathetically, there is manic excitement at landing a job which he soon quits or cannot do anyway. The entire process is hopelessly and irrelevantly charged with emotion. And the pitiful and anxious lies that are written on those forms!

Certainly the current proposals to make the school the employment agency are reasonable; the school is at least familiar, even if the kid hates it and has dropped out.

Our classical ideology is that the job should be looked for with resolution and ambition. But how are these possible on the basis of ignorance and alienation? Here as elsewhere, our problem is lapse of community. Our society has less and less community between its adults and its youth. Traditional and family crafts and trades no longer exist, and a youth has few chances to form himself on model workmen in his neighborhood and learn the ropes and opportunities. The difficulties of getting into a union seem, and often are, insuperable.

Middle-class academic youth in their colleges have at least some contact with the adults who belong to the ultimate job-world, and placement is pretty good. But poor urban youth in schools whose culture is quite alien to them and whose aims fit neither their desires nor their capacities, are among jailers, not models.

These remarks are not optimistic toward solving the problems of employment, and unemployment, of youth. By and large, I think those problems are insoluble, and *should* be insoluble, until our affluent society becomes worthier to work in, more honorable in its functions, and more careful of its human resources.

Chapter 9

AN UNTEACHABLE GENERATION

i

But this is also a hard generation to teach in colleges what I think ought to be taught. I do not mean that the students are disrespectful, or especially lazy, or anything like that; in my experience, they pay us more respect than we usually deserve and they work as earnestly as could be expected trying to learn too much on too heavy schedules. Of course, as I have been arguing, many of the students, probably the majority, ought not to be in a scholastic setting at all, and their presence causes dilution and stupefying standardization as well as overcrowding. But let us here concentrate on several other difficulties that are in the very essence of present-day higher education. (a) The culture we want to pass on is no longer a culture for these young; the thread of it has snapped. (b) These young are not serious with themselves; this is a property of the kind of culture they do have. (c) And as with the lower schools, the auspices, method and aims of the colleges themselves are not relevant to good education for our unprecedented present and foreseeable future.

ii

The culture I want to teach—I am myself trapped in it and cannot think or strive apart from it—is our Western tradition: the values of Greece, the Bible, Christianity, Chivalry, the Free Cities of the twelfth century, the Renaissance, the heroic age of Science, the Enlightenment, the French Revolution, early nineteenth century Utilitarianism, late nineteenth century Naturalism.

To indicate what I mean, let me mention a typical proposition about each of these. The Greeks sometimes aspire to a civic excellence in which mere individual success would be shameful. The Bible teaches that there is a created world and history in which we move as creatures. Christians have a spirit of crazy commitment because we are always in the last times. Chivalry is personal honor and loyalty, in love or war. Free Cities have invented social corporations with juridical rights. The Renaissance affirms the imperious right of gifted individuals to immortality. Scientists carry on a disinterested dialogue with nature, regardless of dogma or consequence. The Enlightenment has decided that there is a common sensibility of mankind. The Revolution has made equality and fraternity necessary for liberty. Utilitarian economy is for tangible satisfactions, not busy-work, money, or power. Naturalism urges us to an honest ethics, intrinsic in animal and social conditions.

Needless to say, these familiar propositions are often in practical and theoretical contradiction with one another; but that conflict too is part of the Western tradition. And certainly they are only ideals—they never did exist on land or sea—but they are the inventions of the holy spirit and the human spirit that constitute the University, which is also an ideal.

Naturally, as a teacher I rarely mention such things; I take them for granted as assumed by everybody. But I am rudely disillusioned when I find that both the students and my younger colleagues take quite different things for granted.

For instance, I have heard that the excellence of Socrates was a snobbish luxury that students nowadays cannot afford. The world "communicated" in the mass media is, effectually, the only world there is. Personal loyalty leaves off with juvenile gangs. Law is power. Fame is prestige and sales. Science is mastering nature. There is no such thing as humanity, only patterns of culture. Education and ethics are what we program for conditioning reflexes. The purpose of political economy is to increase the Gross National Product.

These are not foolish propositions, though I state them somewhat sarcastically. They make a lot of theoretical sense and they are realistic. It is far better to believe them than hypocritically to assert ancient clichés. The bother with these views, however, is that they do not structure enough life or a worthwhile life; that is, as ideals they are false. Or, if they do not pretend to be ideals, what will one do for ideals?

I think that this lack of structure is felt by most of the students and it is explicitly mentioned by many young teachers. They regard me, nostalgically, as not really out of my mind but just out of time and space—indeed, I am even envied, because, although the traditional values are delusions, they do smugly justify, if one believes them and tries to act them. The current views do not mean to justify, and it is grim to live without justification.

There is not much mystery about how the thread

of relevance snapped. History has been too disillusioning. Consider just the recent decades, overlooking hundreds of years of hypocrisy. During the first World War, Western culture already disgraced itself irremediably (read Freud's profound expression of dismay). The Russian revolution soon lost its utopian élan, and the Moscow Trials of the thirties were a terrible blow to many of the best youth. The Spanish Civil War was perhaps the watershed—one can almost say that Western culture became irrelevant in the year 1938. Gas chambers and atom bombs showed what we were now capable of, yes our scientists. The Progress of the standard of living has sunk into affluence, and nobody praises the "American Way of Life." Scholars have become personnel in the Organization. Rural life has crowded into urban sprawl without community or the culture of cities. And the Cold War, deterrence of mutual overkill, is normal politics.

In this context, it *is* hard to talk with a straight face about identity, creation, Jeffersonian democracy, or the humanities.

But of course, people cannot merely be regimented; and we see that they find out their own pathetic, amiable, or desperate ideals. Creatureliness survives as the effort to make a "normal" adjustment and marriage, with plenty of hypochondria. The spirit of apocalypse is sought in hallucinogenic drugs. There is para-legal fighting for social justice, but it is hardly thought of as politics and "justice" is not mentioned. On the other hand, some poor youth seem to have quite returned to the state of nature. Art regains a certain purity by restricting itself to art-action. Pragmatic utility somehow gets confused with doing engineering. Personal integrity is reaffirmed by "existential commitment," usually without rhyme or reason.

Unfortunately, none of this, nor all of it together, adds up.

I can put my difficulty as a teacher as follows: It is impossible to convey that Milton and Keats were for real, that they were about something, that they expected that what they had to say and the way in which they said it made a difference. The students can (not brilliantly) tell you about the symbolic structure or even something about the historical context, though history is not much cultivated; but, if one goes back more than thirty years, they don't have any inkling that these poets were writers and *in* a world. And, not surprisingly, young people don't have ancient model heroes any more.

iii

Since there are few self-justifying ideas for them to grow up on, young people do not gain much confidence in themselves or take themselves as counting. On the other hand, they substitute by having astonishing private conceits, which many of them take seriously indeed.

The adults actively discourage earnestness. As James Coleman of Johns Hopkins has pointed out, the "serious" activity of youth is going to school and getting at least passing grades; all the rest—music, driving, 10 billions annually of teen-age commodities, dating, friendships, own reading, hobbies, need for one's own money—all this is treated by the adults as frivolous. The quality or meaning of it makes little difference; but a society is in a desperate way when its music makes little difference. In fact, of course, these frivolous things are where normally a child would explore his feelings and find his identity and vocation, learn to be responsible; nevertheless, if any of them threatens to interfere with the serious business—a hobby that interferes with homework, or dating that makes a youth want to quit school and get a job—it is unhesitatingly interrupted, sometimes with threats and sanctions.

At least in the middle class, that fills the colleges, this technique of socializing is unerring, and the result is a generation not notable for self-confidence, determination, initiative, or ingenuous idealism. It is a result unique in history: *an élite that has imposed on itself a morale fit for slaves.*

The literature favored by youth expresses, as it should, the true situation. (It is really the last straw when the adults, who have created the situation for the young, then try to censor their literature out of existence.) There are various moments of the hang-up. Some stories simply "make the scene," where making the scene means touring some social environment in such a way that nothing happens that adds up, accompanied by friends who do not make any difference. Such stories do not dwell on the tragic part, what is *missed* by making the scene. Alternatively, there are picaresque adventure-stories, where the hipster heroes exploit the institutions of society which are not their institutions, and they win private triumphs. More probingly, there are novels of sensibility, describing the early disillusionment with a powerful world that does not suit and to which one cannot belong, and the subsequent suffering or wry and plaintive adjustment. Or alternatively, the phony world is provisionally accepted as the only reality, and the whole apocalyptically explodes. Finally, there is the more independent Beat poetry of deliberate withdrawal from the unsatisfactory state of things, and making up a new world out of one's own guts, with the help of Japanese sages, hallucinogens, and introspective physiology. This genre, when genuine, does create a threadbare community—but it suits very few.

In order to have something of their own in a situation that has rendered them powerless and irresponsible, many young folk maintain through thick and thin a fixed self-concept, as if living out autobiographies of a life that has been already run. They nourish the conceit on the heroes of their literature, and they defend it with pride or self-reproach. (It comes to the same thing whether one says, "I'm the greatest" or "I'm the greatest goof-off.") They absorbedly meditate this biography and, if vocal, boringly retell it. In this action, as I have said, they are earnest indeed, but it is an action that prevents becoming aware of anything else or anybody else.

It is not an attitude with which to learn an objective subject-matter in college.

iv

It is also a poor attitude for loving or any satisfactory sexual behavior. Let me devote a paragraph to this.

In my opinion, the virulence of the sexual problems of teen-agers is largely caused by the very technique of socialization, and the irresponsibility consequent on it. (Of course this is not a new thing.) If the young could entirely regulate themselves according to their own intuitions and impulses, there would be far more realism and responsibility: consideration for the other, responsibility for social consequences, and sincerity and courage with respect to own feelings. For example, normally, a major part of attractiveness between two people is fitness of character—sweetness, strength, candor, attentiveness—and this tends to security and realism. We find instead that young people choose in conformity to movie-images, or to rouse the envy of peers, or because of fantasies of brutality or even mental unbalance. In courting, they lie to one another, instead of expressing their need; they conceal embarrassment instead of displaying it, and so prevent feeling from deepening. Normally, mutual sexual enjoyment would lead to mutual liking, closer knowledge, caring for; as St. Thomas says, the chief human end of sexual contact is to get to know the other. Instead, sexual activity is used as a means of conquest and epic boasting, or of being popular in a crowd; and one wants to be "understood" before making love. Soon, if only in sheer self-protection, it is necessary *not* to care for or become emotionally involved. Even worse, in making love, young people do not follow *actual* desire, which tends to have fine organic discrimination and organic prudence; rather, they do what they think they ought to desire, or they act for kicks or for experiment. Normally, pleasure is a good, though not infallible, index that an activity is healthy for the organism; but what one *thinks* will give pleasure is no index at all. There is fantastic excessive expectation, and pretty inevitable disappointment or even disgust. That is, much of the sexual behavior is not sexual at all, but conformity to gang behavior because one has no identity; or proving because one has no other proofs; or looking for apocalyptic experience to pierce the dull feeling of powerlessness.

The confusion is not helped by the adult hypocrisy that says, "Sex is beautiful, a divine creation—for later." It is a pretty makeshift creation that has such poor timing. Is it rather not the duty of society to make its schedule more livable? Consider the following: A psychiatrist in charge of Guidance at a very great university gave a melancholy account of the tragedy of unmarried pregnancy among co-eds. A co-ed asked him why, then, the Infirmary did not provide contraceptives on request. But he refused to answer her question.

v

Still, the chief obstacle to college teaching does not reside in the break with tradition nor in the lack of confidence and earnestness of the students, but in the methods and aims of the colleges themselves. Let me devote the remainder of this little book to this.

Chapter 10

TWO SIMPLE PROPOSALS

i

Jacques Barzun, the Dean of Faculties at Columbia, has predicted for us the end of the liberal arts college; it cannot survive the emphasis on technical and professional education and the overwhelming financing of scientific research by Federal money, corporation money, and most of the foundation money.

I think his prediction is justified—I am not so sure I am gloomy about it; if there is a revival of real education in this country, its form and auspices will not look like what we have been used to. But I do not think that the Dean thoroughly understands the causes, or the extent, of the débâcle. For the same social trend, of vocational training and contracted research, spells the end not only of the colleges but of the Universities as well, regarded as schools for independent professionals, communities of scholars, and centers of free inquiry. The crucial issue is not the change from "general" education to "specialism"; and there is nothing amiss in the

Sciences having a turn as the preponderant center of studies, since that is the nature of the environment. The medieval universities were mainly professional schools dominated by a kind of metaphysical science, according to their lights. The crucial issue is the change from the humanism of independent guilds of scholars, whether in the liberal arts *or* the professions, to a system of social-engineering for the national economy and polity. The medieval professions and specialties were structured in an ideal world that allowed for communication, that was international, and in which—in an important sense —the professions were oddly spontaneous and free. Our learning is increasingly departmentalized and prescribed.

Our educational reality can be seen in operation in the present kind of scheduling, testing, and grading; and if Dean Barzun is interested in making a change, he can start right here.

Let me repeat the facts. From early childhood, the young are subjected to a lockstep increasingly tightly geared to the extra-mural demands. There is little attention to individual pace, rhythm, or choice, and none whatever to the discovery of identity or devotion to intellectual goals. The aptitude and achievement testing and the fierce competition for high grades are a race up the ladder to high-salaried jobs in the businesses of the world, including the schooling business. In this race, time is literally money. Middle-class youngsters—or their parents—realistically opt for Advanced Placement and hasten to volunteer for the National Merit examinations. Negro parents want the same for their children, although the children have less tendency to cooperate.

Disappointingly, but not surprisingly, the colleges and universities go along with this spiritual destruction, and indeed devise the tests and the curricula to pass the tests. Thereby they connive at their own spiritual destruction; yet it is not surprising, for that is where the money and the grandeur are. I do not expect for a moment that they will, in the foreseeable future, recall their primary duties: to pass on the tradition of disinterested learning, to provide a critical standard, to educate the free young (*liberi*) to be free citizens and independent professionals.

The question is, *could* the colleges and universities act otherwise, even if they wished to? Of course they could. Most of them are autonomous corporations. Let me here suggest two modest changes, that are feasible almost immediately, that would entail no risk whatever, and yet would immensely improve these academic communities and importantly liberate them in relation to society.

ii

First, suppose that half a dozen of the most prestigious liberal arts colleges—say Amherst, Swarthmore, Connecticut, Weslyan, Carleton, etc.—would announce that, beginning in 1966, they required for admission a two-year period, after high school, spent in some maturing activity. These colleges are at present five times oversubscribed; they would not want for applicants on *any* conditions that they set; and they are explicitly committed to limiting their expansion.

By "maturing activity" could be meant: working for a living, especially if the jobs are gotten without too heavy reliance on connections; community service, such as the Northern Student Movement, volunteer service in hospital or settlement house, domestic Peace Corps; the army—though I am a pacifist and would urge a youngster to keep out of the army; a course of purposeful travel that met required standards; independent enterprise in art, business, or science, away from home, with something to show for the time spent.

The purpose of this proposal is twofold: to get students with enough life-experience to be educable on the college level, especially in the social sciences and humanities; and to break the lockstep of twelve years of doing assigned lessons for grades, so that the student may approach his college studies with some intrinsic motivation, and therefore perhaps assimilate something that might change him. Many teachers remember with nostalgia the maturer students who came under the GI-bill, though to be sure a large number of them were pretty shell-shocked.

A subsidiary advantage of the plan would be to relieve the colleges of the doomed, and hypocritical, effort to serve *in loco parentis* on matters of morality. If young persons have been out working for a living, or have traveled in foreign parts, or have been in the army, a college can assume that they can take care of themselves.

The American tradition of colleges for adolescents made a kind of sense when the curriculum was largely unquestioned classics, history, and mathematics, taught dogmatically in a seminarian atmosphere, and to an élite that thought it had a justified social role. Present college teaching tries to be something different. It emphasizes method, background reading, criticism, and research, and offers a range of choice or prescription quite baffling to most 17-year-olds. In a curious way, the present dominance of mathematics and physical sciences has resulted in the students being even less mature, yet has obscured the true picture of student ineptitude and professorial frustration. It *is* possible to teach mathematics and physics to boys and girls, especially boys. These abstract subjects suit their alert and schematizing minds, the more so if the teaching treats science as the solution of puzzles. But it is not possible to teach sociology, anthropology, world literature to boys and girls, for they have no experience and judgment. When it is done, the message is merely verbal. The harsh facts and the relativity of morals are bound to be embarrassing and shocking. Regarded as "assignments"—as high school graduates must regard them—the voluminous readings are indigestible straw and are annotated by rote; more mature students might be able to take them as books. In brief, whiz-bang youngsters who have found their identity as mathematicians, chemists, or electronic technicians might well speed on to M.I.T. at age 15. The liberal arts colleges, that are essentially concerned with educating citizens and statesmen, social scientists and social professionals, scholars and men-of-letters, require more maturity to begin with. If the average age of entrance were higher, these colleges would also serve as the next step for the many disappointed science-students, who can hardly be expected to backtrack among the seventeens. (A very numerous group switch from the physical sciences to the social sciences and humanities.)

Throughout our educational system there is a desperate need for institutional variety and interims in which a youth can find himself. If we are going to require as much schooling as we do, we must arrange for breaks and return-points, otherwise the schooling inevitably becomes spirit-breaking and regimentation. In my opinion, however, a much more reasonable over-all pattern is to structure all of society and the whole environment as educative, with the schools playing the much more particular and traditional role of giving intensive training when it is needed and sought, or of being havens for those scholarly by disposition.

iii

My other proposal is even simpler, and not at all novel. Let half a dozen of the prestigious Universities—Chicago, Stanford, the Ivy League—abolish grading, and use testing only and entirely for pedagogic purposes as teachers see fit.

Anyone who knows the frantic temper of the present schools will understand the transvaluation of values that would be effected by this modest innovation. For most of the students, the competitive grade has come to be the essence. The naïve teacher points to the beauty of the subject and the ingenuity of the research; the shrewd student asks if he is responsible for that on the final exam.

Let me at once dispose of an objection whose unanimity is quite fascinating. I think that the great majority of professors agree that grading hinders teaching and creates a bad spirit, going as far as cheating and plagiarizing. I have before me the collection of essays, *Examining in Harvard College*, and this is the consensus. It is uniformly asserted, however, that the grading is inevitable; for how else will the graduate schools, the foundations, the corporations *know* whom to accept, reward, hire? How will the talent scouts know whom to tap?

By testing the applicants, of course, according to the specific task-requirements of the inducting institution, just as applicants for the Civil Service or for licenses in medicine, law, and architecture are tested. Why should Harvard professors do the testing *for* corporations and graduate-schools?

The objection is ludicrous. Dean Whitla, of the Harvard Office of Tests, points out that the scholastic-aptitude and achievement tests used for *admission* to

Harvard are a super-excellent index for all-around Harvard performance, better than high-school grades or particular Harvard course-grades. Presumably, these college-entrance tests are tailored for what Harvard and similar institutions want. By the same logic, would not an employer do far better to apply his own job-aptitude test rather than to rely on the vagaries of Harvard section-men. Indeed, I doubt that many employers bother to look at such grades; they are more likely to be interested merely in the fact of a Harvard diploma, whatever that connotes to them. The grades have most of their weight with the graduate schools—here, as elsewhere, the system runs mainly for its own sake.

It is really necessary to remind our academics of the ancient history of Examination. In the medieval university, the whole point of the gruelling trial of the candidate was whether or not to accept him as a peer. His disputation and lecture for the Master's was just that, a master-piece to enter the guild. It was not to make comparative evaluations. It was not to weed out and select for an extra-mural licensor or employer. It was certainly not to pit one young fellow against another in an ugly competition. My philosophic impression is that the medievals thought they knew what a good job of work was and that we are competitive because we do not know. But the more status is achieved by largely irrelevant competitive evaluation, the less will we ever know.

(Of course, our American examinations never did have this purely guild orientation, just as our faculties have rarely had absolute autonomy; the examining was to satisfy Overseers, Elders, distant Regents—and they as paternal superiors have always doted on giving grades, rather than accepting peers. But I submit that this set-up itself makes it impossible for the student to *become* a master, to *have* grown up, and to commence on his own. He will always be making A or B for some over-seer. And in the present atmosphere, he will always be climbing on his friend's neck.)

Perhaps the chief objectors to abolishing grading would be the students and their parents. The parents should be simply disregarded; their anxiety has done enough damage already. For the students, it seems to me that a primary duty of the university is to deprive them of their props, their dependence on extrinsic valuation and motivation, and to force them to confront the difficult enterprise itself and finally lose themselves in it.

A miserable effect of grading is to nullify the various uses of testing. Testing, for both student and teacher, is a means of structuring, and also of finding out what is blank or wrong and what has been assimilated and can be taken for granted. Review—including high-pressure review—is a means of bringing together the fragments, so that there are flashes of synoptic insight.

There are several good reasons for testing, and kinds of test. But if the aim is to discover weakness, what is the point of down-grading and punishing it, and thereby inviting the student to conceal his weakness, by faking and bulling, if not cheating? The natural conclusion of synthesis is the insight itself, not a grade for having had it. For the important purpose of placement, if one can establish in the student the belief that one is testing *not* to grade and make invidious comparisons but for his own advantage, the student should normally seek his own level, where he is challenged and yet capable, rather than trying to get by. If the student dares to accept himself as he is, a teacher's grade is a crude instrument compared with a student's self-awareness. But it is rare in our universities that students are encouraged to notice objectively their vast confusion. Unlike Socrates, our teachers rely on power-drives rather than shame and ingenuous idealism.

Many students are lazy, so teachers try to goad or threaten them by grading. In the long run this must do more harm than good. Laziness is a character-defense. It may be a way of avoiding learning, in order to protect the conceit that one is already perfect (deeper, the despair that one *never* can). It may be a way of avoiding just the risk of failing and being down-graded. Sometimes it is a way of politely saying, "I won't." But since it is the authoritarian grown-up demands that have created such attitudes in the first place, why repeat the trauma? There comes a time when we must treat people as adult, laziness and all. It is one thing courageously to fire a do-nothing out of your class; it is quite another thing to evaluate him with a lordly F.

Most important of all, it is often obvious that balking in doing the work, especially among bright young people who get to great universities, means exactly what it says: The work does not suit me, not this subject, or not at this time, or not in this school, or not in school altogether. The student might not be bookish; he might be school-tired; perhaps his development ought now to take another direction. Yet unfortunately, if such a student is intelligent and is not sure of himself, he *can* be bullied into passing, and this obscures everything. My hunch is that I am describing a common situation. What a grim waste of young life and teacherly effort! Such a student will retain nothing of what he has "passed" in. Sometimes he must get mononucleosis to tell his story and be believed.

And ironically, the converse is also probably commonly true. A student flunks and is mechanically weeded out, who is really ready and eager to learn in a scholastic setting, but he has not quite caught on. A good teacher can recognize the situation, but the computer wreaks its will.

Chapter 11

A USUAL CASE—
NOTHING FANCY

i

To sum up these dour remarks about American schools in the middle of the twentieth century, consider a usual case. Here is a young fellow in a college classroom. *He* is not usual, for everybody is unique, but his case is usual. His face is pretty blank but he is sitting in a middle row, not, like some, in the rear near the door, ready to bolt. Let me review a dozen important facts about his situation—they are obvious, nothing fancy.

He is in his junior year. So, omitting kindergarten, he has been in an equivalent classroom for nearly fifteen continuous years, intermitted only by summer vacations for play. Schooling has been the serious part of his life, and it has consisted of listening to some grown-up talking and of doing assigned lessons. The young man has almost never seriously assigned himself a task. Sometimes, as a child, he thought he was doing something earnest on his own, but the adults interrupted him and he became discouraged.

He's bright—he can manipulate formulas and remember sentences, and he has made a well-known college. During his last year in high school, he made good grades on a series of gruelling State and National Tests, Regents, College Boards, National Merits, Scholastic Aptitudes. And in this college, which is geared to process Ph.D.'s, he has survived, though the attrition is nearly 40%. He has even gotten a partial scholarship on the National Defense Education Act. Yet, as it happens, he doesn't like books or study at all. He gets no flashes of insight into the structure or the methods of the academic subjects. This isn't the field in which his intelligence, grace, and strength of mind and body show to best advantage. He just learns the answers or figures out the puzzles. Needless to say he has already forgotten most of the answers that he once "knew" well enough to pass, sometimes brilliantly.

The academic subject being taught in this particular classroom is intrinsically interesting; most arts and sciences are intrinsically interesting. The professor and even the section-man know a good deal about it, and it is interesting to watch their minds work. But it is one of the social sciences and our young man does not grasp that it is *about* something; it has no connection for him. He has had so little experience of society or institutions. He has not practiced a craft, been in business, tried to make a living, been married, had to cope with children. He hasn't voted, served on a jury, been in politics, nor even in a youth movement for civil rights or peace or Goldwater. Coming from a modest middle-class suburb, he has never really seen poor people or foreigners. His emotions have been carefully limited by the conventions of his parents and the conformism of his gang. What, for him, could history, sociology, political science, psychology, classical music or literature, possibly be about? (In the *Republic,* Plato forbids teaching most of our academic subjects until the student is thirty years old! Otherwise the lessons will be mere sophistry, emptily combative.)

Our young man is not verbally combative, and he's not a hipster who talks out to show that he knows the score, in order to put you down. But sometimes he is teased by something that the teacher or the book says, and he wants to demur, argue, ask a question. But the class is too crowded for any dialogue. When the format is a lecture, one cannot interrupt. Perhaps the chief obstacle to discussion, however, is the other students. In their judgment, discussion is irrelevant to the finals and the grades, and they resent wasting time. Also, they resent it if a student "hogs attention."

From time to time, the teacher, especially the young section-man, is heartened by a sign of life and does want to pursue the discussion. He is himself given to expressing dissenting opinions, questioning the justification of an institution or asking a student for evidence from personal experience. At once a wall of hostility rises against the teacher as well as the questioning student. Surely he must be a communist, pacifist, or homosexual. Maybe he is ridiculing the class. Feeling the hostility and being a rather timid academic, worried about advancement and ultimate tenure, the teacher signs off: "Well, let's get back to the meat of the course . . . that's beyond our scope here, why don't you take Sosh 403? . . . that's really anthropology, young man, and you'd better ask Professor O'Reilly, heh heh."

Indeed, little of the teaching makes our student see the relevance, necessity, or beauty of the subject. The professor, especially, is interested in the latest findings and in the ingenuity of a new technique, but the student is at sea as to why he is studying it at all, except that it's part of sequence B toward a Bachelor's. The confusion is made worse, as I have said, by the fact that the present young generation, including the young teachers, has at most a tenuous loyalty to the culture of the Western world, the Republic of Letters, the ideal of disinterested Science. But apart from this tradition, the University is nothing but a factory to train apprentices and process academic union-cards.

Yet a college is a poor environment in which to train apprentices, except in lab sciences where one works at real problems with the real apparatus. Most of the academic curriculum, whether in high school or college, is abstract in a bad sense. It must be so. A structure of ideas is abstracted from the on-going professions, civic and business activities, social institutions; and these ideas are again thinned out and processed to be imported into classrooms and taught as the curriculum. To be sure, this ancient procedure often makes sense. It makes sense for aspiring professionals who know what they are after and want a briefing; and it makes sense for the scholarly who have a philosophical interest in essences and their relationship, and want to chart the whole field. But for most, the abstractness of the curricular subjects, especially if the teaching is pedantic, can be utterly barren. The lessons are only exercises, with no relation to the real world. They are never for keeps. And many of the teachers are merely academics, not practicing professionals; they are interested in the words and the methodology, not the thing and the task.

ii

The young man respects his teachers and he knows it is a good school, almost a prestige school, but he cannot help feeling disappointed. He had hoped in a vague way that when he came to college it would be different from high school. He would be a kind of junior friend of learned men who had succeeded; he could model himself on them. After all, except for parents and schoolteachers—and the school-teachers have been prissy—he has had little contact with any adults in his whole life.

He thought, too, that the atmosphere of learning in college would, somehow, be free, liberating, a kind of wise bull-session that would reveal a secret. But it has proved to be the same cash-accounting of hours, tests, credits, grades. The professor is, evidently, preoccupied with his own research and publishing. In both class and office-hours he is formal and stand-offish. He never appears in the coffee-shop, never invites one home. He certainly never exposes himself as a human being. He is rather meticulous about the assignments being on time and he is a "tough" grader, but this seems to be his way of keeping the students under control, rather than due to belief in the system. He does not seem to realize that they respect him anyway.

So, just as in high school, the youth are driven back on their exclusive "sub-culture," which only distracts further from any meaning that academic life might have. As Riesman and others have pointed out, the students and faculty confront one another like hostile, or at least mutually suspicious, tribes.

Also, this past decade, the lack of community has been vastly exacerbated by the state of chaotic transition in which almost every college in the country exists. The grounds are torn up by bulldozers; the enrollment is excessive; the classes are too large; the students are housed three and four in a room meant for two. The curriculum is continually in process of readjustment. Professors are on the move, following the contracted research, or pirated away by salary hikes. These conditions are supposed to be temporary, but I have seen them now for ten years and the immediate future will be worse. A whole generation is being sacrificed.

An even deadlier aspect of the expansion is the unabashed imperialism of the administrators. This leads to entirely phony operations. Excellent teachers and scholars are scuttled for spectacular names that will never teach. A reputation for innovation and daring is sought, but student publications are censored in order to protect the Image. Scores of millions of new endowments are boasted of, but there is unbelievable penny-pinching about deficits in the cafeteria, rent for the dormitories, tuition, instructors' salaries.

Another aspect of transition is the Knowledge Explosion. New approaches and altogether new subjects must be taught, yet the entrenched faculty are by no means willing to give up any of the old prescribed subjects. It is peculiar; one would expect that, since the professors have tenure, they would welcome dropping some of the course load; but their imperialism is strong too, and they will give up nothing. So our student is taking five or even six subjects, when the maximum should be three. Whenever he begins to be interested in a subject, he is interrupted by other chores. Rushed, he gives token performances, which he has learned to fake. No attention is paid to what suits *him*. The only time a student is treated as a person is when he breaks down and is referred to Guidance.

In place of reliance on intrinsic motives, respect for individuality, leisurely exploration, there is a stepped-up pressure of extrinsic motivations, fear and bribery. The student cannot help worrying about his father's money, the fantastic tuition and other fees that will go down the drain if he flunks out; and he must certainly keep his scholarship. On the other hand, the talent scouts of big corporations hover around with lavish offers. In this atmosphere are supposed to occur disinterested scrutiny of the nature of things, the joy of discovery, moments of creativity, the finding of identity and vocation. It is sickening to watch.

iii

Finally, we must say something about the animal and community life from which our collegian has come into this classroom. The college has spent government and foundation money in pretentious buildings with plushy lounges, but the food is lousy and the new dormitories are like bedlam for want of sound-proofing. The values of college presidents are incredibly petty-bourgeois; their world is made for photographs, not to live in.

The Administration has set itself strongly against fraternity-houses because of the exclusion-clauses and to promote cohesiveness of the community. These are excellent reasons, but one sometimes has a strong suspicion that the reality is to fill the new dormitories, built with Urban Renewal funds. If students want to live off-campus in their own cooperatives, they are avuncularly told that, at 20 years old, they are not mature enough to feed their faces and make their beds.

No attempt is made by the University to come to terms with its neighbors. Rather, to expand, it has the neighborhood condemned as a slum and it dislocates residents of many years. Then it asks for police protection because of the social tension. Some students vanish into the condemnable or condemned neighborhood and the campus sees little of them except for classes. Other students more hospitably invite the neighbors to Saturday night dances, with a local jazz combo, but the Dean breaks it up by having a cop ask for ID cards.

There are exquisitely elaborate regulations for sexual and convivial behavior—days and hours and how many inches the door must be open and whose feet must be on the ground. The Administration claims to be *in loco parentis*, yet half the young men and women had more freedom at home, when they were kids in high school. One has more than a strong suspicion, and not sometimes but usually, that all the parental concern is merely for Public Relations. The college motto is *Lux et Veritas,* but there is a strong smell of hypocrisy in the air.

Maybe the most galling thing of all is that there is a Student Government, with political factions and pompous elections. It is empowered to purchase the class rings and organize the Prom and the boat-ride. Our young man no longer bothers to vote. But when there is a need to censor the student paper or magazine, the Administration appoints these finks to be on a joint faculty-student board of review, so that the students are made responsible for their own muzzling.

iv

Our junior's face now isn't quite so blank. It is wearing a little smile. The fact is that he is no longer mechanically taking notes but is frankly day-dreaming, as he used to in the sixth grade.

The prospect is appalling. There might be four or five more years of this, since his father wants him to continue in graduate school, and he no longer has any plans of his own anyway. Think of it! He will now be doing "original research" under these conditions of forced labor, And besides, since he will have a wife, a small child, and another on the way, he will be panicky that he might not get the assistantship.

Of course, many of the unfavorable college conditions which I have been describing can, and should, be improved. There are a number of expedients. The grading can be scrapped, keeping the testing as a pedagogic method. There can be many part-time active professionals in the faculty, to generate a less academic atmosphere. There are several arrangements for teachers to pay attention to students, discover their intrinsic motivations, guide theim in more individual programs. The social sciences can be made less unreal by working pragmatically on problems of the college community itself and the immediate rural or city environment. The moral rules can be reformed to suit an educational community, teaching responsibility by giving freedom in an atmosphere of counsel and support. So forth and so on.

Nevertheless, when we consider those fifteen years, and sixteen years, and twenty years of schooling, we cannot avoid the disturbing question: Why is the young man in such a classroom altogether? It suits him so badly. He is bright but not bookish, curious but not scholarly, teachable but not in this way.

He must be educated; everybody must be educated; but this kind of schooling has certainly not been the best way to educate him. We have seen him in other situations than school when he looked far brighter, both more spontaneous and more committed; when he showed initiative and was proud of what he was doing; when he learned a lot, fast, simply because he wanted to or had to. Maybe, for him, the entire high school and college institution, in the form that we know it, has been a mistake.

If so, what a waste of his youth and of the social wealth! And it is this waste that we are busy expanding to 50% going to college by 1970.

v

The argument of this book is that every child must be educated to the fullest extent, brought up to be useful to society and to fulfill his own best powers. In our society, this must be done largely at the public expense, as a community necessity. Certainly the Americans ought to spend more on it than they do, instead of squandering so much on piggish consumption, hardware, and highways. But it is simply a superstition, an official superstition and a mass superstition, that the way to educate the majority of the young is to pen them up in schools during their adolescence and early adulthood.

The hard task of education is to liberate and strengthen a youth's initiative, and at the same time to see to it that he knows what is necessary to cope with the on-going activities and culture of society, so that his initiative can be relevant. It is absurd to think that this task can be accomplished by so much sitting in a box facing front, manipulating symbols at the direction of distant administrators. This is rather a way to regiment and brainwash.

At no other time or place in history have people believed that continuous schooling was the obvious means to prepare most youth for most careers, whether farmer, industrial worker, craftsman, nurse, architect, writer, engineer, lawyer, shopkeeper, party-boss, social worker, sailor, secretary, fine artist, musician, parent, or citizen. Many of these careers require a lot of study. Some of them need academic teaching. But it was never thought useful to give academic teaching in such massive and continuous doses as the only regimen.

The idea of everybody going to a secondary school and college has accompanied a recent stage of highly centralized corporate and state economy and policy. Universal higher schooling is not, as people think, simply a continuation of universal primary schooling in reading and democratic socialization. It begins to orient to careers and it occurs after puberty, and jobs and sex are usually not best learned about in academies. The bother is, however, that the long schooling is not only inept, it is psychologically, politically, and professionally, damaging.

In my opinion, there *is* no single institution, like the monolithic school-system programmed by a few graduate universities and the curriculum reformers of the National Science Foundation, that can prepare everybody for an open future of a great society.

Thus at present, facing a confusing future of automated technology, excessive urbanization, and entirely new patterns of work and leisure, the best educational brains ought to be devoting themselves to devising *various* means of educating and paths of growing up, appropriate to various talents, conditions, and careers. We should be experimenting with different kinds of school, no school at all, the real city as school, farm schools, practical apprenticeships, guided travel, work camps, little theaters and local newspapers, community service. Many others, that other people can think of. Probably more than anything, we need a community, and community spirit, in which many adults who know something, and not only professional teachers, will pay attention to the young.

But the tendency is in just the opposite direction, to concentrate, aggrandize, and streamline what we have. With the unanimous applause of all right-thinking people, Congress (1963) appropriated another two billions for college buildings. The foundations increasingly underwrite scholarships and professional salaries. Of the fifteen billions budgeted in 1962 by the Federal Government for Research and Development, two billions went directly to the Universities and the rest largely underwrote Ph.D.'s and prospective Ph.D.'s. Fifty millions went to the National Science Foundation just for studies in improving primary and high school courses. There is a vigorous campaign by the President to cajole and threaten the drop-outs back into school, and we saw that the Secretary of Labor asked to extend the compulsory age to 18. And all this goes almost entirely unquestioned, even by know-nothing politicians who refuse to spend anything on any other kind of public goods. In plans to pump-prime the economy, even in such a splendid document as the Manifesto on the Triple Revolution, money for Schools is often Number One, or else Number Two, right after Housing. Among all liberals and champions of the underprivileged, it is an article of faith that salvation for the Negroes and Spanish-Americans consists in more schooling of the middle-class variety. And further, all philosophers, from hard-liners like Rickover, through James Conant, to free-thinkers like Martin Mayer, insist that salvation for society consists in tightening and upgrading middle-class schools, and getting rid of progressive education.

Like any mass belief, the superstition that schooling is the only path to success is self-proving. There are now no professions, whether labor-statesman, architect, or trainer in gymnastics, that do not require college diplomas. Standards of licensing are set by Boards of Regents that talk only school language. For business or hotel-management it is wise to have a Master's. Access to the billions for Research and Development is by the Ph.D. in physical sciences, and prudent parents push their children accordingly; only a few are going to get this loot, but all must compete for it. And so we go down to the diplomas and certificates required for sales-girls and typists. If you are Personnel, you need a piece of paper to apply, and almost everybody is Personnel. Thus effectively, a youth *has* no future if he quits, or falls off, the school ladder. Farm youth can still drop out without too much clatter, but the rural population is now 8% and rapidly diminishing.

If, in this climate of opinion, I demur, I am accused

of being against the National Goals and against suburbia. So I am. But on the other hand, I have been accused of being a racist-élitist who thinks that some people are "not good enough" to go to school. But I am not an élitist and I do not think that some people are not good enough. The scholastic disposition is a beautiful and useful one; we are lucky that a minority of people are so inclined. But I do not think it is the moon and the stars.

vi

To understand our present situation, let us review the history of schooling in this century.

By 1900, our present school system was established in its main outlines, including the liberal arts colleges and the German-imitating Universities. At that time there was almost universal primary schooling in a great variety of local arrangements, yet—we saw—only 6% of the 17-year-olds graduated from high school. Maybe another 10% would have graduated if they could have afforded it. (Recently, Dr. Conant has estimated that 15% are academically talented.) We may assume that that 6% or 16% would be in school because they wanted to be there; not only would there be no startling problems of discipline, but they could be taught a curriculum, whether traditional or vocational, that was interesting and valuable for itself. They were not conscripted soldiers, being chased up a ladder.

Now the 94% who did not graduate obviously were not "drop-outs." They were everybody: future farmer, shopkeeper, millionaire, politician, inventor, journalist. Consider the careers of two master architects who were born around that time. One quit school at eighth grade to leave home and support himself. Gravitating to an architect's office as an office-boy, he found the work to his liking. He learned draftsmanship in various offices, and French and mathematics on the outside (with the help of friendly adults), and he eventually won the Beaux Arts prize and studied in a Paris *atelier*. He has since built scores of distinguished buildings and, as the graduate professor of design at a great university, is one of the most famous teachers in the country. The other architect is the most successful in America in terms of the size and prestige of his commissions. He quit school at age 13 to support his mother. Working for a stone-cutter, he learned to draw, and in a couple of years he cut out for New York and apprenticed himself to an architect. In competition with a room-mate, he studied languages and mathematics. Via the Navy in 1918, he got to Europe with some money in his pocket and traveled and studied. Returning, he made a splendid marriage, and so forth.

These two careers, not untypical except for their *éclat,* are almost unthinkable at present. How would the young men be licensed without college degrees? How would they get college degrees without high school diplomas? But these men had the indispensable advantage that they were deeply self-motivated, went at their own pace, and could succumb to fascination and risk. Would these two have become architects at all if they were continually interrupted by high school Chemistry, Freshman Composition, Psychology 106, at a time when they didn't care about such things? (But they have learned them since, nevertheless!)

It would be a useful study—for a Master's thesis?—to find how many people who grew up from 1900 to 1920 and have made great names in the sciences, arts, literature, government, business, etc. actually went through the *continuous* sixteen-year school grind, without quitting, or without quitting and occasionally returning when it was relevant.

As the decades passed, higher schooling began to be

a mass phenomenon. In 1930, 30% graduated from high school and 11% went to college. By 1963, we see that 65% have graduated, of whom more than half go to college.

Who now are the other 35%? They are the Dropouts, mostly urban-underprivileged or rural. From this group we do not much expect splendid careers, in architecture, politics, or literature. They are not allowed to get jobs before 16; they find it hard to get jobs after 16; they might drop out of society altogether, because there is now no other track than going to school.

vii

What happened to the schools during the tenfold increase from 1900 to 1960? Administratively, we saw, we simply aggrandized and bureaucratized the existing framework. The system now looks like the system then. But in the process of massification, it inevitably suffered a sea-change. Plant, teacher-selection, and methods were increasingly standardized. The "students" became a different breed. Not many were there because they wanted to be there; a lot of them, including many of the bright and spirited, certainly wanted to be elsewhere and began to make trouble. The academic curriculum was necessarily trivialized. An important function of the schools began to be baby-sitting and policing. The baby-sitting was continued into the rah-rah colleges.

Naturally, in the aggrandized system, Educational Administration became very grand. To say it brutally, this was importantly because of the very irrelevance of the system itself, the inappropriate students and the feeble curriculum. Stuck with a bad idea, the only way of coping with the strains was to have more Assistant Principals, Counsellors, Truant Officers, University Courses in Methods and Custodial Care, Revised Textbooks.

Currently we are getting Team Teaching, Visual Aids, Higher Horizons, Programmed Instruction. To compensate for the mass trivializing of the curriculum, there are Intellectually Gifted Classes, Enrichment, and Advanced Placement. And on the other hand, Opportunity Classes for the dull and 600 Schools for the emotionally disturbed. The freshman year in college has been sacrificed to Surveys and Freshman Composition, to make up for lost ground and weed out the unfit.

Correspondingly, from 1910 on, the age of Frederick Taylor, school superintendents have become Scientific Business Managers and Educators with a big E. College Presidents have become mighty public spokesmen. Public Relations flourish apace.

Till recently, however, the expansion was fairly harmless, though plenty foolish. It was energized by a generous warm democracy and an innocent seeking for prestige by parents becoming affluent. These were not new things in America, or elsewhere. By and large, the pace was easy-going. Children were not fed tranquillizers; few adolescents had cause to suffer nervous breakdowns because of the testing; and collegians could get a gentlemanly C by coasting.

The unfortunate part of the expansion was that, insensibly, everybody began to believe that being in school was the only way to become an educated person. What a generation before had been the usual course, to quit school and seek elsewhere to grow up, became a sign of eccentricity, failure, delinquency.

viii

Suddenly, since the Korean war and hysterically since Sputnik, there has developed a disastrous overestimation of schools and scholarship. More basically, there has been a dramatic shift in economic power—climaxing in the Kennedy regime—toward electronic and other high-technological industries, and the ascendancy of the National Science Foundation and the Universities both in and outside of government. Also, since the end of World War II, the income-spread between the haves and have-nots has steadily increased; there is immense new production of wealth, but in the structure of the economy, it does not filter down.

So we see that mothers who used to want their offspring to be "well adjusted," are now mad for the I.Q. and the Percentile. School that were lax, democratic or playful, are fiercely competitive. And an average unbookish youth finds himself in a bad fix. He may not be able to cope with the speed-up and the strict grading, yet if he fails there are loud alarms about his pre-delinquency, and there are national conferences on drop-outs.

We are witnessing an educational calamity. Every kind of youth is hurt. The bright but unacademic can, as we have seen, perform; but the performance is inauthentic and there is a pitiful loss of what they *could* be doing with intelligence, grace, and force. The average are anxious. The slow are humiliated. But also the authentically scholarly are ruined. Bribed and pampered, they forget the meaning of their gifts. As I have put it before, they "do" high school in order to "make" Harvard, and then they "do" Harvard.

I doubt that any of this rat-race is useful. Given quiet, and food and lodging, young scholars would study anyway, without grades. The drill and competitiveness are bad for their powers, and they mistake themselves and become snobbish craft-idiots. There is no evidence that highly creative youngsters in the sciences, arts, or professions, especially thrive on formal schooling at all, rather than by exploring and gradually gravitating to the right work and environment. For some, schooling no doubt saves time; for others it is interruptive and depressing. And on lower levels of performance, do the technical and clerical tasks of automated production really require so many years of boning and test-passing as is claimed? We have seen that the evidence is otherwise.

For urban poor kids who are cajoled not to drop out, the mis-education is a cruel hoax. They are told that the high school diploma is worth money, but we have seen that this is not necessarily so.

Of course, there is no real choice for any of them. Poor people must picket for better schools that will not suit most of their children and won't pay off. Farm youth must ride to central schools that are a waste of time for most of them, while they lose the remarkable competence they have. Middle-class youth must doggedly compete and be tested to death to get into colleges where most of them will doggedly (or cynically) serve time. It is ironical. With all the money spent on Research and Development, for hardware, computers, and tranquilizers, America can think up only one institution for its young human resources. Apparently the schooling that we have already had has brainwashed everybody.

ix

This is the historical and social background out of which our young friend has come to that dazed look in the college classroom. He has been through a long process that has sapped his initiative, dampened his sexuality, and dulled his curiosity and probably even his intellect. He is not earnest about what he is now doing. One would say that he is marking time, except that he does not have any particular ambition to step out.

What to do for him—or at least for the next generation of him?

Maybe the chief mistake we make is to pay too much

direct attention to the "education" of children and adolescents, rather than providing them a worthwhile adult world in which to grow up. In a curious way, the exaggeration of schooling is both a harsh exploitation of the young, regimenting them for the social machine, and a compassionate coddling of them, since mostly they *are* productively useless and we want them to waste their hours "usefully."

X

At the elementary level, especially in urban conditions, baby-sitting the children is indispensable. The schools both relieve the home and rescue the children from the home. But the criteria for baby-sitting are to be safe and enjoyable; our primary schools are safe enough but not enjoyable.

As a means of socialization and democratization, the primary schools have gone much too far toward regimentation. In my opinion, "good deportment" was always overstressed; but in the present conditions, when school is the only serious business of life and the classes are too crowded, it becomes spirit-breaking or a goad to defiance. And of course, in the new extraordinary pattern of suburbia and central city, the public schools are not even socially and racially mixed or equal in opportunity.

There is far too much bother about getting children to learn a set curriculum and to meet certain standards. Not that children are incapable of learning or do not want to learn; on the contrary, all the evidence is that even average children are capable and desirous of much more intellectual stimulation than they ever get in school, and with bright children this is astoundingly the case. Teachers and adults in general have a responsibility to guess, provide means, offer the new, be available.

But this is entirely different from assigning lessons and demanding performance, as if children did not have natural curiosity and wonder. Elementary schooling illustrates at its worst the human propensity to impose an unnecessary system and make it hard for ourselves, and thereby to lose the goods that are easy. Just nowadays, when we could be on the verge of a leisure culture, we would do well to consult the pedagogy of the Athenians, who were very cultivated citizens: they thought it was enough if the children played games, sang and acted Homer, and were taken around the city to see what went on. (Our word "school" is the Greek word for serious leisure.)

Most of these remarks are commonplaces of progressive education, and we should try that. (In fact progressive education has never been tried in this country, except in a few small schools for a few years.) Curiously, this seems to be the better judgment even of the National Science Foundation.

xi

At the high school level, directly useful real activities would be more cultural than the average classroom for the average youth.

The liberal economists who propose using a larger share of production in the public sector are precisely not thinking of employing 15-year-olds; on the contrary, a chief motive of their plans is to diminish the unemployment of adults. But suppose, for a change, we think of the matter directly, without political overtones: on the one hand, there is a great amount of work that needs doing and has been shamefully neglected; on the other hand, there are millions of young people who could do a lot of it and are otherwise not well occupied. Further, it costs about $1000 a year to keep a youth in high school (and more than $2000 in reform school); suppose we paid this money directly to the youth as he worked on an educative job.

Here are four great classes of youth jobs: construction—e.g. improving the scores of thousands of ugly small towns; community service and social work—like the Friends' Service, or working in understaffed hospitals or as school-aides, or janitoring public housing; assisting in the thousands of little theaters, independent broadcasters, and local newspapers, that we need to countervail the mass-media; and rural rehabilitation and conservation. For educational value for a majority of the young, I would match that curriculum against any four-year high school. By and large, too, these are not the areas proposed for big public works to create employment. Most likely nothing will be done about them at all.

Interestingly enough, the retraining and rehabilitation programs of the Departments of Labor and Justice contain better educational ideas, including schooling, than the direct school-aid bills. Since much of the Federal aid to education has been balked by the parochial school issue, some of the money has been better allotted *not* through the school systems!

Vocational training, including much laboratory scientific training, ought to be carried on as technical apprenticeships within the relevant industries. Certainly the big corporations have a direct responsibility for the future of their young, rather than simply skimming off the cream of those schooled, tested, and graded at the public expense.

Another indispensable part of the education of adolescents is the Youth House, the community of youth. This is miserably handled by the present neighborhood high schools, where there is a continual war of authority among school, home, and peer-group. James Coleman has forthrightly proposed that all high school students should be sent to schools on the other side of town, and if possible to be given room and board there. But again the present tendency is in just the opposite direction; to make the colleges community-colleges and commuting schools, so that the young will never get away on their own.

xii

Thirdly, let me fit these ideas for secondary education into the framework of the colleges and universities.

The original purpose of the State universities and the land-grant colleges was to lead their communities, especially in the mechanical and agricultural arts. In this function, they would be admirable centers of administration and design of the public enterprises mentioned above: town improvement, broadcasting station, rural culture, health and community service. The value of any youth work camp depends on the worth of the project; the departments of the University could design the projects and give university-level guidance. Conversely, the students who come to the State universities would have been already working in the field on these projects, and the State universities could soft-pedal the present compulsory academic program that wastefully leads to 50% flunking.

By the same reasoning, the professional and graduate schools could work far more closely with the working professionals and industries in society, with whom their students would already have served apprenticeships as adolescents. This would avoid the present absurdity of teaching a curriculum abstracted from the work in the field, and then licensing the graduates to return to the field and relearn everything in terms of the actual work. And there would be less tendency for the contracted research that is appropriate to these institutes and professionals to dominate the curricula in all schools.

The liberal arts colleges, in turn, could resume their authentic intellectual tradition of natural philosophy, scholarship, and the humanities, without having to flirt with either narrowly technical research or hotel management. Academic high schools would, in effect, be prep schools for these colleges.

Finally, to fill a bad gap in our present framework of higher education, we need colleges for the altogether non-bookish, who nevertheless want to be informed and cultured citizens and to share in the experience of a college community. A model is to hand in the remarkable Danish Folk-Schools, where youngsters who have left school to go to work can return between the ages of 18 and 25, to learn oral history, current events, practical science and the politics of science, and to act plays and play music.

xiii

These are a few speculations of one mind. My purpose is to get people at least to begin to think in another direction, to look for an organization of education less wasteful of human resources and social wealth than what we have. In reconstructing the present system, the right principles seem to me to be the following: To make it easier for youngsters to gravitate to what suits them, and to provide many points of quitting and return. To cut down the loss of student hours in parroting and forgetting, and the loss of teacher hours in talking to the deaf. To engage more directly in the work of society, and to have useful products to show instead of stacks of examination papers. To begin to decide what should be automated and what must not be automated, and to educate for a decent society in the foreseeable future.

To be candid, I do not think that we will change along these lines. Who is for it? The suburbs must think I am joking, I understand so little of status and salary. Negroes will say I am down-grading them. The big corporations like the system as it is, only more so. The labor unions don't want kids doing jobs. And the new major class of school-monks has entirely different ideas of social engineering.

Nevertheless, in my opinion, the present system is not viable; it is leading straight to 1984, which is not viable. The change, when it comes, will *not* be practical and orderly.

The Community
of Scholars

This Book is for
Benjamin Nelson and Harold Rosenberg,
Two Men of Intellect,
My Friends

CONTENTS

for The Community of Scholars

	Preface	161
I	The Community	167
II	The Corporation	190
III	Society and School	210
IV	Co-ordinative Management	226
V	Academic Personality	248
VI	Youth Subculture	271
VII	Reforms and Proposals	295
VIII	A Simple Proposal	323

PREFACE

In the past couple of years I have visited between thirty and forty colleges. These have included big State universities, liberal arts colleges, experimental colleges, and Ivy League; men's colleges, women's colleges, and co-ed colleges; in the East, in the Middle West, and in the West. My trips have had very various purposes—or pretexts; I really go because they ask me and I love colleges. Sometimes to lead a seminar or teach a class, or to shake up the students of a department, or to discuss building plans, or because I am the author of a text, or to be a "resource" for a Campus Conference, or give a reading, or deliver a ceremonial address; and I have led discussions at, I guess, dozens of Christian unions, chaplains' meetings, student forums, peace actions, and fraternity or sorority after-dinners. On a visit of two or three days I might have half a dozen assignments.

I mention these details because they have given me one kind of experience that might be unusual: at many schools I am likely to sit down to dinner one night with administration, another night with faculty, and a third night with students. The students I invariably enjoy; they are all young, and interesting or pathetic. In the nature of the case, the teachers who invite me are the ones who like me; we have common interests, and we often have good talks. My meals with administration are usually more formal—I am usually invited *pro forma*—and usually we don't see eye to eye. However it is, this triple access gives one a peculiar perspective, for one can bring up at one table a subject that one heard at another.

It was from such experiences that I conceived the idea of this book. When I teach at a school for a longer spell, I am too absorbed in my subject to get a glancing view of the community, yet I am never permanent enough to get into campus politics. But from my many brief and busy visits and from the table talk of students, faculty, and administration with a rather brash stranger, I have gotten a more synoptic view.

ii

This book is a little treatise in anarchist theory. It can be regarded as a footnote to a few sentences of Prince Kropotkin on *The State* (1903):

> With these elements—liberty, organization from simple to complex, production and exchange by guilds, commerce with foreign parts—the towns of the Middle Ages during the first two centuries of their free life became centers of well-being for all the inhabitants, centers of opulence and civilization, such as we have not seen since then. . . . To annihilate the independence of cities, to plunder merchants' and artisans' rich guilds, to centralize the foreign trade of cities into its own hands and ruin it, to seize the internal administration of guilds and subject home trade as well as all manufactures, even in the slightest detail, to a swarm of functionaries—such was the State's behavior in the sixteenth and seventeenth centuries.

Looking at our colleges and universities, historically and as they are, by and large one must say of them what Kropotkin said of the towns that gave them birth.

It is impossible to consider our universities in America without being powerfully persuaded of the principle of anarchy, that the most useful arrangement is free association and federation rather than top-down management and administration. Nowhere else can one see so clearly the opportunities for real achievement so immediately available—for the work is teaching-and-learning and *there* in the school are the teachers and students themselves—and yet so much obstruction, prevention, extraneous regulation and taxation, by management and the goals of management. All the philosophical critics see this and say this—for instance, Veblen, Hutchins, or Taylor—but they have other things in mind; they are interested in higher learning, curriculum, individual development. But I am here interested in the naked constitutional question itself: Is this the most efficient setup? how has it come to be organized this way? how should it be done? how could it be done?

Naturally the schools are tightly involved with the performance, and even more with the style, of the dominant system of society. Any significant reform of them would involve a threat to that dominant system. But that also is very well.

iii

I have chosen continually to put the subject in an historical setting. Each chapter has a little history that leads into what I see and want to say. It is the kind of shaggy history that covers eight centuries in four pages, but I return to it again and again. My reason is as follows.

Our good writers have become mesmerized by the social sciences. The most recent encyclopedic volume, *The American College,* is composed, one essay after another, of sociology, interpersonal relations, cultural anthropology. There is little history, almost no politics, *never* biology (but some lovely economics about underpaid instructors). Now the social sciences are obviously essential in discussing educational communities, but they have one defect: they limit the discussion to the arrangement, communication, and culture-pattern of people as they currently appear. An immense and indispensable advantage of history—or poetry—is that it continually presents to us many other possible human ways of being, which might have other arrangements, communication, and patterns. Nevertheless, these strange habits are also perfectly recognizable to us as human. Therefore what these men did, and failed to do, must in some way be relevant to ourselves. But their experiments in our human nature tend to be omitted from the social sciences.

This has a depressing effect. Our ancient colleges, like our other ancient communities, are in sad shape. If we restrict our study to their contemporary personnel, so to speak, we do not have a very lively prospect, even with the application of the social sciences. If, on the contrary, we see them in a broader arc of history and nature, the future is more ambiguous. There have been ups and downs. The universities have been worse off and have come back handsomely. Like any period, our present has its unique menace. Modern co-ordinative management, itself the product of a long history of administration, is really a lulu. So I have thought it wise in discussing it to recall, especially to students, the spotty glories of the past.

iv

My concern is liberal education, the education of the sons of the free, to be free and exercise initiative in the world they inherit. Many readers will no doubt, then, be surprised at how little mention there is of the liberal-arts curriculum, of the well-rounded course of studies as opposed to specialization, the intellectual as opposed to the practical. These are the usual topics, but I do not think that they are important. Curriculum is always given; it is the sciences, mores, and institutions of our civilization. In every part of it, it is possible to find spirit, for it was created by spirit—how else is anything created? The problem of education is how the scholars are to confront that civilization and make it freely their own. I propose an ancient but neglected invention, the community of scholars. Given it, it does not matter much about the syllabus. Without it, nothing will be learned, though many may get degrees.

This book may seem a little preachy and over-earnest. Yes, I am a loyal university man, and I fear —this also is historically familiar—that our culture is in danger of extinction, etc. My fear is exaggerated.

Nevertheless, there is a serious issue. Harold Rosenberg has said that the most important service that we can perform at present is to expose the scandal of the intellectuals, in the schools, the press, the government, etc., playing along with the forces that are senseless. He is right. When, in writing this book, I copy out the Enlightenment sentences of Kant—that the faculty of philosophy is a watchdog, that the young are educated according to the possible future of mankind—I feel a thrill of pride, in him, and satisfaction that I too urge these sentences the best I can.

Besides, just humanly speaking, these days when so many are going off to college and trying to get into college, it is sad to see so much waste of effort, and even unnecessary torture, of both students and the teachers. We—or *they*—must hit on some way for them to get more out of it than they do.

New York City, March 22, 1962

Chapter 1

THE COMMUNITY

i

The 1,900 colleges and universities are the only important face-to-face self-governing communities still active in our modern society. Two-thirds of them have fewer than 75 teachers and 1,000 students, who live with one another, interact, and continually decide on all kinds of business by their statutes, customs, and social pressures. The rural town-meetings that are left are not so close-knit, and perform only rudimentary functions. The congregational churches have come to play only a supportive Sunday role, not much different from fraternal lodges or clubs. Almost all the other face-to-face self-governing associations that once made up nearly all society—the municipalities, craft guilds, and joint-stock companies—have long since succumbed to centralization, with distant management.

In this book on the colleges,* I want to stress that

---

* I shall use "college" and "university" almost interchangeably. Historically, "colleges" were, usually, originally the endowed residence-clubs of students or teachers of the "university," the guild of scholars. In the course of time, teach-

they are communities, really small *cities,* for they have a heterogeneous population and are cut off from their environments as if walled. At present there is a great expansion of education—at least of the number going to schools—and so there have been many new books about colleges; but I do not know one that concentrates on their community. Yet it is remarkable.

Nor is it accidental. With vicissitudes, this medieval community form has persisted for nearly a thousand years because it is, as I shall try to show, a natural organ for the education of youth into universal culture. When writers neglect it, presumably because they take it for granted, they are likely to miss *the ideal of education, which is for animal and social youth to grow up into men and women practicing that culture.** This culture is a peculiar one, and to learn to practice it,

---

ing was done also in the colleges, and often the university became otiose, a place of formal lectures on outmoded texts. So the "college" took over the function of the "university."

In modern usage, a "university" is sometimes the collection of teaching "colleges," sometimes a grander name for a college when new professional schools are added. Since I shall be discussing the community of scholars in whatever form, these distinctions are irrelevant unless the factors of size or dispersion become important.

* All youth, and not only those who go to scientific and literary colleges and study professions, need face-to-face community in order to grow up. They need adults who are attentive, and they need opportunity for self-government. As I said in *Growing Up Absurd,* in this respect our centralized society is a total failure. Indeed, in the present expansion of "education," many thousands of youngsters are going to academic colleges who ought *not* to be academically educated, yet they *ought* to be going to other kinds of colleges. But there are none. I do not think that the desire of these young people to "go to college" is merely because it gives status. They want and need another structure and identity, that only an objective task and some kind of community can give them.

rather than to have it as either a yoke or an ornament, requires a peculiar initiation.

Our university cities comprise teachers and students —and administrators. I separate the administrators from the scholars because their presence raises the first question I want to ask: What are administrators doing there? how did they get in? In any community there must be a certain number of caretakers and functionaries. But the community of scholars is, or could be, quite moderate in size; historically, except in exceptional cases, the number has hovered between 500 and 1,000, and sometimes we shall be speaking of celebrated universities that numbered 100 people! (It is hard for Americans to grasp this.) Such a community seems to require only a handful of unpretentious administrators—a rector unwillingly elevated from the faculty for a short term, a typist, and a couple of janitors. Instead, in the American colleges, the Administration is a vast army and its President is almost regarded as the college itself. How is this?

Another question—closely related, as we shall see— is: If the universities are as if walled, what are the transactions between such walled cities and the rest of society that has a different organization? The wall itself, the separateness, is inevitable—until society itself becomes an international city of peace. For the culture of the scholars is inevitably foreign: it is international and comprises the past, present, and future. The language, even though the scholars speak English instead of Latin, has different rules of truth and evidence that cannot be disregarded when it happens to be convenient. The scholars come from all parts and do not easily abide the local prejudices. They cannot always fly the national flag.

In my opinion, it is finally this foreignness, this humanism, that makes a university; it is not the level of the studies, the higher learning, the emphasis on theory, or anything like that. In the history of universities, we are continually talking about many whose curriculum was far inferior to even our average high schools; and nevertheless they were universities because they crossed the frontiers. Conversely, of our "1,900 colleges and universities," very many are not foreign cities in this sense, e.g., those that are parochial seminaries for their sects, or trade schools to service the economy; and also the important American "community colleges" that have begun to flourish, especially in the West, to give more advanced training than the high schools. The training may be competent and theoretical, but the schools do not transcend their region nor America. (Indeed, they alarmingly repeat a nationalistic *Hochschule* pattern of imperial Germany and contemporary Russia.) * As such, they precisely do not socialize to the universal and potential culture. They are not universities.

In the nature of the case, enclaves like universities must often be in conflict with the surrounding society. Historically this has continually occurred, in doctrine, morals, politics, standards. It is really necessary to make a strong effort of memory—of ages of credulity, prejudice and establishment—to recall how dissensual the university way has sometimes been. Sometimes the scholars have lost disastrously. Teachers have been muffled and excommunicated, students have been punished and expelled, books have been banned, subsidies have been taken away and the communities have gone under. Being essential, the communities have revived.

---

* A recent event was like an amazing parable. The head of the public college of New York City went west to head a great system of public colleges in California. But he soon returned because he could not see eye to eye with them on what a school was about.

(Indeed, they have often done best for themselves when they have been poor and able to pack up and go elsewhere.) This raises another question: What would be the best, most mutually advantageous, *constitutional* relation between the communities of scholars and society?

The present situation in America is extremely paradoxical. The colleges and universities seem to be wonderfully prospering. Since 1930 the schools having 500-3,000 students have doubled in number; those from 3,000-10,000 have trebled; those with more than 10,000 have also trebled; and the University of California has 120,000 under one administration. But are these big numbers of any use for schools of general studies, communities of scholars? I doubt it. They simply indicate that the techniques of self-aggrandizement that are common in American society are being used with success also by the colleges and are destroying them as communities. Put it this way: there are 1,900 colleges and universities; at least several hundred of these have managed to collect faculties that include many learned and creative adults who are free to teach what they please; all 1,900 are centers of lively and promising youth. Yet one could not name ten that strongly stand for anything peculiar to themselves, peculiarly wise, radical, experimental, or even peculiarly dangerous, stupid, or licentious. It is astounding! that there should be so many self-governing communities, yet so much conformity to the national norm. How is it possible?

Or consider it this way: at present, the organization of American society is an interlocking system of semi-monopolies notoriously venal, an electorate notoriously unenlightened, misled by mass media notoriously phony, and a baroque State waging cold war against another baroque State. The colleges, on their part, are powerful and importantly independent. Between such forces one would expect a continual and electric clash. Instead, there is harmony. It looks like harmony but is really a clinch. The scholars are not acting, not being men; and therefore *within* the communities of scholars, there is very little education or growing up.

It is my thesis that the agent of this clinch is administration and the spread of the administrative mentality among the teachers and even the students. It is the genius of administration to enforce a false harmony in a situation that should be rife with conflict. Historically, the communities of scholars have perennially been invaded by administrators from the outside, by Visitors of king, bishop, despotic majority, or whatever is the power in society that wants to quarantine the virulence of youth, the dialogue of persons, the push of inquiry, the accusing testimony of scholarship. But today Administration and the administrative mentality are entrenched in the community of scholars itself; they fragment it and paralyze it. Therefore we see the paradox that, with so many centers of possible intellectual criticism and intellectual initiative, there is so much inane conformity, and the universities are little models of the Organized System itself.

There is a final question: Will the community of scholars survive its present plague of administrative mentality? The *ultima ratio* of administration is that a school is a teaching machine, to train the young by predigested programs in order to get pre-ordained marketable skills; and teaching machines have, of course, made their appearance. Such training can, and must, dispense with the ancient communities, for they are not only inefficient but they keep erasing or even negating the lessons.* In my opinion, the communities will sur-

* Describing the process of teaching by operant conditioning, Professor B. F. Skinner says, "With these techniques a

vive, as they have in the past. Therefore, my real question is: Will the present colleges survive by reforming themselves and purging their own administrative mentalities; or will the communities again have to renew themselves, as often in the past, by quitting and seceding from their rich properties, and going elsewhere in lawless poverty?

Obviously, these are biased sentences. I am a partisan of the scholars and we are losing badly. But I do not think I am unfair. Administrators, administration-minded faculty, and conformist students are of course inevitable products of a long history and the kind of society we have. On the average, I should not be surprised if the universities are better run than the average graft-ridden municipality or big business firm. Nevertheless, it *is* the case that college administrators have a considerable leeway and freedom of choice, more than ward politicians or corporation executives. And—granting their own mythology—they are professional "educators," not merely politicians or businessmen; they have authority to tell their employers what is best, and not to act like hired hands or members of the wolf

---

new form of behavior can be shaped as a sculptor shapes a lump of clay. In a typical demonstration, a hungry pigeon is permitted to move about in a small enclosed space with transparent walls," etc. That is, the situation is set up so that all interesting, novel, or inventive possibilities of the animal are cut off; and then, for want of any other temptation or excitement, it quickly learns Professor Skinner's program, like a lump of clay. Reduced to a low-grade organism, it responds with low-grade behavior.

The reactions of Dr. Skinner himself, as a pigeon conditioned by our society, are well exemplified by the following: "Since it is difficult to write teaching machine programs, bad programs undoubtedly will be written and marketed, but if the market place has its usual effect, we can look forward to the emergence of highly efficient programs in the not too distant future."

pack. Unhappily, what is best is usually for them to reduce themselves to a fairly modest function, and I suppose that this is against human nature.

But in this chapter, let me invite the reader—perhaps a student or a young instructor at a great state university—to imagine the community of scholars as if it were new, before there were any administrators at all, but only students and teachers, they themselves. Ask, what is it that essentially occurs in teaching and learning at the college level? And imagine the relations of the persons in your community if the community were stripped to the essential.

ii The Act of Commencement

"The universities of all countries and all ages are in reality adaptations under various conditions of one and the same institution." By this famous sentence in *The Universities of Europe in the Middle Ages,* Hastings Rashdall means to refer to a literal historical succession from a tiny number of medieval teaching-learning companies, guilds of either the students or the teachers, "the spontaneous product of that instinct of association which swept over the towns of Europe in the course of the eleventh and twelfth centuries." It is remarkable how from the beginning were perfected the only two possible types of schooling: *Either a youth says Show me How, and finds a teacher who will show him*—this is in principle the professional school of Bologna; *or a thinker professes a truth he knows and a fascinated youth latches onto him and asks What and Why*—this is in principle the school of liberal arts in Paris. Ever since, the thousands of *studia generalia* have combined both principles.

The line has never died out. My own doctorate, from Chicago, traces back mainly through Yale, Cambridge in England, Oxford in England, to the Paris of Abelard. In fact, I would not reason as I do if Abelard had not taught there in the twelfth century. Possibly there were similar institutions in the ancient world—in the brotherhood of Pythagoras, the schools of the Academy, the Peripatetics, the Stoa*—but however it may be, the persistence or reappearance of such a community type means that we are dealing with a "natural" convention, an institution that rather simply fulfills an abiding human function. Consider it genetically.

From the elementary grades, the schools as a whole are civilized society's chief instrument for the planned socializing of its young. This means that they must deal, generation by generation, with persons who are growing, indeterminate, and therefore somewhat unpredictably free. And the teachers who concern themselves with this refractory material are themselves not only dedicated to various humanistic or sectarian ideals and not entirely given to ordinary business, but they cannot help being accomplices of the youth. Even in a maximum-security prison, like that described by Sykes in *The Society of Captives,* the guards, despite a pretty absolute power to control and punish, have to come to terms with the inmates against the world. So from the beginning, the use of schools to socialize also produces

* Like medieval schools, some of these owned their property corporately and, since they sometimes chose their Heads, must have been sometimes self-governing. They were also centers of foreigners and must, therefore, have provided some kind of community. But of course the free town of the Middle Ages did not exist in Greece and Rome in the same way. When the *polis* was free and prosperous, it itself was the most important educational institution—at least Plato and Aristotle thought so. During the centuries of imperial bondage, on the other hand, the great centers of scholarship and rhetoric seem to have been so heavily endowed and controlled by the State that it is dubious if they were free corporations.

separate groups and "subcultures," and thus complicates socialization and makes it, fortunately, imperfect.

With adolescence—for comparison, the age of study at the University of Paris in the thirteenth century was 14-21 years, combining our high school and college— the young turn from their natural families, federate in peer groups or youth houses, and transfer their oedipal affections to strange adults whom they imitate and identify with. They look for philosophies to structure their confusion and for careers in order to take part in the grown-up world. This brings us to the college years of American culture, say 17-21, when we put the finishing touches on the socially advantaged, if not intellectually superior,* youth who will then commence into choosing professions, making marriages, and voting in elections. We can regard the college or university as, primarily, *the institution of the act of Commencement.* (The medieval term was *Inceptio.*) *Commencement is the recognition by one's chosen adults that one has become their peer and can proceed on one's own initiative,* much as a knight used to touch the squire with his sword and say, "Rise, Sir Knight." It involves an examination leading to acceptance, and it involves an initial performance for keeps, not an exercise, e.g., giving a real lecture or defending a new thesis, exactly like any other master-piece of an apprentice.

(During this development, the relation of the teacher

---

* It is unlikely that those who have been going to college, at least in the last several hundred years, are even more "academically talented," unless we mean by this that early exposure to books and bookish discipline, and the incentive to succeed in bookish careers, have made them better passers of bookish tests. Experiments in altering the backgrounds and sharpening the motivations of poor youth have made such striking difference in academic performance that it is probable that the average college-selection has been economic through and through.

to the student is also developing. To put it schematically, the teacher teaches a child and not a subject matter. The teacher teaches an adolescent by means of a subject matter. And he teaches a young man or woman a subject matter. Merely to expound a subject matter is not teaching.)

Even in our times we can see that Commencement is an anthropological rite, celebrated with pomp and parties. The details of the medieval ceremonial show how deeply psychological and communal the act of learning was taken to be, and is. The graduate was given a book, the text to lecture from; a ring, to indicate his sworn fealty to the community of scholars; a hat, to indicate his new status in the world; and the kiss of fellowship by a master, by which he is accepted.* There are traces also of an older, more barbarous significance. For example, in Salamanca, "The candidate for a bachelor's degree . . . was to demand it from the doctor sitting in his *cathedra,* which the doctor would thereupon vacate. The bachelor would take his place and deliver a lecture." (Rashdall.) This looks as if the youth once had to wrest his right by force, to be grown up and prove himself. Even today, many an oral examination reveals a certain savagery that seems to go beyond simply testing for competence; it is the masters'

---

* I cannot agree with Professor Haskins that our continuity with the medieval university "does not lie in academic form and ceremony, in spite of occasional survivals like the conferring of degrees by the ring or the kiss of peace, but in the 'institutions' of curriculum, examinations, and degrees." Those institutions are, rather, the academic organs *of* the Commencement, which is the soul: the marriage, the acceptance, the initial performance: the ring, the kiss, and the thesis. One has new identity, a hat, as a way of life in the world. Professor Haskins is wiser when he says that the university is not made of buildings and libraries—nor syllabi and degrees—but it is "built of men," of personal relations.

last chance to take revenge for the fact that they are getting old! One of the oath-bound obligations of the students at Bologna, which was a guild of professional students, was "the attendance and escort of our *doctorandi* to and from the place of examination," as if a young fellow needed protection in such a plight. Psychoanalytically, if entering upon learning during these years is the transfer of oedipal affections, the trial of equal prowess is a means of getting rid of the transference in order to be a free person. It must, then, *be* a trial. The process of academic association must become more and more for keeps, in order to dissolve fantasies by reality. Our own colleges are, on the whole, miserably timid and tame for this.

In an interesting essay in *The American College,* Joseph Katz speaks of the disappointment of the teacher when the alumnus returns and has evidently given up his "rebelliousness"; he has "betrayed" the teacher. But if this occurs, it is because the teacher was not himself a man for real, in the community and in the outside world. The college should have increasingly dissolved the transference. Coping with people who were not merely academic but for real would prevent the later "adjustment," which is nothing but a return to infantile slavishness, now slavish to society because growing up has failed. It is the college that has betrayed the student.

iii

Let us spell out the characteristics of a community of scholars as the organ of intellectual education. Who are the people and how do they live together?

1. Teaching and learning are a personal relation; it is necessary for *both* the student and the teacher. When the tradition is pure, it is a *teaching* master who offers

the kiss or handshake, no matter what dean or chancellor hands out the diploma "by the authority in him vested." For the student the relation is one of identification. As the 1915 code of the American Association of University Professors puts it well: "It is not only the character of the instruction but the character of the instructor that counts. If the student has reason to believe that the instructor is not true to himself, the education is incalculably diminished."

For the student it is an erotic relation as well. Recent studies reviewed by Robert Knapp show that to the student the excellence of a teacher depends on his "interest in students," "fairness," "sympathy," "helpfulness," "sincerity," and "enthusiasm"—about in that order.

It is not surprising, on the other hand, that these students' choices of excellence correlate highly with teachers' ratings of one another in terms of "research" and "originality." The good man *must* teach. This is in part because of a kind of narcissism, by which the skilled artisan needs to show off his skill in his person as well as in his products. More important, perhaps, is the *noblesse oblige* of the strong and competent man, that makes it impossible for him to see the others fumble in ignorance. And also, whatever one's art, just as one received it, so one has to pass it on, if possible improved. As an erotic drive, teaching seems to be a projection of one's own ego ideal, seen as more possible in the young than in oneself; therefore it would tend to be homosexual, in both sexes; but in our culture, of course, not very physical, especially among the males.

Teaching is also said to be an indispensable creative spur for scientists and scholars (in my experience it is less so for artists and men of letters). There is a well-known remark of Veblen's: "Only in exceptional cases will good, consistent, sane, and alert scientific work be carried forward through a course of years by any scientist without students, without loss or blunting of that intellectual initiative that makes the creative scientist." He speaks of the "stimulus and safeguarding that come of the give and take between teacher and student," and Paulsen too, in a similar discussion, stresses the sanity and safeguarding. One has the impression that such scientists are obsessional and a little nutty. Certainly in the eighteenth and early nineteenth centuries, scientists managed to find a community for themselves in adult scientific academies. But I am convinced by the poignant observation of a famous architect and revered teacher of architecture: he needs to teach, he says, because with his students he can propose the ideal solutions of problems, rather than the routine compromises that he must submit to in the world as it is.

2. To his students the elder is a Veteran. He has demonstrated the way of learning in the world. He proves that it can be done. First of all, this may require a proof of moral courage, of loyalty to the university standard of evidence. "Those of us who were at the University of California during the loyalty oath troubles," says Joseph Adelson, "had a unique opportunity to observe how the moral qualities of our teachers could assume overweening importance. It taught us on the one hand that moral courage is possible, and on the other hand that it is uncommon."

But the Veteran is more than a courageous academic; he speaks and applies the university's authority in the world. Let me quote an ancient statute of Alfonso the Wise: "If a doctor of civil law enters a court of justice, the judge is to rise and invite him to a seat on the bench." But more important, this authority resided not in the individual learned man, but in the community of scholarship. For centuries the *faculties* of the great universities "were consulted again and again on vital questions of doctrine and law, and were expected to state their findings and intervene in ecclesiastical and social affairs." (Richard Hofstadter.) It is astounding, and melancholy, that this is just what our modern schools never do. In America, individual professors are free to speak out in public, but the department or the college as such does not commit itself. To the student this must mean that there is no college, but only a framework of courses and buildings.

Most simply, the teachers are Veterans because the doctors and masters are the important professionals and writers in society who *return* to teach. They have the mastery that comes from actual practice, but they teach with the ideality of the future. The teaching professional is neither "academic" nor "tough." The archetype is the Physician: he is still called "the doctor" by the world, but on the other hand we expect, if he is a great man, that he will be teaching at a medical school. Conceive him at the hospital with students, and the event has a curious duality: as an artist he is treating an individual patient; as a teacher he is demonstrating a universal pathology and a scientific method.

(To my mind it is here that the immensely proliferating "contractual research" in the natural sciences is a virulent threat to the community of scholars. It presents a puzzling problem. The idea of scientific inquiry in a university is that the teacher, as an authority, pursues his own researches, taking his students with him, as assistants and finally junior partners; and maybe it is the more inspiring if the research is socially important and is sought for. But this very easily turns into the entirely different situation that the scientist is being paid to pursue some outsider's project—he must produce applicable results; he cannot follow where the inquiry leads; and he cannot question the use to which his intellect is put. Then the student knows that he is no longer in contact with the *master;* and he sees that intellect can be bought, a lesson for which one does not need to go to college. The issue is not whether social need, either beneficent or maleficent, leads to scientific discovery—of course it does—but whether it belongs in the university. When there is a moderate amount of contracting, and the projects are social needs that might spontaneously interest a master, then no problem arises; but when the contracting comes to 25 per cent of the operating budgets of all the colleges, and there are "crash" programs, whether to make war or cure cancer, we become suspicious that science is not free. A similar "contractual" attitude has invaded the social sciences and the humanities, in Russian, African, and Far Eastern "Institutes" which are organs of foreign policy, in Applied Anthropology, in much of the teaching of languages. And in all these subsidized programs, many students take part not because of concern or aptitude but because of the profitable setup.)

3. The guild, whether of students or masters, is the home and brotherhood of its members. As a model, here is a statute from Bologna from which I quoted above: The students swear to each other "fraternal charity, mutual association and amity, the consolation of the sick and support of the needy, the conduct of funerals and the extirpation of rancor and quarrels, the attendance and escort of our *doctorandi* to and from the place of examination, and the spiritual advantage of members." (*Acta* of the German "Nation" at Bologna.)

The scholars, both students and masters, have often been foreigners and their community has provided them with an artificial citizenship in the alien country, as well as protection against the local police. As I stressed above, this makes the communities little cities, places of international and universal culture, rather than indigenous villages. Traditional English and American college paternalism is also protective, but it has the disadvantage—I think a fatal one—of discouraging growing up out of tutelage. We shall see how Jefferson tried to solve this problem at the University of Virginia. The worst possible arrangement, however, is not uncommon in our present American colleges: the college exercises paternal control over the students but then, when trouble arises, it does not protect them from the local police!

With the rise of the national states, of course, the internationalism of the schools suffered a terrible blow. It was a bad day for mankind when, in the time of Hus, the nationalistic Germans seceded from Prague to Leipzig. Yet it has always been felt that the schools must be exogenous. Paulsen boasts that students at least from all over Germany come to every German school; and the admissions policy in American colleges has been to gather students from all parts of the United States. (When just now the provincial Legislature of Colorado wants to restrict the out-of-staters to 20 per cent, the University is protesting it as anti-intellectual.) And now, finally, after so many centuries, we are returning to One World again, and every college again has a beginning sprinkling of many nations and colors.

4. But this international community is also tightly local and mean in size. Until the ruinous gigantism of recent times, the colleges and universities have tended to grow rather by splitting up than by accretion. Except for Paris, which numbered perhaps 5,000, the medieval universities numbered a few hundred to a thousand. The best-known liberal arts colleges in America have between 600 and 1,200 persons. At Harvard, as part of the larger whole, Professors Jencks and Riesman have recently proposed self-governing Houses of 500. With this moderate size and localism, once there

began to be endowed colleges and regular lecture halls, the schools developed their characteristic community planning, the pretty yards, quadrangles, and campuses that have made the colleges the best examples of neighborhood planning in the modern world, and which every city planner ought to imitate. It is lively planning because it directly expresses the real functioning of face-to-face communities. There is no technical reason why a city neighborhood should not be a campus with the physics building replaced by a factory for light manufacture and the library by the local movie.

The term *studium generale* meant at first simply "a place where students from all parts were received." Conversely, a master who has undergone Commencement in one of these international communities has the right to teach at any other, *ius ubique docendi*. Naturally the international authorities, Emperor or Pope, or the national or state authorities, contend that it is they who grant this license to teach; but historically it has been granted *a consuetudine,* by the custom of the scholars. (I have been told that my own doctorate entitles me to enter any college, hire a hall, and lecture for what fees I can get. I don't know, I've never tested it.)

5. But *studium generale* means also a school of general studies, where are gathered the learned professions and the Inferior Faculty of arts. The idea is not, and never was, that a student should study everything and not "specialize"; but rather that *specialization should occur in a community of general studies, a little city.* Let us take it to mean: all possible Man, past, present, and future. The specialists learn to communicate by talking to one another.

I think this is why it has historically come about that the Inferior Faculty, of liberal arts or philosophy, has continued to be the core of the colleges, even when there have been no professional schools. This faculty seems, in some special sense, to meet the need of the community of growing up. It teaches the language of intellectual discourse and the nature (and limits) of the different kinds of evidence used by the other studies.

It has, correspondingly, been the faculty of criticism and dissent. As Kant wonderfully expressed it during the French Revolution, in *The Conflict of the Faculties:* "The superior Faculties, so to speak the Right of the parliament, defend the statutes of the Government. But there must also be in a free constitution a party of opposition, the Left, the bench of the Faculty of philosophy. Such a conflict can lawfully exist if there is an agreement between the citizens [!] and the community of scholars on maxims . . . that can lead at last to the suppression of all limitations imposed on the freedom of public thought by arbitrary power." This is a thrilling thought, of the alliance of the liberal artists and the citizens against the powers that be.

6. Naturally there is a polar extreme from this universalist responsibility and spiritual freedom, that is also necessarily a part of the community of scholars: plain youthful and animal unrestraint, springtime excesses that have been perennial and brawls with the Town that have been pretty bad. Often this energy has expressed itself—or clothed itself (it comes to the same thing)—in dissenting social politics and has spearheaded riots. Away from home and governed only by themselves or adult accomplices, and being out of the domestic and economic mainstream, collegians are indeed indeterminately free. Extramural sports are sham battles of the same origin; being combative, they intensify the feeling of boundary and heighten local patriotism. It is grim that it is just this single aspect of community identity—out of all the possibilities of being

great and proud of oneself—that the American college presidents and alumni have emphasized.

Intramurally, animal liberty takes the expected anthropological form of hazing, to lick the newcomers into community shape, for the freshmen are really nothing but beasts (typically boars) or criminals. And social liberty consists in ridiculing or playing with the studies and lampooning the masters or shouting them down.*

7. The community of scholars is self-governing and has never ceased to regard itself as such. In the twelfth century it is the masters who decide who commences; the chancellor is obliged to come across with the license. And in the most recent and admired manual of Administration, *The Governance of Colleges and Universities,* 1960, John Corson expresses his astonishment at the "ambitious" claims of faculties to have a "comprehensive competence in educational policy."

The students also are self-governing. In the student guilds, like Bologna, students decided the academic policy and held the doctors to a very strict accounting.

---

* Cf., Huizinga in *Homo Ludens:* "The whole function of the medieval university was profoundly agonistic and ludic. The everlasting discussion which took the place of our learned discussions in periodicals, etc., the solemn ceremonial which is still such a marked feature of university life, the grouping of scholars into *nationes* [he means in places where there was no longer an international student body in fact], the divisions and subdivisions, the schisms, competition and play-rules. Erasmus was fully aware of this when he complains . . . of the narrowness of the Schools which deal only with material handed down by their predecessors and ban any point of view in a controversy that does not conform to their own particular tenets. 'In my opinion,' he says, 'it is quite unnecessary to act in the schools as if any infringement of the rules spoils the game. In a learned discussion, there should be nothing outrageous or risky in putting forward a new idea.' "

In the masters guilds, like Paris, the students governed themselves socially and physically in their *nationes*. Sometimes there has been a democratic meeting of both masters and students on all policies, as at Orléans or for a period at Oxford. (Black Mountain College was such a community college.)

The community has occasionally claimed absolute ownership of the property, by-passing bishops or trustees. In the early poor years, this gave them the right simply to pack up and emigrate; but the claim has persisted even when there has been a considerable establishment. Coleridge must be thinking of Oxford and Cambridge when he says, "Those who exercise these [academic] functions possess collectively an indefensible title to a portion of the common wealth." John Bracken asserted the title against the Visitors at William and Mary when he claimed that a teacher had a freehold tenure in the corporation, the argument which Daniel Webster repeated for the teachers of Dartmouth College against the State of New Hampshire. And of course the claim of tenure in at least the professorship is now agreed upon in America, though not always honored.

But indeed, in these communities there is also a persistent *underground* tradition of having no government at all! they are all little anarchies and would as lief decide everything *ad hoc* and unanimously.* Dean Rashdall, who was constitutionally minded, is con-

---

* Unanimity is a hard idea for the modern democrat. Prof. Hofstadter says, "The idea of corporate action . . . implies some sacrifice of individual independence." Not necessarily. Reasonable people who respect each other and have the same ultimate aim are likely to agree. The historian concedes, "As in so many relations of medieval life, the interplay between corporate power and individual freedom was complex." But I doubt that "individual" freedom existed as a thirteenth-century (or classical) motive.

tinually puzzled by this in describing the early centuries. E.g., "If the studium of Oxford was in full working order by 1184 or earlier (1167), while no Chancellor was appointed till 1214, how were the masters and scholars governed?" Maybe they weren't. Or again, in Paris, "the intellectual ferment was most vigorous, the teaching most brilliant, the monopoly of the highest education most complete, almost before a university existed at all." Or again—in a most poignant sentence for our topic in this book—"It was not till 1289 that the university required the names of the students to be inscribed. When a dispute arose as to whether a captured clerk was entitled to university privileges, *the sole question was whether any of the masters would claim him as a pupil*." (Italics mine.)

We need not go back to ancient days. In my own memory I have known examples of a faculty expelling a president as if by right, and of student strikes and protests forcing the expulsion of presidents.

Thus, there is nothing outlandish or untraditional about that eerie sentence with which Veblen ends *The Higher Learning in America*: "The academic executive and all his works are anathema, and should be discontinued by the simple expedient of wiping him off the slate; and the governing board, in so far as it presumes to exercise any other than vacantly perfunctory duties, has the same value and should be lost in the same shuffle." How many an apparently sober professor would secretly agree with this! I do not think that there are any other institutions of established society in which a subversive anarchy is quite so near the surface as in the faculties of colleges. And the students ready to follow hard after.

iv

Taking a clue from the historian's bold remark that "in all countries and all ages" it is in reality the same institution, I have tried quickly to portray this community of scholars.

It is anarchically self-regulating or at least self-governed; animally and civilly unrestrained; yet itself an intramural city with an universal culture; walled from the world; yet active in the world; living in a characteristically planned neighborhood according to the principles of mutual aid; and with its members in oath-bound fealty to one another as teachers and students. This community is the institution of the ritual act of Commencement, the climax of growing up intellectually.

This interesting picture indeed portrays a kind of fact; the Commencement has actually been performed, and it continues to be performed. Nevertheless, our picture is, historically, entirely unreal. The reality of colleges and universities has always—except in momentary flashes that are almost like theophanies—involved a very different set of characters besides the scholars we have mentioned. They are bishops, chancellors, state regents, commissioners of education, trustees, presidents, provosts, deans, and many more. And although, often in fact and sometimes in law, one can reasonably say that the community of scholars *is* the university, we also have to say that the board *is* the university or even, in America, that the president is the university. This is a strange situation.

Chapter II

THE CORPORATION

i The Charter

We have been describing a simple association of students and teachers influencing society by its learning and professional work. In fact, it is always under the direction, regulation, or sufferance of ecclesiastics, state Regents,* lay trustees. Apparently the university was born free and everywhere it is in chains. We must ask Rousseau's question: How does this happen?

The question is important. *For supposing some teachers and students get together to teach and learn: unless they are empowered by their charter, they cannot grant proper degrees. Without proper degrees, the graduates cannot get professional licenses.*

Perhaps the answer is self-evident: every part of society is under the regulation of all society, that sets

* There is a whole history in the fate of the word "regents." Originally the *regentes* were the teaching masters who ruled the guild. In the course of time, when the "university" lectures became otiose and teaching fell to the colleges, the regents became precisely the non-teachers who still ruled the guild. Finally they were not even part of the community, and they still ruled the guild.

standards; and the chancellors, regents, and trustees are the responsible officials. But this idea of a sovereign Leviathan is a prejudice a few centuries old. As W. H. Crowley has put it, in explaining the peculiar dual authority in the colleges, "The problem grows out of the fact that about four centuries ago the paramountcy of the civil state became clear." (Became "clear" by means of cannon.) And if we go back four centuries earlier, to the period of ecclesiastical control, when Dean Rashdall asks in puzzlement about early Oxford, "Did the masters conduct the inception of new masters on their own responsibility?"—since there was no bishop to grant the license—the answer might be, Yes. Who else's responsibility was pertinent?

Or perhaps the answer is financial: the scholars live off society, so society must underwrite and sponsor them. But if we think of the simple university, strong in its poverty, there is no such financial necessity. Students who must learn will always get the money to pay for their learning. We still retain the ideal image of the poor student in his garret—but significantly, the contemporary American variation is the Beat youth living in voluntary poverty, reading paperbacks but unable to find a university to latch onto. Masters, on the other hand, must teach. They do not need charters and endowments.

But the chief argument for the sponsors is really a mystical one: that a corporation must have a charter of powers from the sovereign, otherwise it is nothing at all. As Chief Justice Marshall said in the Dartmouth College Case, "A corporation is an artificial thing, invisible, intangible, and existing only in contemplation of Law. Being the mere creature of law, it possesses only those properties which the charter of its creation confers upon it."

It was this unchartered nothing at all, let us remember, that produced in Paris "the most vigorous intellectual ferment, the most brilliant teaching, the most complete monopoly of the highest education." A functioning corporation is neither fictitious nor intangible, and is artificial only in the sense that its persons associate to produce it; it is a joint effort, like the community of scholars, that institutionalizes itself with customs and rules in order to carry on more securely and permanently. To say it darkly, the sovereign horns in on a going concern to put a stamp on it and collect a tax, and to allay the public anxiety lest a body exist that makes important pretensions and is not officially regulated. As Maitland put it in 1910: "It has become difficult to maintain that the State makes corporations in any other sense than that in which the State makes marriages when it declares that people who want to marry can do so by going, and cannot do so without going, to church or registry." I think he would extend the analogy to teaching and learning.* That is, the State can recognize, control, perhaps protect; fortunately, it cannot always altogether prevent.

It is, of course, useful to be legitimate, to be able to appear in court and market according to the common ground-rules and to have the proud seal of a vested right in the commonwealth. By and large, however, I doubt that it is these civil advantages that have led, over the centuries, to the immense horde of con-

---

* Cf. another of Maitland's instances: "Ignorant men on board the *Mayflower* may have thought that, in the presence of God and of one another they could covenant and combine themselves into a 'civil body politic.' Their descendants know better. A classical definition has taught that 'a Corporation is a Franchise' and a franchise is a portion of the State's power in the hands of a subject." (*Introduction to Gierke's Political Theories.*) Teaching and learning would certainly fall somewhere between the instance of Marriage and the instance of the *Mayflower*.

trollers and administrators that nowadays *are* the colleges. It has been conflict. Conflict, and accommodation, between the communities of scholars and the powers of the world. And the accommodation is proving more fatal than the conflict.

First, throughout the centuries there have been direct clashes, with bishop, king, sheriff, merchant, or state, on matters of orthodoxy, nationalism, absolutism, moralism, fundamentalism, capitalism, militarism, statism and conformism. In such contests with giants, a small community can sometimes win by striking or stalling or making too much trouble, or cleverly playing one big power against another. An ingenious, and perhaps ingenuous, dodge that worked for a time was to say, with the Averroists, that there was a Double Truth: the University truth did not attack true belief, it did not apply—while the scholars prepared new mines. On the whole, the powers have never succeeded entirely in scattering the communities of scholars and consolidating the fragments; and indeed, in succeeding generations, the conflicts have been renewed and the scholars have been proved to be in the right. Usually, however, and in the short run almost always, the external authorities, being stronger, exert their will, punish, fire, and burn books.

Often in such cases "peace" is re-established by grafting *onto* the community some new official, or by imposing new rules and strengthening the existing officials to enforce them. (I shall give some typical illustrations.) And of course such pacification is often accompanied by lavish gifts and privileges for the Corporation, that are quite irrelevant to the community of teaching and learning, but that do seduce it. And so the gulf widens between the community and its Corporation, between the function and the form. As Corson puts it, "Especially in larger institutions, there is a widening gap between the officers and the 'working faculty.' " *

Probably more important than such direct two-way clashes, however, has been the simple greed endemic in all ecclesiastic, political, and economic power, to be still stronger, whether to save more souls, to train more soldiers, or to train more apprentices and sell more textbooks. If teaching-and-learning is importantly going on, somebody will jealously take it over like any other profitable territory, no different from licensing procreation or protecting work and trade. Then, of course, it is given out that without the benevolent sponsorship of these pirates, the natural or social function could not possibly be performed, and the public would not be safe. "Education is one of the major phases of government. It places a larger number of persons under the direct tutelage of the State than any other agency." (John Norton, of Teachers College.) And we are solemnly told that the contractual research now practiced in the universities is indispensable for the advancement of science. Inevitably, when non-educational purposes are imposed on the educational community, there is a further addition of non-teachers and non-students.

But in the long run, even more disastrous to the community has been the imitation within the corporation itself of the styles and motivations of the extramural powers. The college itself becomes a big power and eats up as much as it can, with a galloping multiplication of administrators to co-ordinate the dinner. This is what Veblen was criticizing. But it is not a process peculiar to the times of robber barons and business methods. The history of statism in the ad-

* Cf., Earl Latham of Amherst, "Administrative absurdity increases directly with the square of the distance between context and process."

mired German universities—stemming from the state-endowed professorships of the earliest years—is unerringly reflected in the kind of rules that the Herren Professoren willingly accept and impose. The Dominican genius for putting out the fire of a dangerous idea by introducing lofty irrelevancies—invented in Paris—is still rampant in the style of tolerant bigotry of our American Catholic universities, and inspires even learned journals like *Time*. Oxford and Cambridge in England have been peculiar masterpieces of how to imitate the pomp of a paternalistic Establishment and, loaded with privileges and architecture, to keep one's mouth shut. I have mentioned the above four styles—business methods, statism, putting out the fire, and Establishment—because they are still powerful in contemporary America, in the community-destroying administrative mentality that is the subject of this book.

Our times also have made an important contribution to the academic style: top-down co-ordination or, as it is called, democracy by consent.*

ii Conflict and Pacification

Since the theme of conflict and administrative peace is so important for our discussion, let me, before tak-

* Cf., "In the schools, as in so many other aspects of Middletown's life, criticism of individuals or creakings in the system are met primarily not by changes in the foundation but by adding fresh stories to its superstructure. If teaching is poor, supervisors are employed and 'critic teachers' are added. . . . Between superintendent and teacher is a galaxy of principals, supervisors of special subjects, directors of vocational education and home economics, deans, attendance officers, and clerks, who do no teaching but are concerned with keeping the system going. Thus, in personnel as well as in textbooks and courses of study, strains or maladjustments are met by further elaboration and standardization." (Robert Lynd.)

ing leave of "all countries and all ages," give some tiny histories of a few of the older styles of administering.

Archetypically, in Paris, says Rashdall, "It was the necessity of mutual support and united opposition to the Chancellor [of the Cathedral] which called into existence the university organization." (This was the community that had brilliantly functioned when it did not "exist.") Later, during the thirteenth century, when the university was a hot-bed of Abelardian skepticism and Arabian and Aristotelian rationalism, "the mendicant orders early perceived the necessity of getting a hold upon the centers of education." This led to a bitter struggle, the expulsion of the friars, the excommunication of the masters. But suddenly there was a new harmony: "the mendicants triumphed, but the university too got what it had been contending for"—the university was "consolidated," it was made financially strong, its constitution was confirmed; and "it was from that time," says Rashdall in another context, "that the scholastic method became distinguished by that servile deference to authority with which it has been in modern times too indiscriminately reproached." Another couple of centuries pass and "The effect of nationalization combined with the growth of centralization and absolutism, destroyed the influence of the university beyond the borders of the French church. . . . The great scholastic democracy of the Middle Ages could not live in the France of Henry IV. The functions of the congregation were transferred to what was called the tribunal: the rector, the 4 proctors, and the 3 deans. The university passed into an aggregate of colleges and the colleges of artists sank . . . into mere boarding-schools for boys."

In Oxford, as in Paris, it was a quarrel, between John and the Pope, that led in 1214 to the first administration. Typically, the conflict ended in a "victory" for the corporation over the town and the important gift of the Loan Chest. The bloody Town-Gown of 1355 again ended in a "complete victory," this time accorded by both king and church: "There were fresh privileges for the university, fresh humiliations for the town. The assize of bread, wine and ale, weights and measures, the punishment of both clerks and laymen for carrying arms—all these matters were placed under the exclusive jurisdiction of the Chancellor [the President of the University]." In brief, as the historian says in another context, "There seems to have been hardly any limit to the extent to which the private life of citizens and scholars was liable to regulation in the Chancellor's court." The critical period for old Oxford came, however, in the next century, with Wyclif and Lollardy, when in 1408 and 1410 the students and young masters rose, defied Archbishop Arundel, forced their own Chancellor to resign, and actually fortified the campus. This was one of the human moments in the idiot history of humanity. But the King was too strong. "The issue of the struggle, in 1414, closes the history of Lollardism as a force in English politics and with it the intellectual history of medieval Oxford." The Chancellor became a permanent, rather a biennial, officer, and the Chancellorship, "once the symbol and organ of academic autonomy, became practically the symbol and organ of subjection." And typically, "It is curious to observe how the fifteenth century is the era of 'university buildings.' It is more than an accidental coincidence that this was about the period at which the universities began to lose their independence. In their poverty had been their strength." To give a later stage of the Oxford style of Establishment futility, let me quote from another historian, Richard Hofstadter. Describing the total eclipse in the seventeenth century, he says, "As Chancellor of Oxford after 1629, Laud patronized it liberally with one hand while doing his best to suppress its remaining freedoms with the other. He enriched it with benefactions, adorned it with buildings, and at the same time assumed that it would be 'an institution of orthodoxy, decorous, disciplined, and correct.' From its vice-chancellor he required a detailed weekly report of the discipline and doctrine, for there was hardly a matter so small as to be beneath his notice."

The German universities, by contrast, were controlled from their beginnings by the colleges of masters endowed, and controlled, by princes. Thereby the German professional specialization was established very early—we saw how Kant's claim for the Inferior Faculty of philosophy, because the Superior Faculties "defend the statutes of the government," was a cry of the French Revolution. Inevitably, too, nationalism disrupted university cosmopolitanism very early. In later ages, the pattern of state control and professors has simply persisted (and somewhat crossed the Atlantic to us). For example, the Privat-Dozent, the unsubsidized teacher who, with his following of paying students, is "the living survival of the original French form of the University, in which the faculties, as autonomous teaching corporations, perpetuated themselves" (Paulsen) is precisely not part of the official voting organization. (Freud, with his young band, is an interesting case of a master who could not, in Germany, become an *Ordinarius*.) Then it is no surprise that when German philosophy came to proclaim its famous doctrine of Academic Freedom, of *Lernfreiheit* and *Lehrfreiheit,* it imposed on itself the following ground-rules: "It is necessary to place one restriction, if not upon the thinker, at least upon the teacher appointed by the State and supported by the public funds: he must assume a positive attitude toward the State." (Paulsen.) But this meant, of course, every empowered professor in Germany. Paulsen continues, "Scholars cannot and should not engage in politics. Scientific research is their business . . . and they are bound to develop a habit of theoretical indifference, whereas practical activity, and practical politics particularly, demands a determination to follow one path." * In recent years, this doctrine has given us the atom bomb and continues to improve it with impeccable professionalism.

iii Counterforces

When we consider little histories like the above (and they are typical), we are forced to ask the opposite kind of question: How is it that the communities of scholars haven't been *entirely* swallowed up and consolidated? There have been social counterforces. It is in fact the common sentiment, and has been the common law, that education is something distinct and special and must not be altogether enlisted in the direct service of the sovereign or made to conform to the popular style and mores.

* It is amusing to notice how this philosophical ruling has been transformed in its immigration to America, where we have a different tradition of citizenly freedom. The rule of the American Association of University Professors is that the teacher may engage in politics but "he should make every effort to indicate that he is not an institutional spokesman," for that might embarrass the Image of the corporation. Cf., "The widespread distrust of dissensual knowledge is at the core of the university's 'public relations' problem." (Frank Pinner.) "Such faculty policies [of defending radicalism among teachers] tend to reinforce the isolation of faculties from publics to which colleges must look for support; they add difficulty to administrators' task of coordinating the activities within their institutions with outside groups." (! Corson's *Governance*. This book, underwritten by the Carnegie Corporation, is a real lead-mine.)

In primary education, it has always been felt in America that the school boards should be elected separately from the executive, or at least given a special long tenure, like a high court, free of political pressure. Education is "one of the major phases of government," yet to some degree the State must keep hands off even the elementary grades. The schools, like churches or charities, are exempted from ordinary taxes, and there is currently a general sentiment that tuition fees should be deductible from income, something like primary subsistence.

There is a strong sentiment for local control. E.g., the Regents of the State of New York, established in 1784, were empowered to determine standards for the local schools and to help finance them, but by no means to teach or administer. Jefferson, we shall see, tried to decentralize the local districts even more than was reasonable. When Horace Mann and Henry Barnard crusaded in the nineteenth century against the shameful local neglect, they tried to inspire a more catholic vision but not to centralize control. It is only in the most recent years, in the proposals of social engineers like Dr. Conant, that the dominant style of "centralized efficiency" is taken for granted; yet at this very moment the new reformed Board of Education of New York City is thinking to revive the defunct local boards of the metropolis.

What is the meaning of this localism? It is felt that primary education is something "natural," family-like, psychological, grass-roots, and indeed religious even when secular. Children must not be entirely co-ordinated. The private home will not completely give up its claim to the children—including usually the claim to be as stupid as the day is long. But also, the parents dumbly want for the children a "better" future than the dominant present, including courses in Art and

Music Appreciation. They seem to feel, with Kant, that, "Children should be educated not for their present condition but for the possibly improved future state of the human race, that is, according to the idea of Humanity." Naturally, they translate this to mean that they want their children to make more money than they themselves do, and to be more moral.

The colleges and universities have, in people's feelings, even more right to be special and to waste time on useless subjects. I do not think this is, or ever was, *merely* an elite conception; it has been rather—among the upper class too—an intuition that there are humanities superior to power and success, though they are strictly for Sunday. Legislatures and fundamentalist churches may rage, but few would bluntly deny that there is such a thing as academic freedom. Professors must be allowed to dissent. And as Veblen pointed out, there is among modern people a kind of mystical reverence for Inquiry, idle curiosity. Also there is a belief, grounded partly in this mysticism and partly in abject submission to the vitality of adolescence, that the colleges will, or should, lead us onward and upward. People would piously agree with John Dewey that "at the best, political methods of reconstructing society are compromised by the fact that they are used with those whose habits are largely set, while education of youth has a fairer and freer field of operation." And the Supreme Court of the United States has spoken: "To regard teachers—from the primary grades to the university—as the priests of our democracy, is not to indulge in hyperbole." (Justice Frankfurter.)

It was because of sentiments like these, I think, that the schools were thought to belong properly to the Church. Education, like the Church, dealt with both the natural-creaturely and the spiritual; whereas civil duties and social ambitions belonged to the State. It was not untoward for the Pope and Chancellor to horn in on the tonsured universities; and in this country, Jonathan Edwards was pretty accurate when he said, "The original and main design of colleges was to train up persons for the ministry. Care should be taken that these societies be so regulated that they should be nurseries of piety, otherwise they are fundamentally ruined."

The ecclesiastic power, however, is like any other social power, and from the beginning the community of scholars resisted it, with strikes and expulsions, risking excommunication. *Ad cathedram non pertinet studentium societas:* the community of scholars does not belong to the Cathedral! Paris and Bologna were "founded" without bishop (or king); and Oxford managed to slip into existence, so to speak, when the see of Lincoln was vacant. The universities helped to bring on the Reformation, but then, when the churches were nationalized, it was necessary to attack the government, e.g., Kant: "It is absolutely necessary that the public scientific institution at the University include a Faculty which, independent of the government in its doctrine, has the liberty of giving judgment on everybody whose business contains a scientific part; a place where Reason is authorized to speak out." In America too there was an early restiveness against the control of both church and state. It could be said that the birth of Harvard as a dissenting and democratic community occurred because Increase Mather neglected it and went abroad; while at William and Mary, the faculty extended its freedom by appealing against the Visitors to its Chancellor, a Bishop who lived in London 3,000 miles away.

iv

In this popular sentiment and its history, there is implied a peculiar constitutional relation between the community of scholars and society. Let us try to formulate it. Like the Church, the scholars are special and (ideally) free in society, for they are concerned with matters prior to society and beyond society. Education, concerned with socialization itself, cannot be socialized; and the future of mankind cannot be socialized. But unlike the Church, the scholars do not (ideally) have dogma or mortmain on property and they do not wield a coercive power. As Kant said, they have an "agreement" with the citizens: to free the mind. Also the scholars are this-worldly, not magicians: their rite is the Commencement into society, and the intellectual virtues are active in society.*

* "This-worldly" needs emphasis. For there is a crypto-clericalism that creeps in when one speaks of the intellectual virtues or even, like Veblen, of the higher learning. E.g., the idea of Robert Hutchins is a poor one and quite unhistorical, that "all that can be learned in a university is the general principles, the fundamental propositions, the theory of any discipline." At its best the university has taught also the practice of that theory, through the practical intellect, the moral example, and the public activity of the masters and doctors; and apart from such practice, there are not such principles or propositions.

Hutchins is partly reacting, correctly, to narrow utility, the endless training of marketable skills, often outmoded by the time the youth commences. But I fear that he also has never understood what the active intellect is, that it operates *in re*. Like a Thomist, he seems to think that truths are *applied* to things, something like the modern notion of "applied science." A correct version of what Hutchins is saying is J. S. Bruner's doctrine that the teacher teaches the "structural ideas" of the real subject matter, which become more and more specified and immediately pragmatic as the youth grows up and commences.

An interesting version of this formula occurs in Coleridge, *On the Constitution of the Church and State.* Inevitably he is under the spell of Oxford, the Established style of England in his period; he is unwisely paternalistic and he overestimates the importance of having a permanent endownment; but he gives us a beautiful statement of the notion that there is a special problem in growing up free, that in any society a youth must be socialized and acculturated in such a way that he himself is not lost in the process. (By "Church" he does not mean Christianity.)

"We must be men in order to be citizens. [A portion of the common wealth], therefore, was reserved for the support and maintenance of a permanent class or order . . . to remain at the fountainheads of the humanities, in cultivating and enlarging the knowledge already possessed, and in watching over the interests of physical and moral science; being likewise the instructors of the more numerous of the order. These were to be distributed throughout the country so as to leave not the smallest integral part without a resident guide. This Clerisy of the nation, in its primary intention, comprehended the learned of all denominations, the sages and professors of law and jurisprudence, of medicine and physiology, of military and civil architecture, of the physical and mathematical sciences; in short, all the so-called liberal arts and sciences the possession and application of which constitute the civilization of a country. [Also] the interpretation of languages, the conservation and tradition of past events, and lastly philosophy.

"[This portion of the common wealth] cannot rightly be alienated from its original purposes. Those who exercise these functions possess collectively an indefeasible title to the same. . . . It was consecrated to the potential divinity in every man, which is the ground and condition of his civil existence, without which a man can be neither free nor obliged. . . . The proper object and end of it is civilization with freedom."

v

Now the problems discussed in this chapter, and the main substance of the next chapter, were brought into the courts in 1817-19 in the Dartmouth College Case, the first case on education to reach the Supreme Court of the new republic and democracy. This was not by accident, for in a free republic and in the rising tide of democracy—that was to become the "Jacksonian revolution"—the relation of school and society would have to be considered afresh. But unfortunately, as happens in politics and litigation, the profound issues were treated rhetorically and the crucial issues were evaded, and so the case continues to tease us. I think it is worth still another analysis from the point of view of the community of scholars.

In the formal facts, the democratic state government, on "Jeffersonian" principles, took over the going university corporation to be part of its public system. The trustees objected, and since they were nearly, in persons and in interests, the community of scholars itself, many of the faculty and most of the students seceded, in high medieval style, set up shop in another place, and sued for their Seal and records. Finally, Chief Justice Marshall, the "Federalist," gave them back their Seal and property, on the narrow grounds that the State had unconstitutionally breached a "private" contract between the original donor and the King, namely the charter.

The bother with these "facts" is that all the parties

were acting in inevitable ignorance of what they were doing. First, the "Jeffersonians" did not realize that they were on a tide of mass democracy that would—as de Tocqueville was later to warn—lead, perhaps faster and certainly more thoroughly, to the very conformism and "consolidation" that they feared, and of which Jefferson accused Marshall in a letter of 1819. Secondly, the Corporation's alumnus and lawyer, Daniel Webster, naturally pleaded in the framework of tradition of the English and American schools, a tradition of trustees and "founding" by charters; thus he could not amass the European precedents and arguments that were indeed applicable to the facts, that a school was its faculty, and that a functioning school was a going enterprise not lightly to be interfered with. This would have been a stronger, a more social American claim, than the claim which he did make, that the scholars had a freehold in their Established livings. (Significantly, in our modern Establishment, tenure *is* a powerful principle and would probably be honored in the court.) But thirdly, since he wanted to give the decision to the Corporation, Marshall narrowly confined his decision to a breach of "private" contract, inevitably relying on the theory current in his time that a corporation is a fiction for making contracts. But indeed, a school *is* not, ought not to be, a "private" affair, so his decision is profoundly irrelevant to education. On this ground, the State of New Hampshire was in the right.

As an afterthought, however, the Chief Justice added the following remarkable *obiter dictum* which, if it had been decisive, *would have been* the charter of the community of scholars!— "It is not clear that the trustees ought to be considered as destitute of such beneficial interest in themselves as the law may respect. In addition to their being legal owners of the property, and to their having a freehold right in the powers confided to them, the charter itself countenances the idea that trustees may also be tutors with salaries. The first president [who was a teacher] was one of the original trustees; and the charter provides that in the case of vacancy in that office, 'the senior professor or tutor, being one of the trustees shall make choice of, and appoint, a president.' According to the tenor of the charter, then, the trustees might, without impropriety, appoint a president and other professors from their own body. This is a power not entirely unconnected with an interest. [!] It is by no means clear that the trustees of Dartmouth College have no beneficial interest in themselves. But the Court has deemed it unnecessary to investigate this particular point."

In short, we have a calamitous comedy of errors. Calamitous because just at this point in the new society there could have been given a warrant making it easier for enterprising scholars to go it on their own and fight for their own in the courts; and there might have been worked out a pattern of State education unlike the German or French monolith or the sprawling popular land-grant schools of later in the century. (Calamitous also, if I may say so, for the future educational history of the State of New Hampshire.)

In my opinion, a more correct over-all analysis of the Dartmouth College Case would look like this: There are really not two but three contending principles involved:

A. The Chartered Corporation invaded by the State, and which Marshall dubiously called a private agency.
B. The State's need for a public college, and the reasonable wish to use an existing institution as its basis.

C. The functioning and self-governing community of scholarly interests that was the real Dartmouth College.

Marshall's decision took into account A and C, excluding B. The State, probably rightfully, wanted to nullify A as no longer relevant, but also disregarded the prime educational fact, C. Certainly a more just and far-seeing democratic procedure would have been to respect the real Dartmouth College and to increase its utility to the State of New Hampshire, that is, to embrace B *and* C. Whatever Jefferson thought about this particular decision, this would have been the true Jeffersonian solution, for it is exactly what he planned, and tried to effectuate, at the University of Virginia: a State school with complete faculty autonomy. If this had been proposed by New Hampshire, a useful compromise would certainly have been arrived at.

vi *The Society of Dual Authority*

In our American universities today, the social atmosphere of the Dual Authority is a peculiar one. We are democratic and there is little official pulling rank or subservience—a teacher does not look down on a dean, a dean does not look down on a teacher; yet class lines, of both dignity and contempt, are sharply drawn. With respect to social trappings, top administration is clearly superior. At its dinner the cloth is whiter, the ice shines brighter in the glasses, the chairs are more uncomfortable, and so forth. A faculty meal, even of a department, is definitely middle-class; these are working stiffs, they do not have the aura of decision-makers, or judicial Chancellors. The (infrequent) student who regards the teacher as his father's ill-paid butler does not consider the President in the same light. Besides, the extramural functions of State, the ambassadorial speeches, etc., reside in Administration; it is understood that faculties do not publicly pronounce.

Official salaries are commensurate. College presidents get a median salary 50 per cent higher than full professors. But here, unlike in business firms, there begins to be an ambiguity. Since the teachers have skills, many of them are paid well for extramural consultation, writing, or research. The universities usually take a cut of the loot, yet often a teacher will be better heeled than his boss. In the nature of the case, the teachers must often have more cultured homes and more famous visitors than the boss. And worse, in order to build up his institution, the President must sometimes hire prestigious and highly paid professors who cast him in the shade and prefer the company of their intelligent fellows.

With respect to intellectual authority, administrators might be not so much inferior to their faculties as simply beneath notice. Except precisely when they fear for their jobs or are eager for a hike, professors are likely to shrug off an administrator's academic opinion as if he had not made it. There is no aura at all. Even Educators don't have it. And the situation can be hilarious when the President is, for instance, a military gentleman (retired) who is used to the chain of command and issues a command about Zoology 403, and becomes apoplectic when nothing happens. Rushing to comfort him, his deans urge him gently but firmly that it isn't done this way. The right way, as we shall see, is co-ordinative management.

Nevertheless, the Dual Authority is confusing to students. Sometimes they see their teachers go about their business like men; other times they see them indulge in slavish griping like junior clerks or in the empty smirking that is worse than anything.

Chapter III

SOCIETY AND SCHOOL

Let us now lay the stress the other way, not on the schools in society, but on society and its schools. Education is an instrument of social needs, and by and large—except for the rather large factors of human recalcitrance and ignorant notions of what methods can possibly work—the powers of society get the education they want and that they deserve.

Writers on education can concentrate on social needs that are socially taken for granted: how to teach Reading or Citizenship, or even Driving. More grandly—for the Carnegie Corporation—an author can address himself to the need, in our corporate conformity, to encourage Excellence. More realistically, he can study, like James Coleman, how to manipulate Adolescent Culture so as to achieve goals useful for the adults. Professor Bruner has produced a good book on the current problem, How to educate for science. The advantage of this social-problems approach is that it is practical; the context is agreed, the powers of society need only to be convinced that one has a better technique.

A more philosophical approach is to start with the

proposition that society educates inevitably, to continue itself, and that the kind of education is a function of the kind of society. This is, of course, the line that John Dewey took in *Democracy and Education.* He specified kinds of society; chose more desirable social purposes, e.g., democracy, progress; and so he arrived at the method and curriculum of the best kind of school. With such an approach, the practical problem is to get society to establish or reform its schools for its own good. On the whole, the history of progressive education has not been a cheerful one. Its ideas and methods have been stolen and bastardized precisely to strengthen the dominant system of society rather than to change it.* Nevertheless, it is immortal: in its modern form it has revived for two hundred years and is reviving again with a salutary dash of A. S. Neill to counteract Dewey's propensity for order.

My own bias, however, is that education is going on spontaneously anyway; it is itself part of the kaleidoscope of society. Youngsters are imitating and identifying, aspiring to grow up, asking why, demanding show me how. Adults are demonstrative, helpful, ideal, or seeking to mold, exploit, or get a following. Spontaneous learning-and-teaching can be more or less efficient; it may be better or worse for its participants; but as

* Let me invite the reader to the following: "Schools are the self-corrective mechanism of a democracy. In fitting the young to the culture the converse question of the fitness of the culture for the youth is forever implied. With public control over education, the people have continuous opportunity to change the schools—so as to change the youth—so as to correct the culture. Through the schools, death on the highway is countered with safety education and driver training; shortage of scientists with scholarships and with emphasis on science and mathematics, problems of public health are countered with immunizations, examinations, balanced school lunches, health and physical education." (Richard Wynn in *Administrative Behavior in Education.*)

with any other exciting function, the burden of proof of its defects lies on those who would interfere with it. I have been concentrating on one of its most complex and remarkable manifestations, the community of scholars of a *studium generale*. Such a college or university is a highly artificial product; yet it is profitable, I think, to regard it also as a highly natural convention, as shown by its long history. From this point of view, the practical social problem is often, not how to get society to establish good schools, but, as we have seen, how to keep it from enslaving or destroying whatever good education happens to be occurring. When society's schools interfere too much with education, we must keep open the question whether *they* do more harm than good. *Most of our colleges being what they are, I fear that many of the best youth would get a better, though very imperfect, education if they followed their impulse and quit; and certainly many teachers ought to be more manly even if they risk getting fired.* (In my opinion, the risks are not so great as they fear. They do not push nearly as far as they could safely go.)

Education is motivated through and through by social needs. Culturally, there *are* no nonsocial needs. The professions require licenses; certain skills are marketable; rhetoric and dialectic are learned for leadership; the arts and sciences are useful. Yet it makes an enormous difference if it is directly society that uses the schools to train youth for its needs, or if it is directly the scholars that use the schools to learn or teach what they practically want to know or profess. When seminaries are founded to train ministers or our present universities are heavily subsidized to train military engineers, the social needs exist in the school as "goals of the administration" and this adds many complications: the scholars must be motivated, disciplined, evaluated. But when students who want to be lawyers or doctors find themselves a faculty, or masters with something important to profess attract disciples, the case is simpler: the goals are implicit and there is no problem of motivation. When the goals are in the administration, the teaching and learning are not likely to be for keeps, they are "lessons" (few of us remember many hours in our schooling that were not "lessons"). Teaching and learning for keeps has a very different tone; it can be troubling and even horribly upsetting, but what a pity it is that the nearest that most students ever come to emotional agitation is in cramming for examinations, and that many teachers never come near it at all. At college age, most young people do not know what they want, they must be exposed to new possibilities. But their ignorance, confusion, and seeking are not "academic" and ought to be addressed for keeps. This is what they came for. I remember a farm boy at the University of Vermont, complaining that he had come to college to be shaken in his religious faith, and the school had failed him.

ii

Let us make a list of the implicit goals *of* the scholars and the extrinsic goals of society *for* them.

The implicit aims of the community of scholars have been: (1) To pass on and further, to grow up to and master, the arts and sciences. (2) To advance one's chosen career. Or, in less traditional societies where young people have less sense of vocation, to develop each youth's capacities and powers until he finds himself. (This includes unmaking the limitations and prejudices that he came with.) (3) To learn the philosophical bearings of one's vocation or profession in the universe of discourse, by contact with others in a *studium generale*. For example—a gruesomely important contemporary example—to learn to be not a housing engineer but a master of the social and civil functioning of housing and a lover of neighborhood beauty. (4) Finally, to have a community away from home and out of the economic mainstream, for imitating the veterans, for transferring oedipal affections and getting free of them, for friendship and sexual exploration in favorable circumstances, for self-government. Such are the implicit goals of the scholars.

On the other hand, the goals that society expects the scholars to pursue have been: (5) To fit the young for a useful life by teaching them acceptable attitudes and marketable skills. (6) To continue civilized society by manning its fundamental professions, religion, and government. (7) More narrowly, to train the young as apprentices for immediate service, as, at present, to win a war, to work for the corporations or the State. (8) And indeed, to get the scholars to affirm with their authority the social ideology, whatever it happens to be.*

These two sets of aims, scholastic and social, are not always compatible. The social goals are not always, are even rarely, the ideal goals of culture and humanity. Society is often impatient with the doctrines and morals of university communities. A narrow professionalism is likely to conflict with scientific thoroughness and philo-

---

* E.g., in 1914, the German universities had to affirm the national *Kultur;* in 1916-18, some of the American universities had to affirm our anti-German democracy. Cf., "The state has a vital concern . . . to preserve the integrity of the schools. That the school authorities have the right and duty to screen the officials, teachers, and employees as to their fitness to maintain the integrity of the school as a part of ordered society, cannot be doubted. One's associates, past and present, as well as one's conduct, may properly be considered in determining fitness and loyalty." (Justice Minton, upholding the Feinberg Law.)

sophical breadth. Placement in the workaday world has little to do with a student's capacities or vocation. In all such conflicts, of course, the members of an academic community are also members of society and internally divided against themselves. Students, pushed by their ambitious families and attracted by lucrative careers, may not be interested in the learning that their best professors want to give them. And on the other hand, goal-oriented professors are resisted by students who are not convinced that this academic torture is education for themselves.* Also, professors sell out

---

* Here are examples of the two sides; Medical students who simply want to get out and start practice—and especially since there is really too much to learn in the time that they have—have developed a whole subculture on the examinations. They cannot mix with the faculty, so they guess what "is important for the exam" and they decide that certain questions are "unfair." "What's in the text is important," so a lecturer who strays from the text must have a personal ax to grind and it's a waste of time to follow him. Theory is a waste of time. It's a waste of time to repeat the classical experiments. By a general conspiracy, the students omit handing in reports on "crocks," patients who have only vague or untreatable psychosomatic ailments "from which nothing is learned that might prove of use in general medical practice." This is all deliciously recounted by Hughes, Becker, and Geer for the College Entrance Examination Board.

In another college, however, teachers are dissatisfied with student performance and stiffen the courses. The students respond by passive resistance and minimal acceptable performance, "making life difficult for the individual who threatens to exceed the norm." The teachers become stricter. "Now the students seek ways to hold the faculty stricter to *their* obligations, and to embarrass them by requesting more office appointments, expecting papers to be corrected on time, asking about books they suspect the instructor has not read." This process is described by Nevitt Sanford in *The American College.* Unfortunately, Professor Sanford does not seem to understand that something is missing fundamentally and that the students are importantly in the right. Instead, he treats it with typical craft-idiocy, as sociological game-theory.

both teaching and research to engage in contractual research, and sometimes they follow the grants and leave the community flat. Mostly, however, it is the role of the administrators to see to it that the scholars fulfill their functions as, in Justice Minton's phrase, "a part of ordered society."

When society is wise, however, it tries to use its schools less wastefully, to benefit by the youngness of the young and the independence and learning of the scholars: (9) To prepare in a regular way for society's progressive change, by improving the next generation of the electorate. (10) To have in the disinterested scholars a critical standard for ordinary affairs. (11) And even, to invite the scholars to inquire and pragmatically experiment in social as well as physical problems.

These are the purposes—on which I have quoted Coleridge, Kant, and Dewey—that provide a better constitutional relation between society and school. If the schools are used for free growth, criticism, and social experiment, the socializing of the young becomes a two-way transaction: the young grow up into society, and society is regularly enlivened, made sensible, and altered by the fact that the young must grow up into it. Such social purposes preserve the community of scholars from becoming incestuous and merely academic. And with such purposes, society has its growth as organically part of itself, like the cambium of a tree.

Perhaps this is what Jefferson meant by the need of a revolution every twenty years, every new generation.

iii

It is not an interesting question whether the school system should be harnessed to the "national goals," rather than devoted to individual development, intellectual virtues, or pure research. Any extensive part of society is inevitably harnessed to the national goals. (Even the British public-school regimen of classics and sports was considered, rightly or wrongly, as peculiarly useful for the Empire.) The question is what *are* the national goals, how broadly or narrowly are they conceived and how rigidly must they be enforced?

Let us compare and contrast two philosophers of education, Thomas Jefferson and James Bryant Conant, who are both concerned entirely with the national use of the school system. Both democratically want to educate everybody. Both plan the whole school system, from grade school through high school to college and professional school; providing methods of selection to assure that the acadamically talented continue and the rest are fitted for nonbookish jobs. Both lay heavy stress on professional training, and especially in sciences and technology, in order to meet the national needs. Here the likeness ceases, because their national goals are different.

The difference is fateful for the community of scholars. Dr. Conant is even at pains to disown the implicit aims of the community. E.g., "Some teachers and administrators object at once to any line of argument which starts with such phrases as 'the nation needs today.' Their attention has been centered for so long on the unfolding of the individuality of each child that they automatically resist any idea that a new national concern might be an important factor in planning a program." "College professors of the liberal arts often discuss school problems as though schools operated in a social vacuum. It is convenient for them to assume that a community has no interest in a school except as an institution for developing intellectual powers." (*The Child, the Parent, and the State.*) The bother with these remarks of Dr. Conant is that he himself discusses the "national needs" as if they existed in a social, and human, vacuum. But in his four books on the schools —prepared on a grant from the Carnegie Corporation —he is in fact seeking to mold education merely to bail out an overmature, overcentralized, venal, and conformist *status quo* in the final epoch of the national states: hurriedly to train "scientists" to wage the Cold War, to man the existing and monstrously growing corporations with apprentices and technicians, and to dampen the "social dynamite," as he calls it, of unemployment in the city slums. These national needs he never questions, but he often expresses his impatience with philosophers of education.

Jefferson, however, was concerned with building a new nation by means of a society as open, as unadministered, and as international as he could strategize. These were the national needs. E.g., "We should be far from the persuasion that man is fixed by the law of his nature at a given point, that his improvement is a chimera . . . It cannot be but that each generation, succeeding to the knowledge acquired by all those who preceded it, must advance the knowledge and wellbeing of mankind." Students are to be free of rules and policing, "the rather as preparing them for initiation into the duties of civil life." The faculty, too, must be untrammeled of administration. His Enlightenment idea was that democracy is possible only if the electorate is progressively enlightened, and his political theory was that people learn only by making decisions, including making mistakes. He concluded that it was necessary to decentralize and multiply responsible groups. (Madison explains somewhere that the beauty of decentralization, with federation, is that if a self-governing unit makes a mistake, only a small group is injured; if it hits on something worth while, others can adapt it to their own uses.) Historically, Jefferson's principles have

not won out in America. They have been circumvented
by mass democracy with its tendencies to level, standardize and centralize, and by capitalism with its tendencies to pervert, and also standardize and centralize;
and one of the things we have inherited is the national
needs of Dr. Conant.

In the interests of efficiency, standardization, and
control, Conant would centralize the lower schools as
much as feasible; but he tends to leave the higher
learning to the system of free enterprise in its current
semimonopolistic functioning by which, for instance,
1 per cent of the colleges receive 45 per cent of the
endowments and almost all of the contracts for research. Jefferson, just the contrary, wanted the universal
higher learning, supported by the nation, to be controlled by an autonomous international faculty: Swiss,
French, German, English, Scotch, and Catholic, Jewish,
and Protestant. (When the national plan fell through,
he devoted the end of his life to founding the University
of Virginia.) But the grade schools he planned to be
strictly local; he tried to decentralize them down to
the hundreds that provided the militia, though this did
not fit the conditions of manorial Virginia. And he
regarded this most numerous kind of education as the
most important for the national needs: "Were it necessary," he says, "to give up either the Primaries or the
University, I would abandon the last, because it is
safer to have a whole people respectably enlightened
than a few in a high state of science and the many in
ignorance." *

* This axiomatic proposition of Jefferson's is extremely relevant
today when the great "dilemma" is how to maintain democratic
control when the actual running of things requires such rec-
ondite expertise. But in fact for over a century our political and
industrial arrangements, and for at least a generation our system of communications, have been making the electorate in-

For Conant, the secondary schools are more and more rigidly programmed, since their purpose is either to prepare the nonacademic directly for the labor market or to feed the colleges, which in turn are programmed as training for professional schools. Jefferson left college-preparation to the private academies as they existed, simply providing scholarships for the talented and poor. He seems to have thought that those who wanted to go to college would see to it that they learned what they needed to know. (In his society, the unacademic could fend for themselves.)

In the academic high schools and the colleges, Conant tightly determines the courses and credits, down to almost every hour and point. He is forever testing and grading. He encourages speeding up in getting through. It is a ladder, and the ideal is immediate placement in a job: "There should be a smooth transition from full-time schooling to a full-time job, whether that transition be after grade 10 or after graduation from high school, college, or university. This is an ideal situation admittedly and one which is at present approached only in the learned professions and in a few instances the occupations for which undergraduate courses provide the necessary training. . . . It is in the best interests of both the individual and society. For the college student who has received a general or liberal education, [however,] without majoring in a professional or semi-professional field, many difficulties of finding a suitable job will remain." (*Slums and Suburbs.*) This is a simple theory of education as a branch of social engineering concerned with replacement of personnel, and wisely taking account of individual welfare.

Jefferson was equally concerned with producing

creasingly inept and ignorant. Naturally we have inherited a dilemma.

specialists to meet social needs.* Yet at the University
of Virginia he dispensed entirely with administrative
machinery. Having encouraged the free motives of the
student, he relied on him to rule himself. There was no
taking of attendance and no grading. Following the
Continental model, he introduced an uncontrolled system of electives, the first in America. There were no
degrees, except the M.D. In medieval fashion, graduation meant simply that the faculty recognized the student as a graduate of the University of Virginia, equal
to any in the world. And he urged students rather to
tarry in school another year, if they could afford it, lest
they be merely skilled know-nothings.

Perhaps the chief contribution of Jefferson is his
rejection of specialization in the *faculty*. Since Conant
says nothing about it, we may presume that he ap-
proves, as the license to teach, the modern Ph.D. or
other degree that concentrates on a specific field and the
narrowest possible research in that field. But Jefferson
states categorically, "A man is not qualified for a professor knowing nothing but his own profession. He
should be well educated in the sciences generally, so as
to be able to assist in the councils of the faculty."
This is a profound conception. For the student there

---

* Both our philosophers have a place for general education. For Conant its use is restricted largely to the high school,
as follows: "Talented students should develop specific skills
in high school that, if not developed, restrict their choice of
careers." That is, they must have an adaptable kit of skills.
Jefferson prescribes general education for the "wealthy who
may aspire to share in conducting the affairs of the nation,
or live with usefulness in the private ranks of life." I presume
that in those simpler times this proposition did not yet have
the Veblenian sarcasm. We must remember that leisured
gentlemen did, like Jefferson himself, write great histories,
introduce new plants, practice architecture, and man the
scientific academies.

is no disadvantage in specializing if he is taught his specialty philosophically, in its bearing on the rest of human life and culture, and if he can communicate with students in other specialties. But to have a community of the faculty, it is necessary to have teachers not entrenched in their private thoughts and specialist ambitions. (Later we shall notice the results of the contrary situation.) Jefferson's university was a *studium generale* of a unique kind: it was like Bologna or Padua in being professionally oriented; it was like Paris or Oxford in its notion of a unitary faculty, though not a faculty of liberal arts: Jefferson conceived of Professionals talking to one another.

This brings us to our subject, the fate of the community of scholars. As might be expected, Dr. Conant does not seem to have it in view at all, and says nothing about it. He everywhere implies a powerful administrative organization, and a student body toeing the line, but one has little sense that administration, teachers, and students are groups of persons who form a community or have any transactions at all. Jefferson had the community of scholars continually in view. He was acutely political and psychological. And to him this *was* the University of Virginia. The faculty, once chosen, he made entirely autonomous. We do not know his policy about recruiting and replacement since he died before the problem arose; but he established as strong a rule of tenure as he could get the House of Burgesses to swallow. Against the uniform practice in Britain and America, he resisted as undemocratic the existence of any permanent administration or president beyond the ancient rector annually elevated from the faculty. (As far back as 1779 he had tried to have the presidency abolished at William and Mary, where he had himself been a student during the period when, according to Professor Hofstadter, "its faculty enjoyed more self-government than did the faculty of any other early American college.") There is a touching letter in which he, the Founder and Chairman of the Board, and former President of the United States, apologized for mentioning a text that the teachers might have overlooked; "if you have already discussed the matter, read this letter no further," he said. (To be sure, he intervened strongly in the one issue of the professorship of political science! He was for freedom, but not Federalists.)

The students at Virginia were self-governing, without academic discipline or moral policing: "Pride of character, laudable ambition, and moral dispositions are innate correctives of the indiscretions of that lively age." "Avoid too much government," advised Jefferson, "by requiring no useless observances, none which shall merely multiply occasions for dissatisfaction, disobedience, and revolt." One need hardly make the contrast with the body of students whom Dr. Conant perforce envisages, ambitious for salary and status and cynical about their worth, anxious about grades since they have no other measure of value, yet reacting against the social pressures on them by cheating and withdrawing into an "adolescent subculture" that defies growing up.

As the physical planner and architect of the University of Virginia, Jefferson was again exquisitely aware of the relations of the community.* Confronted with the youthfulness of American collegians, and the Amer-

---

* When criticized for spending so much on bricks and stone—and stringing the Legislature along to get the money—he explained, "Had we built a barn for a college should we have the assurance to propose to an European professor of character to come to it?" Also, the school had to be "eminent in order to draw to it the youth of every State." My own impression is that the narcissism of the architect also had a strong influence in producing that Roman dome and the Vitruvian orders.

ican and British tradition of tutelage, Jefferson undertook to combine the Continental and American attitudes on college paternalism. The students were without surveillance, but in the architectural layout he saw to it that each group of dormitories adjoined a professor's family home; and he provided for the youth to dine there periodically to seek guidance in his anxieties. I have heard the legend that originally the student cells had two doors. Out the rear door, the student would keep his horse, his slave, or his prostitute without public note. When he emerged out the front door onto the Green, he was supposed to dress well and observe deportment.

Even in Jefferson's lifetime, needless to say, the University of Virginia did not live up to the ideal conception. Right off, the House of Burgesses rejected one of his great faculty, Dr. Cooper, because he was an Unitarian. For a time it must somewhat have realized the plan of its founder, for a rival educator spoke of it as follows: "The Jeffersonian University of Virginia is a terror to the land, a curse to education, in fact a nursery of crime and vice." (D. H. Hill, of Davidson.) Yet, in the course of the nineteenth century, Virginia became a fairly genteel Southern college. The present state of things is expressed by the current *Freshman Handbook*: "You would not walk boldly in the temple of a strange religion. It is best not to walk boldly in the temple of tradition—which Virginia thanks her God and her forefathers for the heritage of beauty and freedom." In this spirit, the student liberties, which Jefferson meant to be gentlemanly and revolutionary, have come to a tight little code, prohibiting walking on the lawn and regulating the nuances of getting drunk, and policed by an Honor Court which, I am told, it is taboo to discuss. According to a recent observer, Simon Auster, "The major difficulty at Virginia is that, although formally the school is wide open, in fact the informal regulations are rigid and must be learned quickly or you're in trouble."

iv

With the national needs that Jefferson was thinking of, the relation between the community of scholars and society was a simple one. The autonomous community would be a leader in an open-ended decentralized democracy. This was what Jefferson hoped.

But our present national goals, as conceived by Dr. Conant, are not very humanistic or educative; they are determined not by the scholars but by the administration; and indeed Dr. Conant does not bother to think about the students and teachers at all. Should not this lead to continual conflict?

On the contrary. Thanks to skillful administration, the present climate of our schools is not conflictful but, by and large, a clinch. Our colleges serve *neither* the national goals of Dr. Conant *nor* the ideal aims of the community of scholars. Rather, they are great, and greatly expanding, images of Education, no different from the other role-playing organizations of the modern world. Fortified in their departments and tenure and the kind of academic freedom that is (dilatorily) protected by the American Association of University Professors, the senior scholars are not much disturbed by either the students or by one another or by the administration. And society is satisfied by the symbolic proof that a lot of education is going on, fat syllabi, hundreds of thousands of diplomas, bales of published research. And indeed, the students *are* educated in the process. Most of them learn, in the great colleges, the secret of our uniquely glamorous society, to conform and batten. A few protest. A few dissent. A few quit, like rats deserting a sinking ship (and they also are drowned).

Chapter IV

CO-ORDINATIVE MANAGEMENT

> "A university that rests on a firm financial foundation has the greater ability to unleash the minds of its students."
>
> —John Henry Newman

i

In the previous history we saw that society has oppressed the community of scholars by imposing external demands and restrictions, and has burdened it with pomp and size that are irrelevant to education. These doings continue at present. But the peculiar disease of modern Administration is that it replaces, in a formal and functionless way, the community of scholars itself. It is able not only to lodge in the college but to take it over and make it hardly distinguishable from the extramural world.

Between the college and society, facing in both directions, stands the President with his staff. Vis-à-vis society, represented by the legislature, the trustees, the alumni, the parents, so long as there is no offense and the college is successful and prestigious, the president has a remarkable freedom to determine policy, whether educational, architectural, or financial—he is more independent than a tip-top corporation executive. Vis-à-vis the college, however, his position is more problematic because of the community. Administration is strong when it can attach to itself the voting senior faculty and also the official student government and press, and can see to it that neither teachers nor students disturb the public relations with the legislators or donors. In effect, it is the genius of strong administration to weaken the community by keeping the teachers out of contact with the students, the teachers out of contact with one another and with the world, and the students imprisoned in their adolescent subculture and otherwise obediently conformist. Our theory has been that the university *is* the personal relations among veterans and students in a *studium generale,* as a climax of growing up and commencing. Modern administration isolates the individuals, the groups, and the studies and, by standardizing and co-ordinating them, reconstructs a social machine.

The machine has no educative use, but it occupies the time of the students (in a period of youth unemployment), it pays the salaries of scholars, and it manufactures licenses and marketable skills. Yet these are not its purposes. Like the American economy itself, the system of universities is really a machine for its own sake, to run and produce brand goods for selling and buying. Utility is incidental. More revolutionary products like free spirit, individual identity, vocation, community, the advancement of humanity are, rather, disapproved. But frictionless and rapid running is esteemed; and by clever co-ordination of the moving parts, and lots of money as lubrication, it can be maximized. As John Corson puts it, the idea is to get "a working consensus among all members of the institution, trustees, officers, faculty"—in this model the students are called the clientele—"about what purpose is to be achieved. Like other governments, the university cannot afford order or certainty at the cost of the freedom of those governed. It must obtain the consent of the governed."

The above paragraph must seem to be a sarcastic exaggeration, but I mean it quite simply. If teaching-and-learning is in fact a process of contact among the veterans and the young, and what is to be taught and learned is disclosed in that contact, then the smooth functioning of the academic machine and the democratic consent to its preconceived goals are simply irrelevant to education. This is no exaggeration, but of course one cannot help being sarcastic.*

In order to explain the nature of modern academic administration, it is necessary briefly to trace two distinct lines of evolution: the evolution of the idea of the American College President and the evolution of the idea of modern co-ordinative management. These two lines have crossed.

ii

From the beginning, the American college president has been ambiguous. Is he the chief and spokesman of the scholars, or is he the henchman of some outside power, state, sect, or donor?

When the primitive American societies of the seventeenth century needed professionals and higher learning, there was neither a pool of masters to combine and set up shop, nor a separate ecclesiastic to carry

---

* Books on the colleges tend to this style; one falls into it. It is partly because of the contrast between the actuality and the names incised in stone above the library.

on higher education as a traditional function. We saw how eventually Jefferson tried to overcome these lacks by bodily importing a guild of great Europeans and giving them autonomy. The more primitive societies appointed a board to provide a headmaster or president and three or four poorly paid young tutors for a few dozen juvenile students. In such little colleges the president was, by his office, on the board, but he was also likely to be the only experienced and permanent scholar, for the tutors were in transit, they were young ministers waiting for livings, etc. The problem at this stage was to build up faculties at all.

When in the course of time there began to be little faculties, there is evidence that the president sometimes regarded himself as their teaching fellow rather than as a servant of the trustees. In the replacement of Mather at Harvard, Leverett, an ex-tutor elected by his ex-students' votes on the board, was a faculty man. We have mentioned the free faculty at William and Mary during the time that Jefferson was a student there, and the charter of Dartmouth that provided for faculty appointment of the president. At Yale there was a revolt of faculty and students against the tyrannical Clap, forcing his departure. Other times, however, the trustee-president was in control. The conflict involved in the ambiguity of the presidency had begun.

Certainly by the time Jefferson addressed himself to the problem toward the end of the eighteenth century, it was already likely that the presidency was dangerous to the community of scholars, and Jefferson tried to abolish it. But instead, the sectarianism and Jacksonian populism of the next half-century produced the nadir of monolithic control by the trustees and almost the strangling of the scholars. Describing the period, Professor Hofstadter says, "The trustees prescribed the work of the classroom, wrote the laws of student government, shaped the curriculum, subjected the private lives of teachers to scrutiny and espionage." The president was nothing *but* their henchman. Naturally, so much outside interference led to student disobedience and faculty revolt. Following the theory of Jefferson, which he had absorbed as president at Charleston, Jasper Adams remonstrated, in 1837, that "the purpose of incorporating a college was to assemble a learned faculty, and therefore to make the faculty subordinate to the trustees was to exalt the means above the end and subvert first principles."

Lo, in the decades of economic expansion after the Civil War, emerged a new figure, the President as free enterpriser. Many schools had suddenly become great and replete with erudite scholars. Faculties were now important bodies. Except on critical issues like Darwinism or the rising labor movement, trustees could not simply intervene in academic matters. On the contrary, the president was beginning to tell the trustees what to do and sign, to prepare the budget, to hire and fire. Did this mean that he had resigned from his ambiguous eminence and become a mere community spokesman like a European rector? No, he had now become an Educator, a new breed: not a teacher but a philosopher of teaching, one who understood the "goals of education" and could bulldoze trustees and attract donations from alumni, and could also (pretend to) organize the faculty and the students according to the right principles known to himself.

This is the type, at its most robber-baronial in multi-million-dollar endowments like Stanford or Chicago, that was anatomized by Veblen in *The Higher Learning in America*. The Captain of Erudition. But still the old dilemma of the presidency persisted. For, having shown how colleges could successfully become great by skillful business administration by the president,

Veblen was nevertheless forced to conclude: "But no standardization can finally be worked out so long as the executive is required to function as the discretionary employer of his academic staff and hold them to account as agents for whom he is responsible, at the same time that he must, in appearance, be their confidential spokesman and their colleague in the corporation of learning. It is impossible to forgo either of these requirements, since the discretionary power of use and abuse is indispensable for the businesslike conduct of the enterprise, while the appearance of scholarly co-partnery with the staff is indispensable to that prestige on which rests the continual exercise of that power."

With this agonizing contradiction, Veblen gave up the President altogether and dropped him down the drain. He did not know an administrative secret that we know, which is able to resolve the contradiction and save the President by vanishing the corporation of learning instead.

The first generations of the twentieth century saw the working out of Veblen's dilemma, now in the form: Is the captain of erudition a businessman or an Educator? (Note that in this formulation we are far from either social needs or education altogether.) Sometimes the presidency was split into two persons, a business President and something more cultural, like a Chancellor, a title apt for very *big* fund-raising, a kind of Talking Chief. Other times there was a feud: cf., Harold Taylor: "It is said in justification of the manager-president that his skill in public relations, fund raising, business management, and general administration is needed so that the university can gain the financial backing it must have for the improvement of educational quality. This argument contains a dangerous fallacy in its separation of financial policy from educational leadership. The function of a university is to educate and the head of the university must be an educator." This is the captain of erudition as Philosopher.* According to the anarchic and poverty-stricken criterion of the community of teaching-and-learning, however, such Educators must seem very like dictators co-ordinating the scholars.

(I do not mean to say, by the way, that Sarah Lawrence, St. John's of Annapolis, or any other of our colleges run on an educational idea have been worse than the conventional schools. On the contrary, they have been better, because they have had at least the dynamism of a person with an idea, a free enterpriser, rather than no dynamism at all. They have not been conformist. Nevertheless, a President's *a priori* conception of the goals of education is not a simple community of scholars. One cannot help thinking back to Jefferson's modest claim: "We shall allow students uncontrolled choice in the lectures they shall choose to attend. Our institution will proceed on the principle of

---

* Naturally Harold Taylor or Robert Hutchins would vehemently deny any similarity with Veblen's figure of fun because they are *serious* educators and not ambitious stuffed shirts. And let me say that the three famous Educators whom I have known are all trim, slim, and handsome men, younger than their years, and *not at all* like the repulsive figure whom Veblen portrays in his notorious footnote.

Ex-President Taylor is very conscious of the community. He explains that "the strength of a college depends on the way in which every one connected with it—students, faculty, alumni, and administration—identify themselves with the institution. . . . My own view is that the only way in which students become seriously identified with their college is by personal relationship with the faculty and other students." That is, the administrative sequence is as follows: there is an Institutional Idea—the teachers have it presumably by selective hiring and firing—and the students are inoculated with it by identification. This seems masterly administration. It could, however, reverse itself and turn into a dissenting community and, I think, Taylor wants this *too*.

doing all the good it can, without consulting its own pride or ambition.")

The high modern theory of the presidency, especially for great institutions, *is* more modest and less eccentric. It eschews philosophical preconceptions or, indeed, any thoughts as proper to the executive. He is rather an "educational statesman" and, intellectually, a "generalist." This is, as Harold Dodds points out after his many years at Princeton, a deeply satisfactory role "in a world in which specialists are a dime a dozen." It is the virtue of a generalist to put (and put down) each scholar in his place—in terms of co-ordination, period. Nobody can legitimately object, because no one can understand the necessities except the co-ordinator; and he does not have to explain, because he is a generalist. It is, you see, a matter of weighing, and of measuring incommensurables, and of understanding the national needs.

iii

But to take the final step in our history of the presidency, into the present when the administration takes over the school, we must turn to the parallel line of influence, the science of modern management.

Veblen did not, in his time, understand that it is possible for administration to process not only the products of education but also the producers, the teachers and students. If this can be done it immeasurably diminishes the pressures of the corporation of learning that, as John Corson laments, "add difficulty to the administrators' task of coordinating the activities within their institutions with outside groups." By the proper sociological and psychological techniques, such pressures can be practically nullified, leaving the president with a free hand to aggrandize his institution. Put it this way: Veblen's model is drawn too closely from old-fashioned *business* administration, with its chain-of-command bureaucracy and arbitrary hiring and firing, a situation in which scholars are resentful, insecure, and restive. But our modern model is drawn from both *public* administration, developed for a placid civil service, e.g., by Woodrow Wilson, and from *scientific business management,* with its philosophy of harmonious belonging, as developed by Elton Mayo and others. The satisfied senior worker, with tenure, adequate salary, and rational rules of promotion, is unlikely to complain that the whole enterprise is useless. He can be privately vocal; and on all matters that are not essential to the essential business, the prestige and growth of the college, considerable authority of tinkering is granted to the faculties, so that it is easy to gain their consent to everything else. Meantime, a judicious mobility and competition among the younger workers guarantee their good behavior. And since in the expanding system the colleges are a seller's market, the students are speechless—as well as being obedient by artificial selection.

In this new climate of consent, many of the old trouble spots of the community of scholars tend to vanish. "Decisions relative to student admissions, discipline, recreation, government—fields traditionally subject to faculty control—have been turned over to administrative supervision. Deans of students and their staffs, armed with an increasingly extensive knowledge of psychological tests, have taken over the direction of student affairs." (Corson.) "The evolving role of the college professor in America has been characterized by a progressive decline of his character-developing function . . . which is taken up by specialists in guidance, counseling, and psychiatry." (Robert Knapp.) And in strictly curricular matters, by the multiplication of departments and entrenched specialties—"our Milton man," "our man on population statistics"—and by "the strong tendency for the research and informational functions to part company and form two separate callings" (Knapp), one can keep the faculty out of touch with one another on any real issue whatever, whether what is happening to particular students or what the school is about.

In a remarkable proposition in ethics, John Corson tells us that "Decision-making is the central and continued business of every human enterprise." It is the task of administration. One would not have thought to define a community of scholars in exactly this way, or to name the administrators as the chief *dramatis personae* in it, but let us follow along with the modern theory and spell it out. In *Administrative Behavior in Education,* Roald Campbell of Chicago explains: "The reaching of a decision is the core of Administration. 1. The first step of rational decision-making is a clear comprehension of the purpose or goal to be served by the decision. 2. All possible facts, opinions, etc., are assembled. 3. Analysis and interpretation. 4. Formulation of alternatives. 5. Evaluation in effectiveness toward reaching the purpose or goal. 6. Selecting the particular alternative." All of this occurs on three Levels: "1. Organizational purpose and over-all program and personnel policies. 2. Specific objectives and coordination of efforts of staff. 3. Operational: individual staff-members deciding on what is professionally and technically correct." But the most important part of this theory of Professor Campbell's is Communication: "Communication is the process by which directions, information, ideas, explanations, and questions are transmitted from person to person or from group to group. When communication is adequate, the organizational purposes are likely to be commonly understood, and the members will tend to act in a cooperative and coordinated manner toward the accomplishment of the purpose." This is a sublime belief; but some people, the more they understand, the more they tend to say Naa. But let me spell out these ideas of one syllable a letter further; I quote from a 1955 statement of the American Association of School Administrators: "The constituents of the process of Administration are: 1. Planning, to control the future in the direction of desired goals. 2. Allocation of human and material resources in accordance with the plan. 3. Stimulation or motivation of behavior toward desired actions. 4. Coordination of groups and operations into an integrated pattern. 5. Evaluation."

I have taken the reader through this paragraph on the modern science of administration in order to show how a community of scholars can be harmoniously replaced by an organization whose operations at least apparently implement the ideas of the President that at least apparently fulfill the mandate of his Regents or Trustees. Given so much communication (in this language), the collection of "all possible" opinions, and co-ordination, stimulation, and motivation (by muted bribes and threats), it is quite unlikely that there will not be, if only out of weariness, consent. Or identification with the institution.

iv

Education is a relation of a fairly specific kind between students and teachers, though it includes many factors and has many useful and baneful varieties. But scientific administration, including the administration of schools, is a technique of personal relations in general, to make any enterprise whatever run smoothly; any specific task or function of it, e.g., education, is likely to be fairly incidental. A study of twenty superintendents of elementary and high schools, conducted by New York University, lists their functions as follows: "1. Working with people. 2. Business Management. 3. Developing plant. 4. Improving the educational program. 5. Serving the profession, by lecturing, teaching, etc. Of these, number 4 is the most neglected responsibility." * (Reported by Robert Fisk.)

College Presidents, of course, perform these activities at a more exalted level. They are Educators and importantly make public appearances as public spokesmen. But the general pattern is much the same. Corson estimates that the average college president spends less than one-fifth of his working time on educational matters. His direct involvement with the students consists of four areas: athletics (games and coach); discipline (liquor and sex); problems arising when controversial figures are invited to the campus; problems when students want more self-government. It is evident that the President's real function is to encourage extramural interest in the college and to discourage intramural incidents that might arouse extramural antagonism. He is not a teacher. His relation with his teachers is, as a generalist, to allocate their skills, as Corson says, "to meet society's changing needs. Teachers themselves are subject matter specialists. They think in bits and pieces." Finally, the President's most important role is dealing with the trustees and selling them the budget, for, as Veblen demonstrated long ago, it is usually the

* Correspondingly, the requirements for selection of superintendents in Texas are, "Personal appearance, agreeableness and friendliness, ability to work democratically with staff; personal integrity and fairness; ability to supervise instruction; experience as superintendent of schools; aggressive leadership in improving school programs; ability to discipline students and teachers; personal habits; skill in financial matters; skill in working with parent groups and spokesmen." (Reported by Hall and McIntyre.)

President's office that handles the business, despite the popular wisdom that the trustees must be businessmen.

My argument, then, is a simple one. The colleges and universities are, as they have always been, self-governing communities. But the personal relations in such communities have come less and less to consist in growing up, in the meeting of veterans and students, in teaching and learning, and more and more in every kind of communication, policing, regulation, and motivation that is relevant to administration. The community of scholars is replaced by a community of administrators and scholars with administrative mentalities, company men and time-servers among the teachers, grade-seekers and time-servers among the students. And this new community mans a machine that, incidentally, turns out educational products.

v

The advantages of this take-over are, for the President, very great. He is the master in his own house. He is freed from headaches in his dealings with legislators, the press, parents. He can control the student organizations and newspapers. He can wangle the appointment of prestigious and congenial professors and get rid of trouble-makers. He can alter the character of departments and the proportion of faculties in order to meet society's changing needs. This might involve a great increase in teachers of remedial English or Language Lab; or acquiring a hotel and giving a Master's in hotel management; or, most important at present, taking on government contracts for research decided not by the scientist but by government. Government and government-sponsored projects now carry nearly 25 per cent of the operating budget of the colleges and universities. President Pusey says that at two unnamed great universities in the East four-fifths of the budget is from such sources! Columbia gets $20 millions annually.* Further the President can garner research from foundations, and arrange for "co-operative education" and merit scholarships by which corporations dodge taxes by defraying the tuition of prospective and part-time employees. And he can get new buildings. It is very thrilling to take part in building operations, to be in on the architectural planning, to be all about while the buildings rise, to survey the enlarged estate.†

Besides, he can make the actual classroom education more lucrative by standardizing courses and increasing enrollments, and by dispensing with courses that are not really solvent. As John Corson has expressed it, "Increasingly businessmen incline to examine the administrative efficiency of universities to which they make donations." As Jacques Barzun has more tersely expressed it, "Columbia is run like a bank." Meantime there are overcrowded classes making office hours impossible for the teachers, and large lectures that should be seminars. There are underpaid tutors instead of professors. Nevertheless the tuition increases. It was on

---

* The President's Report explains that, "The increase in government-sponsored research has come about because every one recognizes the importance of great research programs to the national welfare and recognizes at the same time that the universities . . . are best qualified to execute a significant part of these programs." I am told that there has occurred an interesting change in the use of language. It is only this contracted research that is called "research." What a free scientist does in his laboratory according to his own interest is not considered as "research." It has not yet been named.
† Private donors prefer to give buildings. I am impressed by Ullmann's Brass-Plate Theory that the exposure-hours of immortality of a named building per dollar is greater than lectureships or student aid. In my opinion, old-fashioned book-plates have a deeper penetration; but it depends on what you want.

these issues that 2,000 students of an Eastern school staged an angry demonstration last fall.

It is iterated and reiterated that these factory-like and businesslike ways are inevitable under the modern conditions with which administrations must cope. Harold Taylor, who deplores them, nevertheless explains, "The most important reason [for the lack of educational responsibility] is the drastic increase in the number of students and the consequent growth of mass educational needs . . . to be met in a hurry. The major forces are all in the direction of submerging the individual teacher and the individual student in a mass of rules, formulae, administrative authority, and academic bric-a-brac." Maybe. The fact remains that the administrators engage in a tooth-and-nail competition to aggrandize their institutions and produce these very conditions. *They* are among the major forces. We do not hear that they have gotten together to decide on a judicious policy for distributing the different kinds of goods of education, during a period of increasing population, affluence, and youth unemployment. They do not propose nonacademic colleges for the nonbookish. They do not encourage new communities and differentiation. Instead they behave like department stores opening new departments and sometimes branches, and increasing efficiency by standardizing the merchandise and the sales force.

It is not necessary to spell out the disastrous effects. Veblen explored them fifty years ago and they have been reviewed annually ever since. But let us keep clearly in mind that winning the competition does pay off—in its own terms. As mentioned above, "18 institutions (only 1 per cent) receive nearly 45 per cent of the total endowment, $314 millions in 1954. 805 institutions had no endowment at all, although they enrolled one quarter of the students." (V. C. Blum.)

"Seventy-five institutions do virtually all the research. These are, hence, able to attract the best graduate students." (Corson, 1960.)

Finally, there is an immense increase in the number of administrators themselves. With centralization, standardization, and "efficiency," the ratio of teachers to students may fall. But the ratio of administrators in the population will rise *perhaps even more than proportionately*. This is the familiar American style. As Gale Jensen of Michigan has broadly hinted, "Some observers of this breeding process of administrative roles say that it is a reflection of Americans' need to produce evidence of their personal success." In any case, within our school system there are more administrators in New York State alone than in all of Western Europe; the ratio of administrators in America is 30/100, in Israel 3/100, etc., etc. Besides, we must add the army of para-collegiate examination boards, scholarship boards, accreditation associations, processing billions of documents with business machines. Since 1955 the number taking College Boards has increased from 250 to 850 thousand; National Merit Scholarship from 50 to nearly 600 thousand; so with American College Testing, etc. A high-school graduate may take three or four of these national tests. The expense, however, is usually borne by himself, so it does not appear in the costs of the college system.

My guess—perhaps it is a prejudice—is that the more "efficiently" the academic machine is run, the more expensive it is per unit of net value, if we take into account the total social labor involved, both the overt and the covert overhead. Consider the following simple-minded comparison:

If students paid their teachers directly, without administrative intermediaries, then an average annual salary of $10,000 per teacher (the American median salary is $10,000 for a full professor), with a teaching load of twelve hours, averaging twenty students in a class, and each student taking five courses, would be paid by an annual tuition of $625. Add to this $25 rent for a classroom (urban middle-class accommodation). That is, college would cost him annually $650, plus books and necessary apparatus.

At Columbia, with comparable conditions for teacher and student (it is impossible to make exact equivalents), the tuition is $1,450, plus books and some fees; but this sum includes classroom, Gymnasium, and Medical.

Now what is astonishing is that at Columbia, according to the President's Report of 1960, the tuition amounts to little more than half ($13½ millions) of the total sum spent for "teaching and educational administration" (nearly $25 millions.)* That is, education at the great university costs about four times as much as is needed directly to pay the teachers and the rent! This seems to be an extraordinary mark-up for administration and overhead. Is this the most efficient way to run a *studium generale*?

Columbia College is again about to hike its tuition —the fifth time in eleven years—to $1,700 in September 1963. The publication of the Dean and Alumni explains the increase in part as follows: "Competition from state universities, private colleges aided by foundation grants, and big businesses for America's finest thinkers and researchers has become increasingly fierce. Columbia with its traditional emphasis on research and on graduate and professional training is a prime hunting-ground. It must continue to raise faculty salaries in order to retain its scholars and maintain academic excellence." I do not see how this is an argu-

* This sum does not include Student Aid, $2,700,000, or Library, $1,800,000.

ment for increasing tuition in the undergraduate College; but the fact is that, at the same time, Columbia is introducing a new bottom level of low-salaried preceptors, and I bet these will be teaching a section and marking papers of undergraduates! Also, "As the University has grown in size and in number of activities, it has been necessary to hire not only more administrators but men of more outstanding breadth and ability. University executives traditionally work for less than they could earn in business, but occasional increases for the best of them are necessary so that the disparity between University salaries and those offered elsewhere is not too great."

These remarks speak for themselves, in content, in tone, and in the character of persons described at Columbia and among its competitors. It is an interesting thought that the scientific centers of Western culture have become hunting grounds. And that the Dean regards this as just the way it ought to be.*

* Our interest is in the fate of the community of scholars. Let me quote at random from a report on the hunting by the education editor of the *New York Times,* June 10, 1962: "Little short of piracy." "The gentlemen's agreement to halt raiding not later than May in the interest of campus stability, has been abandoned." "Observers call most serious the fact that many of the outstanding faculty members devote less and less time to the teaching of undergraduates." "He was given a one-year leave of absence by Yale as his first year there. Thereafter his teaching schedule was to consist of one seminar." "Weaker institutions, intent on improving their image rapidly, buy prestige by using a few prominent scholars as window-dressing while the rest of the faculty continues to be underpaid." "Institutions with sizeable foundation or Government grants lure talent away from rivals that have slowly and laboriously built up departments of quality but lack glamorous crash projects." "Indiana's move toward an outstanding department was supported in part by a $2,300,000 Ford Foundation grant for graduate international studies." "Although administrators like to boast about new appointments, they are reluctant to talk about the terms,

vi

Let us leave these economic questions, however, and return to our proper subject, the *style* of the administrative community compared with the (ideal) community of scholars described in Chapter I. In principle it is impersonal, like any machine. Here are half-a-dozen illustrations of how it can work out in fact:

A State university in the East is going through a period of random expansion and the administration has as yet no clear notion of what the school is about. Many students are confused about the program. They are allowed, therefore, to enroll in the division of Counseling, and are not restricted to the curriculum of any one school. The number of such students has been steadily increasing and they have begun to resemble a college of general studies. (Simon Auster.) That is, the young people are allowed, if they are psychological cases, to do what might be best for many of them normally—just as "occupational therapy" usually means a schedule of work that would suit everybody if we had a better society.

A small new school in Canada is due for an immense and perhaps necessary expansion, with provincial money, and a large and rather pretentious academic building has already been constructed. The students complain that the new building has spoiled the spirit of the school. In the old, more informal setup they were closer to the teachers; they say that the money—they are poor boys and girls—should have been spent to reduce the price of tuna-fish sandwiches, which are cheaper in a neighboring school. A consultant advises the administration not to build the new elaborate

lest they make the next foray more costly or lower the morale of the home forces."

dormitories, but to provide barracks for the youth or rent old houses that are available in the neighborhood; and to spend the money on teachers and scholarships, books and scientific equipment. But this proposal is unfeasible, for, in fact, the school will not get the appropriation from the legislature except for the elaborate buildings, even though they damage the community.

On a large campus, the students have elected a liberal government that embarrasses the administration by campus criticism and political activities that might offend the donors. The administration handles this by separating the graduate students from the general student association, so as to make sure that the less intellectual and more pliable younger students—and especially those organized in fraternities—can recapture their traditional leadership. (Christian Bay.) This is a brutal example of keeping the young from growing up by isolating them from their models.

At a school I taught at recently, I kept receiving a vast quantity of letters from the office, continually slipped under my door by messengers. Since they might be relevant (one once was), I had to go through them all before depositing them in the waste basket. This took up about ten minutes of my well-paid time twice a week, so I demurred to the administration, but I was told that, since they had bought the new machine, it was more efficient to circularize everybody.

A large State university has a useful program of freshman-orientation weekends in the mountains. At one, a professor of biology lectures on the usual subject of "The Nature of Man and Woman," and his theme is that some of our mores and taboos are not physiological but cultural. The details of it reach another professor, who throws a paranoiac fit and demands his colleague's expulsion. The administration, however, does not want another to-do like the expulsion of Leo Koch from Urbana. How does the Administration cope with the dilemma? By calling off future freshman-orientation weekends! This is a classic.

But here is a grimmer case of the same. At a great university a young woman consults the medical center because she may be pregnant. The next week she is dropped from the school on a scholastic pretext. The worst here, of course, is the breach of medical ethics, which must soon render medical service impossible on that campus. But there is also the smooth avoidance of the real issue by the dean. She cannot openly say that premarital sex will be punished, for that would raise a derisive howl among the students. Yet she can hardly say that it is punishable just if the woman becomes pregnant. The policy is not to provide contraceptive information.

At a small State school noted for its high academic quality and close faculty-student relations, a new president decides that "society's changing needs" require changing the character of the school toward engineering. His first step is to dissolve the three-faculty division of the school, claiming that it is divisive, and to establish in its stead twenty-two discrete departments. He can then proceed to hire and fire more freely.

A most prestigious Eastern university invites a teacher from a distant city to take over one weekly joint session of some seminars—the fee is good and all expenses paid. After two hours of the session, the discussion has become very lively and questions are flying thick and fast from many of the fifty students, who are themselves paying good fees. But the lights blink, it is 10 P.M., and they must break it up so the janitor will not have to be paid overtime.

Finally, let me tell a story that is not especially academic, but it is a lovely thing. In a great city in the East, a great Bank, having moved into new and larger quarters, has a lot of old-fashioned furniture to dispose of. The second-hand dealer offers only $25,000. But an "appraiser" values it at $300,000. The great Bank happens to have connections with a great University, so it donates the furniture to it and is able to deduct the entire $300,000 as a charitable contribution. The University, in turn, now has to dispose of the furniture piled in its corridors. It is said that the furniture was to have been used for the new Law building; but the architect of that building, although a relative of the same Banking family, did not want it in his building either.

From these examples, it is clear that the administrative college is indeed a self-governing community, but it is hardly a city walled against the dominant society. On the contrary, it conforms nicely to the Organized System, and the American College President is a real promoter.

In the interests of the image of the institution, and busy with buildings and grounds, contractual research, syllabi, policing, and prestigious personnel, the administration only incidentally disrupts the community of scholars and students. The president cunningly protects his institution like any top manager, faithful to the firm and competitive to aggrandize it. He does no deliberate damage except in personal issues, but it is just in its persons that a community exists. By weakening the community, the President avoids conflict. Trustees and donors have special interests; many professors and the organizations of professors are prestigious and vocal, and anyway they have tenure. It is growing up and teaching-and-learning that are the easiest sacrifices.

Chapter V

ACADEMIC
PERSONALITY

i

A teacher is a veteran of an art, profession, or science who teaches because he ought to and must. By this standard, American college teaching, like the college presidency, suffers from an historical flaw. We saw that the poorly paid young tutors of early days were usually marking time till they could begin in some profession. This situation is still not uncommon—a young fellow makes a poor living as an instructor until he can make pay what really interests him—but mostly, nowadays, the "profession" that he is waiting to begin is precisely to be a senior teacher. Is this a profession? what has he practiced?

The senior teacher, or headmaster, of early days, was a proper teacher: a mature man, probably a parson, who took over the school. But of course he was the President, responsible to his board and lording it over his tutors. In such a situation, the bother may not be that the board interferes but that the headmaster has been chosen according to their conception; he is safe. He is not a free master who attracts students or is chosen by students. And historically it worked out that this ambiguous president chose to go it alone, not as a teacher, but as an "Educator."

In the process of time, American colleges began to have strong and numerous faculties of older men. But these were not only subservient to a president who transmitted outside commands, but also they were usually only the former tutors grown older. They were "professional" teachers who had never known any other competence or sphere of life. Such a combination of circumstances has been disastrous for American college teaching and its ideology. It has led to its being timid, unworldly, lacking in community, and not confronting the extramural society with authority. In a word, our teachers are academic.

I do not think that *college* teaching is a profession, for it has no proper subject matter. The sciences that are taught really exist in the practice of them. The youth taught are too old and independent to be objects of professional attention like children or the sick; yet they are not like the clients of a lawyer or architect who are given an objective service. Pedagogy, child-development, *is* a profession, for the children are real matter and the subjects taught are incidental. (Indeed, if we treated the reading and arithmetic as incidental and did not spend so much time and organization on them, perhaps they would be picked up more spontaneously and better. This was the Greek way.)* But at the college age, one is teaching young people by means of proper

---

* Sloan Wayland of Teachers College points out that, in cases of necessity, kids pick up in a few months the reading and arithmetic that was supposed to have taken eight years to acquire. It is ridiculous to structure elementary education around such "subjects," as we do.

cultural subjects, or even teaching proper subjects *to* them. There is no way to be a master of subjects without nonacademic practice of them; and it is in that practice, and not as a teacher, that the college teacher is a professional. John Rice says it well: "Teaching is a secondary art. A man is a good teacher if he is a better something else; for teaching is communication and his better something else is the storehouse of things he will communicate. I have never known a master in any field who was not also a master teacher."

Everybody knows this and we emphasize the need for research as essential for a teacher; but there is considerable confusion as to what is involved. In the physical and biological sciences the university pattern of research-cum-teaching works well. The professor uses his advanced and graduate students as proper apprentices, laboratory technicians and junior partners, on real projects. Historically, in both America and Europe, the scientific academies have come to lodge in the schools in a viable symbiosis. Also, in our scientific and technological society, there are plenty of extramural markets for such practice, in case a scientist does not take to teaching.

In the social and political sciences, the pattern works much less well. Usually the research is not—it is not allowed to be—a pragmatic addressing of real problems, whether in extramural society or even among the students and teachers. (I shall mention exceptions in a later chapter.) And the kind of questionnaire-and-analysis research that is done is precisely academic and largely futile, though it has flooded the popular culture as social science. But even academic daring in the moral sciences is "dissensual knowledge," as Frank Pinner calls it, and there are attempts to muffle it. In such circumstances, there is a great need for practiced veterans of moral sciences to man the schools. Are there any? A certain number from politics and public administration. The real veterans who could teach are few; few of the few would teach honestly; and almost none of these would be hired! It is not surprising, then, if the most gifted academic social scientists devote inordinate attention to Methodology, as if sharpening their tools for some use that is not yet. Needless to say, this theoretical methodology is irrelevant to our ongoing society whose needs, rather, are glaring and hardly require so much subtle documentation and analysis before getting to work. And as always, the *avoidance* is more influential than the attention. Also, the social scientists themselves become safe spectators. Typically, there will be subtle and widely published analyses of the sexual pathology of the movies, but there will be deathly silence about the sexual bondage in the primary schools and playgrounds.

But the case of the humanities is even worse. The very notion of a nonacademic practice of history, philosophy, or humane letters has nearly vanished—whether in statecraft, serious publishing, criticism, the pastorate. There is no humanistic attempt to improve the public tone. History and philosophy do not exist except as school subjects; there are certainly no paying jobs. Journalism and both popular culture and earnest art and writing have divorced themselves (wisely) from university standards. Therefore a journalist or writer does not seek to teach, and if he teaches it is not as a scholar. The more impressive results of academic humanities sometimes get abroad as conversation pieces that cannot make any difference; they do not help to shape social policy. Free and learned thought is simply not a social force among us; therefore, strictly speaking, there are no veterans and the humanities cannot be taught in colleges at all. Naturally there are sage and learned men in the colleges, but they are there just because they are salaried there; they would do as well on Guggenheims.

The learned professions, of course—medicine, law, and engineering—are still importantly taught by veterans. But inevitably the teaching is enfeebled, both in the knowledge of the teachers and in the readiness of the students, by the absence of the moral sciences and humanities. There is no philosophy of medicine, and little attempt to treat the soul and body as one; law is not ethical and neglects political theory; and engineering is not sociological and aesthetic. And the social sciences themselves are made narrow by the academism of philosophy, literature and history; they keep counting and analyzing men as they appear, without belief in what they could be or knowledge of what they have been. But there is not much future in men as they appear.

Academism has emasculated the humane disciplines also academically. Classically—e.g., for Aristotle—there was no such *subject matter* as "philosophy." Philosophy was the heuristic, critical, and methodical part of any proper science, relating it to the system of sciences and to man. But once having concurred in the opinion that "philosophy" is the preliminary vague stage of the various sciences, professions, and arts, academic philosophy has pompously set itself up as a special Department dealing with important remnants that have no scientific or professional bearings. The linguistic analysis, that is currently the rage, is more modest; but what is it doing in the Department rather than in each field? how can one specialize in analysis as such? The result is a series of academic exercises, in ethics, language of science, etc., which are disregarded where they should be relevant. History has allowed itself to be maneuvered into being documentation of the past as such, giving up its power both of genetic explanation and of artistic reconstruction. Without genetic understanding, the unfinished situations in the present are unrecalled and left unfinished; the social-scientific handling of them is short-sighted and superficial, and *therefore* it is neither conservative enough nor radical enough. ("Conservatism" means going back thirty years; "radicalism" means adding on a new governmental agency.) Without artistic reconstruction, we imagine that the rag ends and bobtails of men in the specious present are all the mankind there has been; and especially in the secondary schools, history degenerates into "social studies," as if to give examples for present use (which history cannot), or to give symbols for citizenship (which it does falsely). And the notion of literature as the activity of men of letters—the concrete blending of observation, memory, criticism, reasoning, imagination, and reconstruction in order to find-and-give human meanings—this is no longer thought of. Instead, the Department falls into two parts: reading Great Books, a useful enterprise which is properly a part of history, except that the books tend to be read unhistorically; and Composition, the teaching of a lingua franca or pidgin-English that, neglecting the fact that speech is an action of a rational social animal, reduces every "communication" (as it is called), on whatever subject and in whatever communal situation, to an otiose tinkle.

Finally, the academic "professionalism" of the professors is accurately reflected in the kind of union they have. In ordinary political theory, we would expect college teachers to form a union of the *studium generale,* since they are a community, and to include the students, the alumni, and the local learned public. Such a union could exert power in the kind of immediate crises that in fact arise on campuses.* Instead, the American Association of University Professors is a national craft union, largely of entrenched seniors, that copes with distant crises by dilatory committee work. According to its rules, it will not protect freedom in cases of pragmatic action, but only academic "inquiry" and teaching—but what kind of inquiry is it that is not essentially involved with pragmatic experiment and risk? And it explicitly enjoins against involving the name and strength of the community of scholars in any action that one may take as an "individual." Such limitations would have been unthinkable in the medieval, nonacademic community of scholars.† The AAUP is useful in its code of tenure and academic freedom; but we must remember that it is the pure style of the dominant Organized System to establish status and to transform intellect into conversation, with the proviso that nothing is in danger of being changed.

* This seems to have been the idea behind McKeen Cattell's proposed university, in 1906: The corporation would include all the professors, officers, and alumni, and all the members of the [extramural?] community who would pay dues. The corporation would elect the trustees, whose primary duty is to care for the property. The professors would elect the president.— This is a fine thought; I wish I had studied with him.

† Cf., Rashdall, "It is probable that it was the masters of arts and their pupils who were particularly interested in resisting the oppression of the ecclesiastical authorities. It was not the elderly and dignified doctor of divinity, but the young master of arts and his still younger pupils who would be most in danger of having their heads broken in a tavern brawl, or being lodged in the Chancellor's prison for breaking other people's heads." I do not think that we can advocate our own "pragmatic" privileges to the point where Theory becomes quite this tenuous, but we certainly can push them further than does the AAUP.

ii

It is in this context of the academic, that we can understand the administrative mentality among teachers. The teaching-and-learning is not for keeps. It does not, immediately or ultimately, meet any intrinsic test of making a difference or exercising mastery. Instead, there are credits and grading.

Academic exercise, like the old disputations and *philosophare,* is a useful means to unblock thought and deploy the possibilities of a subject. It is play and has game rules, and might lead to serious insight or decision. (In the Middle Ages it rarely did.) But the academic exercises in our colleges are neither play nor earnest, but a third somewhat. The rules are not intrinsic to the subject, but are an imposed schedule of courses, grades, prerequisites, and departments that satisfy—at least symbolically—a social need for degrees, licenses and skills. The examination is neither play nor a trial of strength and proof of adulthood, but one more detail of the format. Thus, neither the students nor the teachers become personally involved, as if they *were* somewhere. But indeed, a major advantage of the schedule-and-grading game for academic personalities is that it keeps them out of embarrassing contact with the students. Unfortunately, however, the social pressures, of conforming, competing, and fear of failing, *are* for real, they cause anxiety; so that the academic process, which could at least be a refined way to waste four to seven years in an economy of youth unemployment, is not even painless.

Why do the teachers grade at all? (It happens that a few schools do not grade and manage well enough, and some teachers in many schools nullify the process by giving all A's or C's. We know that the grading is dispensable.)

I remember an incident at a big Western university, where I sat at lunch with six senior professors, including chairmen of departments. The subject of grading came up, and all were unanimous in the opinion that grading is injurious to both teaching and learning. It does not work, they said, as competition, but rather alienates the peer group and makes for cheating and sabotage. At the very first lecture, the student will ask, "Are we responsible for that on the final examination?" and the teacher's heart sinks. Grading destroys the use of testing, which is a good method of teaching if one corrects the test but does not grade it. Students like to be tested, to give structure to their studying and to know where they are; if tested but not graded, they are eager to learn the right answers and they ask how to solve the problem. But if graded, they are either puffed up or they are crestfallen and gripe that they have been badly treated. The teacher uses tests as a diagnostic, both of what is blank to the student and of what he himself is failing to get across. Even pass or fail are not necessary grades, for if a student isn't working, he should be fired out of the class. So they talked on.

Finally I intervened and said, "Here you are six voting members of the faculty. Why is there still grading?"

At this, I was treated to a puzzling display of administrative mentality and evasion. They explained that there would be no other way to determine progress, scholarships, admission to graduate schools, although they knew that some colleges do not grade and manage by means of recommendations. (But this would involve the faculty's talking to one another about the students and even talking to the students.) They explained that if grades were dropped, the parents would complain and the students would become intensely anxious. This was true, but wasn't it their problem as teachers to overcome such attitudes? A couple were at least uncomfortable, but were not going to cause trouble. In fact, no one had any intention of changing the *status quo*.

Fatherly advisers tell students to take the grading in stride, to pay it no mind and get by, because it is unimportant. But it is important because it is structural. There is grading because it is what the teachers are conditioned to as a way of life. It dates back through endless eras of schoolteacherly "strict discipline" in boyish academies. Rationally no one believes in the discipline; yet one is astounded to find apparently intelligent adults holding adequate students to purely formal rules, e.g., making up every missed assignment, and actually flunking them if they do not comply! Surely some taboo is operating. Further, to drop the grading means to be thrown into a series of personal contacts, to be willing to claim the students as one's personal responsibilities. But the academic seems, rather, to fear for his own authority and to use the grading to keep the students in control. That is, the administrative method is injurious to the teaching-and-learning, but it does protect the individuals from one another. For the student, it at least establishes a rule. We saw that when the students rated their teachers, they put "interest in students" in first place; but they chose "fairness" as a good second best.

What clear and distinct idea is expressed by the grading? Take the best instance, mathematics, since it has definite answers and right methods and can at least be accurately marked. Say that out of five problems in elementary algebra, the student muffs the permutations and progressions. Does he then understand 60 per cent of algebra? But it is permutations and progressions that he doesn't understand. What is the use of "passing" or "failing" him on his 60 per cent or wherever the dividing line is? How will that further his progress? The teacher might guess that he doesn't grasp factorials. But it is too late! the term is over!

Or take another common case. There is a vast class and the test has to be scored by machine and so is tailored to the machine.* This has become customary from the lowest grades to the highest. Now any one who has had the misfortune to teach the freshman course in composition knows that most of the students can't write an English sentence. How should they have learned? One learns to express a thought by writing something one knows, e.g., "The mass of the moon is a cause of the tides." One cannot learn to write sentences by correctly marking a multiple-choice questionnaire. It is too late to learn it by struggling with compositions on My Trip in the Subway (Columbia), because narrative is too hard if one can't write a declarative sentence. A basic ignorance is built into the young by the system. But the system is efficient: it allows for the economy of big classes, grading on the curve, and large samplings for scientific evaluation of the teaching.

Faced with the above problem of student composition, a young English teacher at a great school used his class time to correct the students' reports for their other courses, psychology and history. This led to his

---

* The machines have strong personalities. I have recently heard of two contrasting cases. At one college, the teachers were told to drop the plusses and minuses from their A's and B's because the machine would not score them. But at another college, the teachers were told to *add* plusses and minuses because *their* machine could score them, and presumably it was necessary to put the capital investment to maximum use. What we need is a machine that declines to grade, and then we shall win the battle against grading.

making inquiries, and he was reprimanded for going across departmental lines!

Why do they departmentalize? From the student's point of view, departmentalism may look like this: A young lady is busy working on an essay on Genet, but she "ought to" leave off and study her German or she will flunk out. According to his best judgment, the professor of literature thinks that the professor of German would do well to excuse her till the next semester, but he can hardly approach him and request it. Administratively, however, the issue is simple: German 201b is prerequisite for the junior year.

Theoretically, there are two viable procedures. On the one hand, one can adopt the European system, as Jefferson did, in which the student follows his own interests and submits to a comprehensive examination when he is ready. He is left to himself—or abandoned to himself—and learns the hard way by his mistakes. Perhaps this is best, though it must of course result in dilatory exploration which does not fit with our contemporary notions of scheduling from the cradle to the grave. On the other hand, there might be a small staff-meeting of the student's teachers to advise him. This perhaps fits better with the younger age and relative immaturity of American collegians, and certainly with the abysses of ignorance that they bring with them. One can conceive of a judicious mixture of the two procedures. Our administrative mentality, however, inevitably chooses a third, unviable, alternative: it decides *beforehand* what the "goal" is, according to some Educator's theory of the well-rounded individual, the intellectual virtues, or the national needs; or perhaps simply according to the existing personnel and their vested rights in prescribed courses. The pattern is then imposed on the student. If the effect is spectacularly bad, he is referred to Guidance, which is another branch of the administration. In the course of time, as we saw in the last chapter, this branch can become a whole new *studium generale* of the confused.*

At actual faculty meetings, of course, no real students are discussed. But even changes in the curriculum or credits are hard to discuss, since each teacher, even if he has tenure, is unwilling to take a disinterested view, lest his own specialty be diminished; and all protect all by departmental courtesy. John Corson is right, "They are subject-matter specialists. They think in bits and pieces." But his remedy, the intervention of the administration, is likely to be more calamitous than the disease. One can think of a couple of remedies that are relevant to the causes. The first would be to transform the Ph.D., the license to teach, from a piece of narrow research to a philosophical and historical handling of the subject. This would at least give the young instructor, in his first uncertain year, something to *teach*. (The research thesis is, historically, the master's thesis.) It might also enable him to communicate with the other teachers.

But the second remedy is deeper; it is to get rid of departmental courtesy and let argument be vigorous and *ad hominem*. This is difficult but it is not impossible *if* there is no administrative pressure and threat of reprisal. We must assume that the teachers are fundamentally well intentioned toward the students and toward the community; therefore, they must finally be willing to listen to one another and take all good reasons into account. It is the community that educates. It

---

* In any institution there must be a casuistry to make it livable for individual persons. Now consider how this works at a famous progressive college: A student may "petition" to be exempted from certain work. The petition is passed on not by his teachers, who might know the *casus*, but by a Board manned by other teachers.

does not make any difference if a man comes as a craft-idiot or even a technologist; it is the exchange of reasons that makes a humanist. Narrow specialist pride is really a species of timidity grounded in distrust of the others and fear of the supervisor, so a man is afraid to make a fool of himself or make a slip by speaking in broader terms. The remedy for specialist pride is community and autonomy.

As it is, the credits, grading, 54-minute scheduling, departmentalism, narrow expertise, and bureaucracy constitute an administrative mentality in the faculty that divides teacher from teacher and teacher from student. It is a system that serves well enough to produce paper degrees and even bales of publications; and it is by such success that institutions acquire prestige, grants, and the pick of students. But it is not a system calculated to elicit original genius, to help the young find vocations, or to encourage the exploration of nature. E.g., if a student's experiment in chemistry does not come "out," he will not, according to this system, devote the rest of the semester to discovering *how* it did not come "out" and exactly what did happen, but he will see to it that he has gotten the "correct" reaction that satisfied the requirements. The students who fall by the wayside in this obstacle course are not necessarily the least gifted. Nor is it surprising if teachers regard the process as a waste of time and devote themselves to outside research, neglecting especially the elementary teaching. The reality that can be hoped for in colleges is the occasional meeting of spirits confronting an objective subject matter. Such occasions are cleverly balked by the schedule and the bell that rings the end of the hour.

iii

The academic situation is paralyzing in its tensions. In my opinion it is not true that "Those who can, do; those who can't, teach." Academics are not only more learned, but more intelligent and inventive than the average in their fields. The pressures of modern society are at least as debilitating as those of modern colleges. Often it is because the extramural opportunities are so low-grade, the standards so base, that teachers linger in schools. But this makes their situation all the more frustrating. They know, but they are not sure; they have not tried. Therefore they become obsessional about their footnotes, in order not to be tripped up. (Paradoxically, it is easier to make mistakes and admit being in the wrong when the activity is for keeps and mistakes are expensive!) And because they are not sure of themselves, academics are in a false relation with their students and become sticky about petty observances as if to compel respect.

It is galling, too, to have to suffer administrative fools politely. "Tenure by rank instead of by constant ingratiation," says Professor Metzger, "[has] made professors more independent and willing to take risks." Yes, but— The bother is that achieving the tenure may involve playing it cool and, especially, creatively faking it, which is the worst possible expense of spirit in a waste of shame. For instance, the rule is Publish or Perish; but in fact professors have nothing to publish if, as academics, they have had no world to pose a problem; so they invent academic problems. And this becomes a habit of life; as Christian Bay points out, "The race to publish tends to be a life-long one, with pay-hikes, prestige, and self-esteem dependent on it." Yet none of it may be real.

Meantime they must avoid the one reality that exists in colleges, and to which they are continually exposed, a personal relation with the students. We may assume that most teachers would not linger in colleges if they did not have an interest in the young and an aptitude for teaching them. This again makes their situation the more frustrating, if personally they cannot or do not dare to teach them. "Tenure is normally granted," says Christian Bay, "only when the instructor is too old to take a renewed interest in his students." When Corson and Knapp point out that character-developing, discipline, recreation, admissions, etc., have been progressively abdicated to Administration, we may be sure that the teachers have chosen it so. Not altogether to their discredit, contact with students has become too hard for academic personalities. Consider the question of a teacher's beliefs, and the contradiction between belief and action. When the teacher could believe in the official norms of character and virtue, it was still possible for him to exhort the students and to impose discipline. But now the teacher knows better or is skeptical, and he is too honest to be as pompous as the dean. Yet, not being a veteran, he cannot simply take himself for granted and teach the best way he knows.

Even good academic teaching becomes impossible in these circumstances. In a fine analysis Frank Pinner speaks of the passive resistance of students to the dissensual ideas of the teacher; it is unreachable, and "most likely to result in the severance of all possible community ties between teacher and students; it makes communication impossible." In my opinion, it is the *teacher's* holding back that leads to the students' passive withdrawal. He can state his wicked propositions abstractly—usually, but not invariably, without interference by the dean; this makes the youth anxious and puts them on guard. But he cannot make the personal reference or express *ad hominem* the emotion that must lead to action here and now. Because he is himself afraid of anything happening.

Extracurricular "college paternalism" is excluded *a fortiori*. (Let me say, by the way, that in its negative form of policing, college paternalism is at best a poor idea. The argument that, as the youth are, they are unable to discipline themselves, is self-defeating. If they are as they are after so much previous tutelage, why continue the same in college? It is weird how in America we keep youth in social and sexual bondage till eighteen, nineteen, and twenty years. At one university, the house mothers told me that they opposed co-operative houses for the young women because the "girls," averaging twenty years old, could not be trusted to keep the places neat and get their own meals. At twenty-one, however, they are supposed to get jobs and marry.)

To the extent that the college must be *in loco parentis,* the administration would seem the poorest possible choice for parent-figure, since it has no direct or exemplary relation with the sons and daughters except precisely in emergencies of discipline. The teachers seem to be the only possible candidates as campus parents, since they merit authority by respectful acquaintance. Yet we see that the teachers do not want, or they are too honest, or they fear, or they are embarrassed to be cast in the role. But perhaps, on closer consideration, the administration *is* the right "parent." For if nobody believes in the moral standards, there really is no personal issue after all. Paternalism is an administrative procedure for maintaining appearances. I have given illustrations above to show how it may work out in a crisis.

To sum up: the young people come to college vaguely hoping to meet veterans who will show them a path; instead they meet academics who interpose the administrative framework of instruction to prevent personal contact, and an impersonal morality not different from that of the world outside. To anticipate the next chapter, it is in this context that we must explain "youth subculture": it is nothing in itself, it is reactive to rejection and disappointment.

iv

As might be expected, the chief complaint of students in colleges across the country is that there is no contact between the students and the faculty. Cf., the brief chapter on Professors in the "Harvard" issue of the student-run literary magazine *i.e.,* 1956: "The average undergraduate has no contact with them, and realizes that is the way things should be, when he does talk to them. There are rare exceptions—about two or three —who happen to be men too—as a hobby, you might say."

The lack works the other way too. If in these colleges the teachers are isolated from the students, why are the teachers there? Like other company, faculty company is empty unless the day's work has been full. Without contact, the teaching must become either cut-and-dried or narcissistic display. And let me repeat a poignant anecdote that I have published elsewhere. At a small prestigious liberal arts college, a respected teacher was not-promoted (read dropped). The students who, by waiting at tables, etc., know everything, indignantly told me the details. But the professor said to me, "How did *you* find out about it? And did *they* really care? If I had known they cared, I should have put up a fight."

"The rules in force in our universities," says Frank Pinner, "separate students from faculty both in mind and in action." Lack of communication is often built into the architecture. A new building will have a good cafeteria for the students and a sumptuous common room for the teachers, yet there will be no place on the campus where a professor can have his cup of coffee with the students, signaling by his presence that he is available to chat. At some places, e.g., Carleton, they have tried to initiate a regular common coffee hour, but few attend, it is too stiff. Scheduled office hours are also contactless, because they are structured to "important questions," something to justify taking the teacher's time. (A student has remarked that he has to invent a "personal problem" if he wants an admired teacher to pay attention to him.)

The embarrassment of older-younger relationships is deep in our society and not restricted to colleges. Like other young people, students are afraid of being rebuffed and "rejected." Teachers are afraid of becoming "emotionally involved." At its best, too, teaching-and-learning is erotic and so always threatens to seem, or to become, sexual; and in America this is a very big deal. The imputation especially of homosexuality is wondrously horrible. So American sexual mores and the postures of academic self-defense combine to a paroxysm of timidity. As it works out, it is an unusual scholar who can ask a student a fatherly question as a matter of course and follow up with practical concern.

To be sure, young people are cannibals and will mercilessly devour the time and exhaust the attention of their respected elders, who have family and business of their own to take care of. Yet apart from the needs of the young, and the graceful and grateful rewards that they know how to give, there is not much in teaching at a college. Teaching is worth while if it is pursuing a subject matter *with* some one, or teaching it *for* some one. (In a very personal relation, it can be teaching some one by means of the subject matter.) If it is merely lecturing on a subject matter or hearing lessons, it is better done by tapes and films and teaching machines.

In the absence of personal contact with the students, also, I wonder if the academic soul must not generate a good deal of spite and envy of them. The complaint of unfairness is a common one; sometimes it may be justified. The finicking exaction of the tithe of the tithe often looks like a need to punish; and the "recommendations" that are written by professors for their best students are frequently hair-raising in their malice. We do not need to look in colleges to find irrational vindictiveness and resentment of other people's good times, but the academic syndrome is also specific: The young are lively, beautiful, and callous. In Nietzsche's sense, they are excellent, and there is nothing to do but love them. If this is impossible, the next thing is to resent them.

Besides, there are teacher-student embarrassments for which neither teachers nor students are responsible— problems of placement, recommendations, etc., which belong to the processes of any society. A typical recent plague, however, is the proliferating interference by security agents and business corporations invading the campus and questioning teachers about the youth's draft status, loyalty for classified work, qualifications for employment. Let me quote a good sentence on this theme by the American Civil Liberties Union: "Those who think of education primarily as the delivery of information by teachers to students will find no danger here. But if probing, sharing, and hypothesizing are regarded as essential; if education requires uninhibited expression and thinking out loud; if tentative and spontaneous questions are to be encouraged as conducive to learning . . . then questions relating to the student's patriotism, his political or religious or moral or social beliefs and attitudes, his general outlook, his private life, may well jeopardize the teacher-student relation and become a threat to the educational process."

v

Like other face-to-face neighborhoods, the community of scholars is disrupted by our new economic policy of mobility of personnel. The Ph.D. from Berkeley becomes an instructor at Cornell, Cornell goes to Iowa, and Iowa goes to Berkeley. These first moves involve breaking with old friends, dragging the oldest child out of nursery school, and finding a new house. One had been on a graduate committee for revising the Ph.D. thesis, but that must be given up. Is this move necessary? The question is not simple. Academically, the incestuous staffing of departments can be deadly. Also, a young teacher might learn something from new superiors. Yet the new man rarely lives up to his promise. And there is no use of new superiors if one never comes into intellectual contact with them. In a new place the move is repeated—it may be seven, eight, nine years before one gets tenure—and again there is camping in the New Faculty housing, the children dragged from higher grades in school. The wives adjust as best they can, in the peculiar tight and transient community life that has become common for the wandering families of junior executives promoted from one branch office to another.

Whatever the academic merits of the policy of mobility, for the community of scholars it is an unmitigated evil. It is impossible to develop loyalty, whether to the welfare of the school, of the seniors to the younger men or the younger men to the seniors, or of the seniors to one another. For a faculty to be strong and willing to fight an issue to the end, the members must be able to count on one another, and this requires an acquaintanceship of many years. Likewise, a teacher will not befriend students if he is going to leave next year, and this year and next year make two out of the student's four or five.

Conversely, those who stay, get tenure and seniority, and become chairmen, will usually be precisely the safe and the amiable who get on with the other chairmen and the administration. In a devolution by artificial selection the voting seniors become adjuncts of the strong administration, whose opinions and disposition they share. Thus, both mobility and stability conspire to weaken the community of scholars. Of course, some of the oldsters who have no fight left in them are simply tired, or they are still fighting the battles of the American Association of University Professors when new issues might demand new means of action. But most of the powerful seniors were company men to begin with; and further, the increasingly abundant technologists, even some of the scientists, tend to be morons about community tradition. The wanderers, the great men, have more vitality and independence, but they care nothing about improving the schools through which they are transient.

In a moderately big school, then, one might see the following fragmented forces: A small band of young instructors and assistant professors are intent on re-vising the curriculum, methods, constitution, because they are still fired by the adventure of teaching and are trying desperately to make their life-work worthwhile, though they everywhere see portents of futility. Others of the younger men are so busy publishing instead of perishing that they have no time for either their students or the college. The younger men are separated from the older faculty by the chasm of tenure and a quite different life-style. Some of the seniors are independent great men; others are administration men, maintaining the *status quo* or revising it in the direction of image, efficiency, expansion to meet "society's changing needs." Except for some of the graduates, the students do not mix with young instructors, who are recently married and have the young-married social life; they are isolated from the middle-aged faculty by mutual embarrassment and because the professors are busy; and the more fatherly older faculty are likely to be squares. And the undergraduates themselves are sharply divided between the liberals and the fraternities, between General Studies and the College. Last but not least, there is a small army of administrators with whom everybody communicates on a formal, and rarely pleasant, basis.

Chapter VI

YOUTH SUBCULTURE

In 1929 Robert Lynd quoted the President of the School Board as saying, "For a long time all boys were trained to be President. Then for a while we trained them all to be professional men. Now we are training boys to get jobs." Extending the series to our era of co-ordinative management, we might say, "We train them to be contented individuals useful for the national needs." This is concurred in by the parents who say, "I don't care what he becomes as long as he is happy."

Like the college president and the college teacher, college youth has always had an ambiguous status in America. The colleges are special, and there is a hopefulness reposed in the young far beyond what a traditional European society would consider reasonable. Yet, maybe just because of this high expectation, the Americans have tended to keep their young in anxious tutelage, both protective and restrictive, far beyond what a traditional society would consider necessary. The young, especially if they are upper-class and/or gifted, must not be cowed or whipped into shape by patriarchal discipline; yet they are precisely not allowed to grow up, take risks, leave home, learn something different, and improve the democracy. A strong demand is made on them to excel their parents, yet they are not supposed to change any of the ground rules. There is a premium on energy and vitality, yet there must not be any new ideas or displays of intellectual virtue.

In the "frontier" society, there was plenty of opportunity to go further than papa and become President, although remaining in the same framework of ideas. And during the great immigrations, when there was a difference between the culture of the first-generation parents and the American model, the freedom of the offspring was even an inspired recipe to achieve rapid assimilation and man the growing cities with ambitious graduates. It broke the parents' hearts and roused their pride. But what when the places filled up and replacement tended to become routine? Then, if we exclude heterodox careers—fostering individual talent, making innovations, working perhaps radically to improve the quality of the whole system—the drive to advancement could mean only sharpened competition. In our own times, all of the older motives, getting rich, achieving status, beating out the others, are still evident. Yet it is evident that they are, for the many, unrealistic: there is also need for the mature system to slow down and become established, for people to be content just to do their jobs, as if we had a traditional society.

But this is lifeless, because we do not *have* a settled culture that would pay off in all kinds of quiet satisfactions. And our present effort at Establishment is largely panic. Far from being settled, our society is patently in rapid change. There is need for initiative, adaptability to meet the new, and intellect and freedom to make the most fundamental overhauling when necessary. Instead, the panic of the adults now tries to discipline the young more rigidly, to tighten the credits and grading, to stimulate and bribe scholastic achievement!

These ambiguous tensions all come to a crisis in adolescence. The considerable animal freedom and spontaneity permitted to childhood have made for an exciting and fairly happy childhood community. But when the time comes to break with the family, what social meaning can the youngsters achieve to replace their family identifications? They have not been disciplined into the grown-up ideas willy-nilly; yet they have been interrupted in becoming independent and taking on the grown-up culture, economy, and politics on their own initiative and in their own way. Rather, the grown-up world stands in the background, alien and waiting. It is not attractive. To enter it means the end of freedom. Yet there begins to be a pressure *to* conform to it and even to excel. And suddenly, in recent decades, this pressure is increased.

It is resisted. The resultant of all the forces—of the spontaneous community of early adolescence, of the interruption of growing up further, and of resistance to the pressure to excel in "their" way—is the formation of the Youth Subculture that is now written about.

In my opinion, this subculture is constructed by the active community of youth *against* the adults. It is a substitute to fill the soul. Its rudimentary contents, cars, games, sex, simple music, being popular, are things that are spontaneously attractive to adolescents, but they do not go far. Its motivation and style, however, are both against the adults and inevitably imitative of them. There is plenty of spiting, rebelling, and delinquent reaction-formation. But in cultural format and economic style, the youth culture is only an absurd imitation of an absurd adult culture; the youth craving for popularity is only a pathetic imitation of a bathetic adult sociality and craving for celebrity; and the youth sexuality is as bad as the grownups'. The tone of the whole is not improved, either, when the adults in turn imitate the youth. That is, there is nothing authentic in the youth subculture except its youthful vitality, its disappointment in being cut off from the adult world, and its spite against the adults' demands. Meantime, waiting and in the background, is the real world of the Organized System to which most of the youngsters will inevitably conform.

Writers about the youth culture tend to overrate its contents and underrate its importance. It has no cultural value; it is base rather than juvenile. The valuable juvenile is the adolescent-romantic, the crush, the stupid-stubborn honest, the daydream, the religious conversion, the frantic daring, the unbelievable loyalty, etc.; and these probably exist as much as ever and the same as ever. The way to tap these values is to let them grow up further. But the attempt to manipulate "adolescent society" as such for adult purposes—as proposed by James Coleman and others—can lead only to trivial and base results. But the importance of youth-culture is its protest, that the adults are alien and that they are not worth growing up to. The problem it raises in education is a simple but hard one, how to make the adult culture more available, more useful, and more noble.

By and large, the youth coming up to the colleges have a youth culture. This was always so in England and in earlier America, among the classes in which youth were favored and kept in tutelage. Tom Brown had a youth culture. But it is immensely more so in present American society (and spreading to European modern societies). And in the colleges, this alienated youth meets, devastatingly, the academic personalities of the teachers that cannot and dare not pierce to the reality of growing up, and the venality, conformity, and impersonality of Administration which confirm and reconfirm youth's worst picture of the adult world. We can predict that most of these youths will not respond to the universal culture available in a *studium generale*.

ii

In the colleges we can observe both aspects of the students' alienation: the isolation of their personal lives from the teachers and studies, and their passive conformity to the values of the waiting extramural world. In an essay in *The American College,* Theodore Newcomb says, "Most students develop friendships with others whom they know as persons but not as students. If peer groups of importance to their members include individuals who are sharing the excitement of academic-intellectual discovery, it is almost a matter of chance. It has become less and less probable during recent decades that students who know each other well and are important to each other outside the classroom, experience shared excitement in the same classroom. . . . Teachers operate in social systems such that whatever excitement they offer tends not to be caught up, reinforced, and multiplied by being shared outside the classroom."

Newcomb seems to think that this is importantly a matter of social *arrangements* and he offers the remedy of smaller subcolleges allowing for more frequent intellectual contact; I doubt that this would amount to much unless the teachers themselves became less academic and more for real. Our *prima facie* inference from the split between the social and the intellectual must be that the studies are not vitally important, or they would be the basis of friendships. Rather, what *is* transmitted by the academic teaching is just the split itself, between lively interest and studies for credit.

Yet the students must obey the administrative rules in order to pass, and so in a pinch they sacrifice their friendships. Thus, the ultimate effect of what college teaches is to slight *both* friends *and* serious intellect! and to end up with the compromise-formation of business-friendships plus conformist thinking and conversation pieces. This is socialization with a vengeance.

But secondly, since the students really consider that the extramural values of society are the only possible ones to live by (rather than to be an academic), the experience of college as a whole is not for keeps. Describing the young women at Vassar, Professor Newcomb, again, points out that they come with a firm sense of the "social stability": "Since the monolithic social order has jelled, there is little point in engaging in activities toward social reform. They have now learned that a Utopia is an impossibility and are convinced that the wrongs in our society will right themselves without direct intervention on the part of college students. . . .* Future husbands should work directly toward a niche in the business and professional world which provides adequate remuneration and status, but a rise to the top is neither demanded nor expected."

Such views at Vassar are not quite so sickening as they would be in a men's college, since most of the women are looking forward to motherhood. But there is no doubt that the great majority of male collegians are equally resigned and conformist, and, having noth-

* Let me mention an incident from that campus, however. There was an attempt to raise funds at Vassar for the Lincoln Square Music Center, a pretentious and worthless commercial enterprise. This was objected to by some of the students as commercial soliciting. Thereupon the Administration had Lincoln Square included in the list of recipients of the annual Community Chest charity drive! Students leafleted, but I don't know whether it came to anything.

ing real to look forward to, they are more anxious and one-upping.

Given this alienated youth and the academic teachers, we must conclude to Professor Newcomb's catastrophic anthropological error, that "Students and faculty are two societies occupying the same territory"—cf., Jencks and Riesman, "Professors and students know one another . . . as ambassadors from mutually fearful cultures": the scientists then try to work out a method of college education in terms of acculturation of the tribes. But it is an error. The anthropological truth about colleges is that they are the scene of the climax of growing up, of the personal contact with learned veterans, and commencing into careers and citizenship. The young ought to, and confusedly *do,* come for this purpose. The teachers ought to be veterans, and they *know* that they are timid and failing. The students are not another society but the *same* society younger and learning. To regard them as another society is to avoid the hard task of unblocking, touching, and really teaching.

iii

My view that the youth culture is only a reaction to interrupted growing up, is against the consensus. It is also against the apparent facts of American life, the teen-age heroes, the dating patterns, and the ten-billion-dollar annual teen-age market. So the reader must allow me to run through the argument again. It is a crucial issue, for if these facts cannot be reduced, we are faced with the following dismal picture: the young people come to school conforming to one empty culture; they endure five to ten years of grading and acquiring credits in high school and university; and they depart conforming to another empty culture.

In *The Adolescent Society,* James Coleman of Johns Hopkins applies an admirably delicate statistical analysis to the apparent teen-age facts in ten assorted high schools, and he seems to prove them conclusively. His typical finding is: "What disapproval would be hardest to take?—Parents, 53%; Friend, 43%; School, 3%"— where Friend means the complex of teen-age culture. Correspondingly, a Brilliant Student is not a star or member of the Leading Crowd; such benefits come from sports, clothes, cars, knowing the songs. The problem for the educator, accordingly, is to avoid the disruptive effect of such competition, and Coleman recommends various stratagems for manipulating the teen-age culture for adult purposes, for the youth's own good. This is administration at its most intelligent.

But the bother with Coleman's work is not in its analysis but in its questionnaire, what it takes for granted. He assumes in his questions exactly the worthless and impersonal adult values which the kids turn from as unattractive. He never asks a question that takes a youngster seriously as a human being. By a Brilliant Student, he means the ideal of a superficial teacher. Such a lad is likely to be sexless, ruly, unaware of others, narrow, and even supercilious—why should he be chosen? There is never a question asking whether a *study* or *idea* was ever thrilling, moving, or important; a "student" is a kind of role. Further, when Coleman asks questions about sexuality, it is appallingly the titillating and symbolical sexuality that the adults recognize and suffer from themselves; naturally such sex is distracting, so that our author even contemplates giving up coeducation. Yet significantly, the progressive school of Coleman's assortment shows far less distraction by "sexuality." My guess is that this is not because it has less sex, but because it has franker sex, that can be integrated with the rest of life. (So

Russell decided in his school: let them copulate so that they can attend to mathematics.)

In most such studies the questionnaires are poor and reflect a stereotyped life. Perhaps the foundations that sponsor the studies would not tolerate more earnest questions. In *The Adolescent Society,* Coleman asks, "Different people strive for different things. Rank 1— 4: Pleasing my parents. Learning as much as possible in school. Living up to my religious ideals. Being accepted and liked by other students." A question like this is so irrelevant to the confused crisis of a youngster's day-to-day life that it *compels* a reactive, defensive, or stereotyped answer. What is tested is not what the youngster *could* be, or even is, but the system of his defenses. Worse; the possible life presented in the choices is so predigested according to the norms of *Life* or Hollywood that a youngster must respond with profound unbelief and the feeling that the future offers no exit. E.g., the fantasies offered by Coleman are: "If you could be any of these things—Jet Pilot. Famous Athlete. Missionary. Atomic Scientist." (This is really base.) The quality of friendship offered by Coleman is: "Which is necessary in order to be popular in your crowd? Be a good dancer. Have sharp clothes. Have a good reputation. Have money. Smoking. Know how to dress (or, for boys, Know about cars). Know the movie stars." Would any of these be important choices in *Huckleberry Finn, The Catcher in the Rye,* or even *Penrod*? (Perhaps smoking, in 1890.) But they would fit *Tom Brown* or *The Rover Boys*.

On the other hand, there is never a question on actual sexual practices or vices, on prejudices, on actual ambitions, admirations, or guilts. There is no way offered to express one's real sentiments on loyal friendship, love, knowledge, pride in a useful job, moral courage, radical dissent, fear and trembling. Yet if we take friendship seriously, these are the topics we try to probe. What strikes me—and what must vaguely strike the teen-ager—is that the *avoidance* of these questions is a signal. It means: this is the typical stupid grownup, therefore be resigned to continue as a typical stupid teen-ager.*

The avoidance of human contact—and the replacement of it by attention to superficial consent—is the prerequisite of co-ordinative management. What Coleman puts into the hopper is what he comes out with.

Human contact destroys standardization. It sometimes explodes, often produces novel responses, is always messy. It is more worth while and efficient in the long run, but that long run may be lifelong and hard to evaluate. The response to human contact may not immediately satisfy an administrative goal. Conversely, the persistent and regular avoidance of direct contact can discourage any deep hopes of worth or happiness. Therefore it makes conformity and consent to the second best, and a gradable performance, much easier to attain—in the short run. It is only in the long run that there is evident a waste of humanity and a foolish citizenry; but these cannot be directly imputed to school administrators. They are secure.

---

* The comparable questionnaire for *What College Students Think*—underwritten by the Carnegie Corporation—is somewhat inferior to Coleman's, for it tends to by-pass the concrete experience of school altogether, whether intellectual or personal, and to concentrate on extramural opinions ranging from Republican to ADA and from *The Reader's Digest* to *Harper's*. To be just, its title promises no more; "thinking" means the manipulation of acceptable stereotypes. The authors allow, however, the expression of an indefinite dissatisfaction or unease to test for *anomie,* which is shared by the reader.

iv

At college, the friends are different, the subgrouping persists and still excludes the studies. The house mothers at Cornell tell me that their chief problem is that the social life of the girls is incompatible with their schoolwork; and fraternities expound the doctrine of the Gentlemanly C. "There are three things we try to teach our men to handle moderately: liquor, women, and courses." (Quoted in *What College Students Think.*) In colleges, as in high schools, this attitude leads to cheating to get by and co-operative sabotage to keep down the averages on the bell-curve. The conspiracy described by Nevitt Sanford above (footnote to page 51) is reported also by James Coleman. Neither of these authors, however, entertains the obvious hypothesis that the classwork may indeed be a useless torture from which the students are wise to protect themselves, although in ordinary labor relations most reasonable observers would agree that the workers are prudent to keep production down.

The ironical case is the contrasting one cited in the footnote to page 51, the conspiracy of the medical students described by Hughes, Becker, and Geer. For here it is the students who are accusing the professors of sabotage, of not being earnest with their highfalutin' academic standards and scientific scrupulosity. Having gotten to this point in their studies, when they are about to embark on actual practice, the students feel that *they* are in earnest, they have put away childish things like medical science. In brief, they feel they have wasted their five to seven years at a *studium generale,* but they have acquired a marketable skill and they want to get the license and make money. From this point of view, many of the bright younger students are also most for real when they cram for grades in order to get scholarships. They tell you how the National Science, the Woodrow Wilson, the Regents Teaching, etc., are good loot—and easy work— if one has the knack. To say it brutally, in our society commercial lust might make a more authentic university than Robert Hutchins' training of the intellect, for at least career and money are for keeps.

It is all topsy-turvy. Youth at this age need a structure of objective meaning to replace the families they have left, and a practical human community in which the structure is embodied, so that they can identify with it by their own actions and affections. Sciences and arts are wonderfully such an objective structure embodied in scientists and artists and in conversation with fellow students in a *studium generale*. (As I have shown in *Utopian Essays,* the case is no different for nonbookish youth who find, in a work camp, an objective structure in socially useful projects for which they have aptitude.) Growth occurs by losing oneself in some objective world and finding oneself again, larger. In the presence of the objective, the relations of persons, whether emulation or resistance, mutual aid or competition, serve as a support to let go of the past and risk growing.

But in our colleges, in average cases, the studies are courses for credit; the teachers are instructors rather than embodiments of what they are teaching; learning is motivated by extrinsic superego demands and ego re-enforcements that could apply in any other task-work; and the society consists of interpersonal relations to which being in college is quite incidental. There is no reason why these parts should cohere any better than they in fact do. Growth is incidental, though, having gotten older and having been occupied, the students do grow. Graduation does not mean having achieved a new objective size and commencing; it means having surmounted (or avoided) a number of obstacles and survived. A youth is not *in* high school, college, and graduate school, taking them along when he leaves (they are *alma mater*); but he *does* Bronx Science, M.I.T., etc., in order to land in Westinghouse.

Schools have always been a mixture of a community of scholarship and an obstacle race. Cribbing and cramming are nothing new. But when they become as predominant as they seem to be with us, there must be some simpler and more efficient device than colleges to train and eliminate.

v

An experiment by U. E. Whiteis, "Poor Scholarship in the College" (*Harvard Educational Review,* Winter 1962), tries to test whether the increasing failure of learning and the high rate of drop-out are due to "lack of disciplined intelligence" or the interference of "emotional maladjustments" of the students. Professor Whiteis employed a kind of Rogerian and Sullivanian psychotherapy in one class but not in an equivalent class that was used as a control. The results were fairly spectacular. The therapeutic class had almost no absences, while the control had the usual sharply rising number of absences; the therapeutic class scored progressively better on academic tests; only two of its members were dropped from the college as against nine; etc. One is reminded of the identical results of other more extensive "psychological" experiments to improve learning, e.g., the Higher Horizons program in New York schools that aimed to open the future for underprivileged children, or the Banneker program in St. Louis schools that soft-pedaled training altogether and worked on integrating school, home, and com-

munity. My guess is that the success of all such programs comes from taking the students seriously as
human beings, with sentiments and purposes that make
up a whole existence.

What was the "therapy" employed by Professor
Whiteis? It was non-directive interpersonal contact. In
his words, he gave "acceptance and understanding"
rather than "cajoling, coercing, ordering, forbidding,
threatening, advising, etc." He allowed the students to
express their hostility, guilt, secret wishes. In this atmosphere, it seems, it was possible for the students to
feel again the spontaneous interest that any young persons might take in a reasoned subject matter and to
exercise what intelligence they had. It does not matter
if this is called "therapy" or not; I would prefer a use
of language that would call it precisely the normal state
of things: the lively response of normal students to a
teacher who knows something and who pays attention
to them as human beings. Rather, it is the disposition
to teach and grade like a machine, and to try to achieve
in a human vacuum, that is emotionally maladjusted.

vi

In their dealings with one another, the students are
still rather raggedly communal. Most are apathetic
about the official student government for the sufficient
reason that it has no powers. To run the dances, to
decide which firm of jewelers will make the regalia,
are not worth campaigning about. At Columbia this
year the collegians suddenly voted three-to-one to
dispense with the government altogether and have anarchy. Fortunately, on most campuses the more conventional and popular students who like to make petty
arrangements and be big shots, are members of Greek-
letter societies that are political blocs adequate to keep

them in charge. Student agitation for meaningful campus reform, on the other hand, is less likely to be constitutional—or even allowable. Protests against high fees, the prices at the bookstore, or the dormitory rules, do not get on ballots.

It has been thought to give students more power by a national association of the student governments, even though the governments represent no live opinion. That is, typically, to add another administrative story to the superstructure. My guess is that this does little for each community. Students are in college only a few years; their problems are local and transient. Problems can be usefully met only on the spot and at once, as when recently the students of New York State at Oyster Bay struck and got rid of the new president who had taken away their privileges, subdivided the faculties, and removed a well-liked dean. (The school had been run by its faculty and there was good contact between teachers and students.) But like young Socialists, young Democrats, or young Birchites, national student associations tend to pass resolutions about China and Katanga, even though the constituents are too young to vote, and avoid the hard task of democracy, which is to react where the shoe pinches, on the campus. (The peace movement and the fight against racial segregation are special cases, to which I shall return later.)

College newspapers make the same mistake. Mostly, of course, their aim is to make like newspapers, with due sensationalism, lofty editorials, etc.; this is to be expected, student papers are play. But it has become customary, also, to print some national or world news, to avoid covering just Home news, which is "trivial." The editors could not be more in error. Real home news cannot be trivial. The paper can be the voice of its community. If the editors would publicize ways to improve life on the campus and document the abuses that exist; if they would smoke out the professors and make them commit themselves or be quoted as refusing to commit themselves; if they would editorialize in order to have an effect, then the papers would be lively, and the editors would find themselves expelled. (*Mutatis mutandis,* the same could be said of the *New York Times.*)

By and large, administrations are liberal about controversial off-campus issues, including inviting Communist speakers. This is innocent debating and patently educational. Unhappily, Administration is then hit from the other side, by the American Legion and the State House.

If, however, the student organization or the press becomes very controversial about an issue *on* campus, one can be sure that before long they will be muffled not because of the content of what is said or done, but because something is in Poor Taste. And the conforming majority of the students will agree that it *is* in Poor Taste. If a professor takes part, he will be disapproved as unmannerly and disloyal, washing dirty linen in public. To be sure, if he does not come to the rescue publicly, his protest will be privately swept under the rug.

vii

Very many students are utterly confused. Our American society is peculiarly lacking in moral justification, in its mores, its culture, its economy, or its government. Those who, like Professor Newcomb's students at Vassar, have come to college convinced of the "social stability," are upset by the "dissensual opinions" of many of their professors. Social criticism by Mills, Whyte, Riesman, or myself, are widely used as texts. But this is not part of an orderly debate, for we have little literate opposition. Authors who can write an English sentence are not inclined to defend the present stability; nor if they were so inclined would they have much to say. Besides, the young people's own Beat and Hipster writers range from the unsparingly cynical to the devastatingly apocalyptic. Nevertheless, while the system is subjected to such attack and has no moral defenders, the students' academic teachers, and of course the administrators, offer the astonishing spectacle of behaving as part of the system without batting an eyelash. This is utterly confusing.*

There have been more hypocritical and oppressive regimes than ours. But in such periods the free scholars were fired or muffled, and the official spokesmen were rabid in their loyalty and vindictive in their thin-lipped piety. In our colleges the contented professors give their students as little support as do the dissenters. The situation is morally confusing, yet the teachers do not even take the students' moral confusion into account!

Most of the students perform as required. Some get satisfaction from the beautiful subjects and are patient about the conditions of learning. A few are cynical about their performance. Many are simply obedient, as they have been since childhood. But many who conform and perform because it is prudent and acceptable to do so, are embarrassed to explain themselves and are made anxious by interrogation, as if it did not stand to reason to do what is approved and profitable. More alarming are those who conform and take it out on themselves. There is a large consumption of stimulating and tranquilizing drugs, even more among the women

---

* An interesting situation—I am thinking of one of the smaller Ivy League schools—occurs when a traditionally complacent body of students is persistently crossed by a new, more earnest group of teachers. This leads to a noticeable atmosphere of somber depression, whose outcome I cannot predict.

than among the men; and there is a dreamy clique life of sexual hangups and endless self-analysis of the kind that discusses "I" and "you" and "how we relate" as if they were discussing third persons. Here is the breakdown of youth subculture and the onset of *anomie*.

It is only the great history and the great society that can provide meaning. But if the young come to college to find themselves by associating with learned adults, they are bitterly disappointed. They do not easily see how the texts are a tradition for themselves; and the professors who profess the tradition do not, by the example of their own lives, make it seem very relevant.

I ask some seniors what they intend to do next year. Several say they are going to graduate school. In what field? They say it doesn't make any difference, they just want to stall another year. Another says he is going to join the marines to get his military service out of the way. Out of the way of what? (A depressing variant is, "I'll join the Air Force for four years and take courses. Since they're going to get you anyway, you may as well make it work for you.") It is clear that there is not going to be any real Commencement this June.

Perhaps those who do not or cannot perform are less confused. At least they are not daily contradicting themselves, but just balking. But of course college is not for them and they have to leave. It is a pity that among so many possible friends in such pretty neighborhoods, they cannot find anything to do. As might be expected, some of these college drop-outs have been the chiefs of the Beat generation. Unable to make out in the academic culture, they have opted to do without teachers and to try to find universal culture in their own guts and in Experience. I have described the vicissitudes of this experiment in *Growing Up Absurd*.

···
viii

In crucial academic areas, there have been signs of student rejection of the pattern of the "national needs." For instance, in the East there has been a marked falling off of enrollment in Engineering, even though the demand for this kind of training continues to increase. Partly this is because the candidates with aptitude prefer to go into the "pure" sciences and mathematics, where there is more prestige and even higher salaries; but there is some evidence that the less conformist Eastern students are unhappy with what Engineering itself has come to mean. And Edgar Friedenberg of Brooklyn College has reported remarkable interviews with students who have switched from the physical sciences to the social sciences and the humanities explicitly because of the inhuman, useless, and uncreative way of life of young physical scientists at present, highly rewarded as they are.

The picture is more definite in such a field as Advertising. Whereas a generation ago this was a favorite choice among bright young fellows on the make, now it is avoided by precisely the bright and verbal. Perhaps *Mad* magazine is having a subversive effect; perhaps the TV speaks for itself. "The anti-advertising prejudice induced in young people will, if not checked, destroy advertising. In our public schools and universities, advertising is becoming a dirty word." (Walter Guild.) But how to check such a prejudice? The experts in public relations recently thought up a campaign to polish the tarnished image in the colleges; but it was abandoned because its effects might be still more disastrous. "Just about the worst thing the advertising business could do," said Neil Borden, professor emeritus of advertising at Harvard Business, "would be to approach academic people to tell them what the facts are. I am skeptical whether any sort of public relations can help in this situation." (*New York Times,* June 24, 1962.)

One has the impression in the colleges—and indeed in the country—that *very* much of the conformity is half-hearted, if not unwilling. How much? That is what is hard to know. Maybe there is no conclusive rejection of the present pattern simply because there do not seem to be any alternatives. And of course it is the genius of any tightly organized system like ours to make it seem that there *cannot* be alternatives to itself, and to discourage their invention and proposal.

There is certainly a very important new factor of clarity and community, the "politics" of rejecting nuclear war and rejecting racial segregation. These movements are not properly political because they are only negative, but they are clear-cut and lead to action. By their nature they belong to youth as well as to everybody else; and they generate themselves and do not need extramural propaganda. There are, and continue to be, sporadically but more frequently and with increasing numbers, remarkably spontaneous direct actions. And they have been a powerful force to bind the fragmented community of scholars. Senior professors, younger teachers, and students join in. Especially in peace actions the professors have led, as they must since they have more expert knowledge. The authority of the teachers and natural sympathy for the students have had a strong influence on outside society. But it is noteworthy that the administrators have not played much part. The departments and names of the colleges have not yet been heard.

Consider the following from a report of L. and W. Biddle of Earlham on a project to foster integration and prevent neighborhood deterioration in a nearby city: The staff of the project went to the President of the university in the area—"He was friendly enough to give time to the conversation, but reserved in response. Staff members tried to interpret the contemplated activity as a community service opportunity for the university, which opened up new vistas to the social sciences and gave pertinence to religion. The President made clear that he regarded such projects as 'do-gooder' activity in which the university officially could have no part. He would not, however, stand in the way of his faculty who might give extracurricular time[!]. He made oblique references also to money-raising campaigns which might be jeopardized by discussion of controversial questions. Throughout the project, faculty members from the social sciences, philosophy, and religion have been active. The university administration has taken no part in and given no recognition to the neighborhood activity."

Of course, when the Corporation is itself importantly a real estate operation and run as such—like the University of Chicago whether in the time of Hutchins or today—the Administration plays a more active (negative) part; and we see the students sitting-in in the President's office, with their dinner in paper sacks and their bedding. Similarly, we can hardly expect the Administration to be enthusiastic about reasonable international policy at the same time as it is dickering with the Air Force for many million dollars of Research.

In my opinion, many administrators are making a personal mistake. They are bigger than they allow themselves. They destroy themselves and trivialize their enterprises by an impossible moral position. The future will be otherwise, or there will be no future.

ix

Let us sum up. When there is a rigid system of society, imposing impersonal managerial aims, youth at once becomes an exploited class. For it must give up the genius of novelty that belongs to it, in order to implement the preconceived aims, and in fact to provide replacement and labor for the dominant system, whatever it happens to be. The *liberi,* the sons of freemen, effectually become slaves. Instead of a liberal education in arts or professional education in a *studium generale,* schooling becomes merely apprentice training. The idea of education is to bring up the young to be new centers of initiative; they are not merely trainees. They grow up by identifying with the adult society and culture, taking it over, renewing it, and transforming it. In an important sense, the educated—those who have commenced—make their own careers, because education has made their careers their own. A trainee does not have the chance to commence. He is stamped for a predetermined use. He must be motivated and disciplined.

Sometimes socialization fails. The young resist preformation and become class-conscious of themselves as exploited. And occasionally, instead of succumbing to confusion, they develop their own rebellious ideology. French Romanticism after the Congress of Vienna is a good example; or the flocking of the bohemians to Mazzini and Garibaldi in Rome. Their principle is that the enemy is the illiberal grownups who are in power. Their problem, however, is to find their own grownups, in order to learn something and become grown-up themselves.

In this light we can make sense of the American student attitude toward Castro. Reporters have had difficulty in finding the class basis of the Cuban Revolution. For instance Theodore Draper shows that it was not the industrial workers, not the farmers, not the middle class. But perhaps it was just the youth, rallying to this young leader, with the complaisance of the dis-

gusted elders. Indeed, Castro makes not a bad Garibaldi, he is even younger. The bother is that there was
no Mazzini, only Che Guevara (or, as it now seems,
Blas Roca in the shadows). But whether or not this
was importantly the case in Cuba itself, there is no
doubt that among the Beats and on our American campuses, Castro had this meaning. Our youth were not
much interested in Cuban economics and not at all in
Cuban civil liberties, nor that Castro broke the University of Havana. But they were enthusiastic over a
young fellow with a beard who licked the old squares,
and our own squares had better observe fair play. The
young were enraptured by every display of uninhibited
personal contact between Castro and the people that
defied protocol and public relations. Castro "paid
attention."

Mary Bunting of Radcliffe makes the same point in
another way when she says that at present the youth of
the world regard one another as an international class
and do not take their separate intervening governments
with equal seriousness.

In simple conditions, the young grow up among adults,
model themselves on adults, are included in adult activities, and become adults. But if, for good reasons, the
young dissociate themselves from the grown-up world,
they are faced with a peculiar problem. In order to learn
something and finish growing up, they must find and attach themselves to grownups who can be respected because they know something or have some other value;
who pay attention and let themselves be attached to; and
who play an exemplary role in the world that youth
can learn to share. These are the needs that express
themselves, in the colleges, as the complaint that there
is no contact with the teachers.

The first requirement can be met, for the teachers
can be respected. Most of them know something and

are not bad on their home grounds, in the classroom. And the students are touchingly respectful, except for a few cynics. The second requirement is harder, for it is just in their personal relations that the colleges have become poor communities. Guidance comes from impersonal administration; sympathetic clarification of the students' confused ideas comes from nobody; and the teachers brush off attention to themselves.

But it is the third requirement—the teacher as veteran—that is most necessary and most unavailable. Most necessary because it is only if the ideals and wisdom of the classroom make a difference in the intramural community and in the world that the student can understand that college is *about* something, it has a connection, rather than being merely a step on the ladder when there isn't much at the top. The student must learn that the intellectual virtues are active virtues. But this learning is unavailable because it is just the confrontation of reality, whether in the community of scholars or in the world, that is strongly discouraged in our colleges.

Chapter VII

REFORMS
AND PROPOSALS

i

Most of this critique is not newsy. Teachers thoughtfully worry about the frustrating conditions in which they have to teach, and I could have written the last three chapters mostly by quotations from them, instead of merely peppering the text with quotations in order to prove my unoriginality. We are unhappy about the swollen institutions, the business and government financing, the divisiveness of administrative rules, the lack of personal contact, the irrelevant methods of accountancy, the specialist pride of faculties, the closed minds and conformity of students.

My idiosyncratic emphases have been that college teaching is not itself a profession, but a college teacher is a professional who teaches; and that the community of scholars must confront society, often in conflict; a university is not a monastery but a walled city. Let me try to explain these odd personal emphases. I am a man of letters pretty busy in the world, but sometimes

I teach in the Inferior Faculty of arts. But it is just this faculty that, unlike Law, Medicine, Theology, or Engineering, has tended to become academic, consisting preponderantly of "professional teachers" (except for the natural scientists). Therefore my view that the professional historian, humanist, or philosopher is not an academic seems unusual. But it is ancient.* Secondly—and perhaps it is the same thing!—as an anarchist I feel that our association of scholars, like any other association that does real work, has an independent voice in the common council of society and is duty bound to tell them off when they behave like fools. This view is ancient too.

Yet apart from this theme of the nonacademic and the socially conflictful, the contemporary critics of the universities are looking to the same traditional ideal of teaching-and-learning that I sketched in the first chapter of this book. In terms of it they have proposed fairly radical reforms, and have sometimes tried them out. This is a difference between the usual social criticism and the social criticism of the colleges; and proves that the colleges are still living communities, though sadly fragmented. In no other area in our society, not in urbanism, economy, popular culture, or politics, does radical criticism lead to continual efforts at remedy. The principles of college reform are clear-cut: to get back to teaching-and-learning as a simple relation of persons, and to make the teaching-and-learning

* Medieval schoolmen were, rather simply, also political and ecclesiastical figures. But from the Renaissance through the Enlightenment, humanists tended even to avoid the universities. Bacon, Descartes, Spinoza, Leibniz, Voltaire, Gibbon, were moderns and worldly, whereas the schools were ossified. Erasmus and Locke were in and out, and in trouble. Kant was a remarkable exception, but even he finally ran into trouble. After the French Revolution, however, the scenery begins to look like our own.

more committed, more for keeps. Is reform of this kind significantly possible within the framework of our present colleges and universities? I think so, but it will require more revolutionary courage than most of the collegiate critics seem to exude. In this chapter let us review a dozen recent proposals to reform the size and centralism of the institution, the conception of the teacher, the conception of the students, and the curriculum and methods. In the final chapter I shall suggest a more drastic experiment not in the framework of the present schools.

ii

Since persons are lost in the sheer quantity, diversity, and massiveness of the universities, and especially during the present period of expansion and excessive mobility, critics propose setting up smaller "colleges," relatively self-contained and self-administering, within the larger administration. How is the mean size determined? It must be small enough for face-to-face relations; to insure frequent meetings of students and the collegiate teachers, and conversation and commensalism of students with the same studies; and also to recruit by acquaintance rather than records. It must be large enough to have a well-rounded assortment of teachers and students, enough for a couple of years. The purpose of the small experimental college within the larger college, says Christian Bay, is "protection against the consensus . . . and vigorous exchange of intellectual stimuli." Jencks and Riesman hope that each college will, by self-government and self-recruitment, develop a unique "tone." They propose Houses of 450 plus 50 teachers. Theodore Newcomb estimates that 300 to 400 is the optimal size, and he mentions a common coffee bar for faculty and students. The independent experimental colleges of recent times, Sarah Lawrence, Reed, Bard, St. Johns of Annapolis, etc., have tended to be larger by a few hundred because they do not have the university professors in the background to fill out the program; but the Black Mountain community never had more than 150 all told. (It was, however, intensely communal: one could not always tell apart the students, the married students, and the teachers. This made for a fuller life and for trouble.) The medieval universities were usually well under 500. The older American liberal arts colleges, Amherst, Carleton, Knox, Haverford, Swarthmore, etc., have usually grown larger, but they too set a limit: 1,200 seems to be a sticking point, very hard to maintain when there are so many applicants to these prestigious seminaries and so much loose money abroad for new buildings and grounds. It is a badge of honor if they stay fairly small.

Balancing the mean size is a principle of federation. When small colleges are set up in the larger college, the central administration is their federal union. (Cf., a similar proposal for mass urban lower schools: "The solution lies in the development of a philosophy and administrative procedure which retain the advantages of centralization but which regain those of decentralization."—J. K. Norton, of Teachers College.) Independent colleges, on the other hand, form regional Conferences, like Grinnell, Knox, Carleton, etc., or Mt. Holyoke, Amherst, Massachusetts State, etc., which can exchange books, use common expensive scientific equipment, have equally matched games, and perhaps exchange teachers. Needless to say, this excellent Jeffersonian idea of local autonomy and federal co-operation could be profitably applied in our society elsewhere than in schools. Ancient universities, of course, were nothing but such a vast federation; their masters were licensed to teach everywhere; the students wandered from one university to another and brought new texts that were immediately copied; there was a *lingua franca*. And it was out of this anarchic universalism of local associations, communities and scientific academies, that, as Kropotkin liked to point out, there grew the amazing consensual system of modern science. They were all entirely lacking in "organization"; they unanimously sought a common truth. In fact there was an exquisite voluntary organization, of conferences, correspondence, exchange of students, rapid publication. So Jenner wrote to Paris in the midst of the Napoleonic war, "Science has no nation." But the style of our generation is tightly to organize local science, even to make it irrelevantly competitive, and at the same time to forbid the universal exchange of knowledge.

Honors programs, within departments or cutting across departmental lines, are analogous attempts to escape the impersonal mass. These are set up for a small group of selected students and a few teachers, dispensing with credits and grading, providing more "integrated" studies, and allowing more intellectual sharing. An Honors group may have a small library of its own, a lounge with a coffee urn, and so forth. At a big state university, Honors is likely to be a pathetic tiny "college" of intellectuals in a busy crowd of mining engineers, aggies, and practical nurses.

In general, I am not convinced that any merely sociological or administrative arrangement like Colleges or Honors can profoundly enhance the spirit of a community of scholars or its use in the world, any more than busy and lighted streets make for safe and happy neighborhoods. Most collegiate plans are borrowed from the colleges of the English universities, and their example is not impressive. To the extent that colleges provide more intellectual contact, it is likely to be more incestuous. To heal the split between the "social" and the "intellectual" experience of college will still not lead to a committed life that will withstand, on graduation, careers of status and salary or again becoming an academic. Indeed, it is said that the big corporations prefer to hire the graduates of liberal arts colleges rather than those trained specially for the corporations, because they are more intellectually alive. But we often see on campuses that those who are in fact more earnest, spontaneously seek one another out at a peace rally, the literary magazine, the odd-ball fraternity. They form their own college, and perhaps it is an advantage for them to mix and fight democratically with the mining engineers, etc. What is lacking is teachers.

Perhaps it would be possible to heighten the *esprit de corps* of a group of willing students by stripping away the conventional middle-class architectural framework and reducing their little community to the poverty of its scholarly functions. Quonset huts, wooden barracks, or an old house in the neighborhood serve well enough for dormitories and classrooms. (Robert Hutchins somewhere recommends tents.) A sandlot and a river are sufficient for games. Money could be spent only on books, scientific equipment, and scholarships. The fees could be lowered. Possibly, though, our society being what it is, such a poor college of a prestigious university would at once become the swankiest and most prestigious part.

iii

Let us turn to the teachers. It has become customary in schools great and small to invite outside experts, professionals, and authors to lecture, take a day's class, lead a seminar, take part in a "campus conference." Sometimes an individual professor or a department extends the invitation—there are special funds for the purpose, distinct from the more ornamental convocation lectureships—and the purpose is to stir up the students, to confront them with the author of their text, to bring a little of the world of practice into the academy. Often it is the students or student organizations that set up the conferences, sometimes with the fairly obvious purpose of getting a dissenting voice on the campus to annoy the professors. There is also a vogue of writers or artists "in residence," as if the ordinary faculty feel that there is a creative life to which the students should be exposed; but the artists, on the other hand, must not limit themselves to being teachers. In the professional schools, whether of medicine, architecture, or business, veteran practitioners exist more officially on the faculties as part-time teachers; inevitably, for the practice of the art is the immediate aim of the studies. But by and large these part-timers also regard themselves as outsiders performing a service to the profession, rather than as members of the community of scholars.

The essential purpose, of learning from the veteran, is not realized by these means, for the veteran is not, and is not allowed to be, a scholar. (Yet it is easily realized by the assistants of a scientific researcher when he is engaged on his own, not some outsider's research; or by the medical students who follow a physician in the hospital; or by the students in an architect's atelier.) Rather, the effect of inviting the outsider is to make the academic seem even more academic. He himself is likely to be a poor scholar, but he is a being from another world to which the students look even more wistfully. And the part-time engineer or lawyer also confirms the academism of the academy, by both the hard practicality of his practice and the narrowness of his unscholarly intellect.

How ponderously we defeat our purposes! We start with the fact that there are professions and tasks in the world that require learning, and they are performed by men. We make an abstraction from the performance of these men; those who can meet these "standards" will be licensed. We then copy off the license requirements as the curricula and departments of schools; and we man the departments with academic teachers. Naturally, at so many removes, the students do not take the studies for real; so we then import veterans from outside to pep things up! * Would it not be more plausible to omit the intervening steps and have the real professionals do the teaching? But they don't know anything,

---

* The same procedure is followed, of course, in primary education. In a simple farm and village society, a child went to school for a few hours to learn the three R's that he could not pick up in the barn and field. What is the school now? Take the old primary curriculum of Franklin Babbitt and the National Education Association as typical: "Fundamental processes. Health. Home. Vocation. Citizenship. Leisure. Ethics." An abstraction is made from ordinary life; it is set up as the curriculum; and departments are manned to teach ordinary life—across four distorting reflections.

Recently, at a teachers college, I proposed two experiments to leave out most of the mirrors. (1) To have a class not go to school at all, the only principle of selection being to choose kids whose homes are not so disastrous that the children need school as a necessary refuge. The prediction is that they will learn just as much. (2) Dispensing with the building and curriculum, to use the city as the school, by having classes of tens wander about the city accompanied by a guide and interpreter, somewhat like the Athenian pedagogue. A judicious mixture of these methods, I urged, might save a lot of money which could hopefully go into teachers' salaries and smaller classes. Nevertheless, my proposals were received with varying degrees of lack of enthusiasm.

they are narrow practitioners. Of course they don't, of course they are! They are not the faculty of a *studium generale*.

For the sake of *both* the university and the professions, the professionals must return and assume responsibility for the history and humanity of their arts by taking real places again on the faculty of the university. Responsible teaching of the young is always teaching of the more ideal, for the young must transform practice in the world. If the young are free, they will not put up with narrow practical teaching; it's too boring; it's not worth studying; they ask far-reaching and embarrassing questions. On the other hand, only real practice is believable and authoritative.

At present, there is no philosophy of medicine, no jurisprudence, and no social theory of engineering. The social consequences are disastrous. And in my opinion, it is importantly because they are not on the faculty that artists and writers are so individualistic and fragmented as to be almost treasonable in their co-operation with *l'infame,* and in their failure to defend the plain sense and beauty that they know. On the other hand, if they were regent masters they could set the conditions of freedom under which they are willing to assume responsibility.

The university must incorporate veterans so the teaching-and-learning can be for keeps. We can conceive of a faculty with a permanent staff of full-time tenured teachers, people who have a special calling for teaching and veterans who have retired to it. To these we must add many practicing veterans who also have a permanent association with the university, some temporarily teaching full time, some teaching part time. And through these, the faculties can extend out among all the artists and the professionals in the region.* Since

* At Columbia, largely through the efforts of Frank Tannen-

historically our universities have taken over the science of the learned academies, which are now largely ceremonial, they must assume the social responsibility of being the concourse of the learned. And especially in the present expansion of the colleges, we ought not be so wasteful of our intellectual resources. The present restriction of faculties to professional academics almost guarantees that they will be manned by inferior professionals. But many of the best, who are now outside, would join the guild if they had freedom and some power.*

If the faculties were composed in this way, they could not easily be controlled by administrations. There would be too many distinguished independents; the combined voice would be too authoritative. More important, they would become a force to be reckoned with in society. The University is the *amicus curiae* of society, the disinterested professional knowledge that advises and warns. Who else? We have had miserable evidence that the Bar Association, the Medical Association, the Institute of Architects, etc., will not play the role because they are too concerned with licensing and often with their members' own financial interests.

---

baum, there are so-called University Seminars on various broad topics, composed of Columbia professors and scholars of the region, some teaching at other schools. The monthly meetings are profitable for the members, but they could also perform a teaching function, e.g., as advisers and critics of theses. It is a pity that so much scholarly power is not put to more academic use. Yet, if it were put to use, there is a risk that these voluntary clubs would soon be administered to death.
* Cf., Robert Lynd, "As a growing number of more highly paid occupations are drawing men and women from teaching, emphasis comes to be laid on the perfection of the system rather than upon the personality or qualifications of the teacher." By the same token, the recent Schinnerer report on the New York City system pointed out that the bureaucratic selection drove away the good candidates!

Traditionally it is the university that, just because it has no direct social power, is the voice of universal reason and criticism. When Kant said it, he was reaffirming the ancient *ius respondendi*. Let us be specific. Conceive of the scholars—the veterans banded in their conservative and future-making function exercising their appropriate right in the world as the loyal opposition and watchdog of society. The physics department will notify the public that scientific secrecy and competition rather than co-operation in exploring space* are incompatible with science as taught in the classroom and laboratory. The school of architecture will speak up about the public housing and the absence of any philosophy of community in the civil engineering in cities like New York. The departments of physiology and psychology will have much to tell the police and the legislators about the narcotics and sex laws, laws which it seems will never be changed unless by the intervention of informed professional opinion from the universities, because it is clear that neither the churches nor the important professional associations are able to come across. (Local bodies, like the New York Academy of Medicine, have tried.) The departments of English and the school of journalism will co-operate in criticizing the inadequacy—one might almost say the lying—of the *New York Times* and the nauseating tone of the advertising. (Isn't it odd that the Federal Communications Commissioner can call the TV a wasteland, but the English Department of Harvard cannot?)

My point is not that the university is to take political

---

* Prescott tells the story that when Columbus was returning from his first voyage, he put in at Lisbon. John of Portugal corresponded with his Secretary of State as to whether it was possible to annihilate the expedition and all traces of it. But it was already too much abroad—the Admiral of the Ocean was not a bashful man—so the King received him with honor.

positions. On the contrary, it must be apart from politics: politics is too transient, not important enough. But it must affirm intransigently the maxims that are categorical imperatives for the teaching, the ideal, of each department of learning, and the public insult to which, indeed, undermines civilized society.* And it must try as much as possible to express these home truths not through the isolated voices of individual professors, but as the consensual voice of all the scholars in the departments, and in the name of the university. If governments have to cope with practical emergencies by devious means—and they do have to—let them hear also the concerted opinion of the university goading them to get out of it quick. It is not the violation of civilization that is the scandal. This is what power is made of. But it is the fact that it is allowed to pass as the regular course of things.

Young people would then be proud of their elders and their school; and I think the teaching-and-learning would be more for keeps.

iv

The more profound critics see that the present task is to help the young to achieve identity, to discover and accept who they are, and to explore and find real opportunities to realize themselves. *Identity and Anxiety* is a typical title. Education must unmake the *anomie* and anxiety caused by the standardizing socialization

---

* In an interesting footnote, Professor Hofstadter mentions "the recent tendency to propose more rigorous academic self-discipline or self-censorship in return for an anticipated broader respect for university independence from the community." This is the German philosophy. It misses the point. Self-censorship on what? Respect comes not from discipline but from power, where there is relevant authority.

that has replaced a more viable traditional socialization. The problem is anthropological in the classical meaning—the question being, "What is Man?"—and the authors are influenced by psychoanalysis and a kind of existential theology.

In the colleges it is proposed to make at least the freshman year an exploration. (In principle this is the opposite of the administrative idea of freshman orientation to the environment provided by the adults, but in practice they can amount to the same thing if there is plenty of free choice, including the choice to do very little. In both cases there have to be adult attention and following-up to give support to the panicky.) At Harvard—largely, I think, through Professor Riesman—freshmen can register in the Seminar as their first-year course of study. This is a year-long bull session, frequently provoked by ringers from outside, hopefully leading to fields of interest and specific reading and reports. At Sarah Lawrence the essence of the freshman Exploratory Course is a weekly individual conference* to try to tailor-make a course of reading and reports that might catch fire in the student's interest that has been well swamped by past miseducation. When I myself teach freshmen, I find myself trying to fill, with little encyclopedic lectures, the abysses of ignorance that they reveal on the most common subjects—what a jury is, where the liver is—because I feel that otherwise they are lacking in confidence in any conversation or reading whatever. Professor Nelson,

---

* I do not think the *individual* attention is such a good idea. The girls become too isolated. I would prefer seeing three for an hour and a half together to seeing three for a half an hour each. There is as much "individual" attention, and very soon as much "private" revelation. Also, there is not much that a teacher can tell one student that is not profitable for a couple of others to hear.

the historian, on the other hand, has a knack for calling attention to their actual things and behavior—a cut of clothes, a piece of slang—to make them aware that they have a past in time and a place in the world.

At the other end of the college years, I have proposed to various administrators, so far unsuccessfully, a course of group therapy for the senior year, when the young people are about to choose careers (or to stall) and to marry (or not marry)—they rarely know why. As seniors they are in a position to become economically independent enough to risk finding out something about their relation to Papa. I envisage groups of less than ten for a two-hour weekly session. Of course such a course must not be called "psychology" but preferably be put in the Humanities, where indeed it belongs.

The attempt to pierce to common humanity by self-awareness in groups is more realistic, I think, than the curricular program of Robert Hutchins and his friends to establish communication by teaching the common great books and philosophy. With adolescents, a great-books program is almost sure to result in merely verbal wisdom and, in fact, a superior kind of withdrawal from the world, rather than courageous initiative. Neither Hutchins nor his mentor Mark Van Doren ever seems to remember that the course of study they advocate was explicitly postponed by Plato till age thirty to thirty-five, when a man had some practical experience to be scientific and philosophic *about*. (The Greek ephebic education was heavily weighted toward character-training and war.) In his aim to restrict the college to the theoretical, Hutchins can go to absurd lengths. E.g., "A modern heresy is that formal education must assume the total responsibility for the development of the individual. The Greek notion that the city educates the man has been forgotten. . . . Their elders spend no time in school, yet, we hope, they are constantly gaining in practical wisdom." Of course he is not serious, but he is even less serious than he thinks. There *is* no city. The kind of practical wisdom that one needs cannot be learned from the city, for it is how to cope with the kind of city there is. The elders of most of these youth are *not* constantly gaining in practical wisdom, but in fact are constantly discouraging mature men and women from existing.

Rather than use the language of Identity, I should prefer to say that the academic problem at present is to *unblock* the intellect in the young, to prove that it is possible for persons to display intellectual virtues without embarrassment or punishment, and to use them in the community and the world without futility. For this we need the community of scholars, of other students and of veterans. As Frank Pinner puts it, "Education is the same thing as the creation of the academic community." He then speaks movingly for the teacher's revealing himself to his students as a fallible man, a hard prescription for an academic. Having more non-academic professionals on the faculty, as I have advocated, would show the strength and the weakness of the intellect in the world—and this might well be embarrassing for the nonacademic; he may cow the students with his tough low-down and know-how, but they may also quit his class in droves. The presence of veterans would serve also to dispel the bugaboos of close contact with the students that now make academic personalities so timid that there is no contact at all. A man who has a grounding in the big world can let himself be in his personal relations; he has more perspective and can rely on probabilities, his feelings, and his judgment. For the young just this attitude clears away ambiguities and is fortifying.

Finally, there are proposals for student freedom. At some places the students have spokesmen in the faculty meeting, so they have a measure of control or at least of veto of the college environment that they are subjected to. I do not see why in matters of behavior, e.g., dormitory rules, they should not have preponderant control and keep their own peace, as Jefferson prescribed. A recent student proposal at a big Eastern school seems to me to be statesmanlike: to divide the dormitories into three voluntary groups, one without (sexual) rules, one with liberal rules, one with the present rules. This would have the immense ethical advantage of making the law jibe with the facts. In other matters, the students should at least have the right to talk back. The idea of the "Harvard" issue of *i.e.* was a good one, a critical review of the university by the graduating class. Students at Columbia are pushing an even brasher proposal, to review the teachers and courses at the end of each semester.

Simply as education, freedom is indispensable. Consider the following from Dewey's *Experience and Education*—he is talking about children making noise in class; but the same holds for the social freedom of collegians: "Let me speak of the advantages which reside potentially in increase of outward freedom. In the first place, it is practically impossible for a teacher to gain knowledge of the individuals without its existence. Enforced quiet and acquiescence prevent pupils from disclosing their real natures. They enforce artificial uniformity. . . . The other important advantage is found in the very nature of the learning process. There cannot be complete quietude in a laboratory or a workshop. Periods of genuine reflection occur only when they follow times of more overt action and are used to organize what has been gained in activity in which the hands and other parts of the body besides the brain are used." *

Something should be said, too, about Admissions. Since higher education is at present a seller's market, there is a great to-do about whom to admit, and high-school students live in anxiety lest they be rejected by this or that "prestige" college. (Their anxiety is misplaced, since there is not much significant difference between the best of the schools and the average. A youth is lucky if in his four years he meets three or four teachers who communicate to *him,* and this is as likely at the University of Nebraska as at Yale.) Administrations fear that, if they go by academic records, they will collect too many "intellectuals"; their policy is to try to get "well-rounded" individuals—an interesting breed that, according to one theory, tends to be pre-psychotic. Recently, Professor Kemeny of Dartmouth has suggested a more rational idea that it is the college and not the individuals that should be "well-rounded." Being a mathematician, he proposes a quota system, 5 per cent to satisfy alumni, 5 per cent in hopes of future endowments, 5 per cent of screwballs, 5 per cent from west of the Mississippi, etc., etc. (But he

---

* But Dewey, as usual, backtracks with an unnecessary restriction: "There can be no greater mistake, however, than to treat such freedom as an end in itself. It then tends to be destructive of the shared cooperative activities which are the normal source of order." This is so only if the environmental and social structure, which is disturbed by commotion, are *themselves* not subject to experimental change. It is the rigidity of the background structure which makes for "individualistic" high jinks and disruptive fooling around that do not exhaust themselves. If a society is fairly open, free agents have a pretty good tact for it, and there is also no need to tease and torment it.

does not suggest that Dartmouth become co-ed.)* I wonder if we cannot propose something simpler. If the syllabus of a college were scrupulously honest, if it listed what was really taught and how, what the teachers were really interested in, and perhaps included a fair sampling of student critical reviews of the kind mentioned above—then the prospective students could make enlightened free choices and each college might automatically attain its proper center of gravity. If public relations were forgotten and the notion of "prestige" absolutely discouraged, there would be a lesser problem of Admissions.

v

Proposals and reforms in curriculum and methods have, of course, been legion. They are the craftwork of academics and get most of their attention. What is most objected to is the quantity of chopped-up courses and the departmentalization, causing confusion and imposing pressures that the students cannot meet. So there are proposals for Integration and Sequence. To me, these are not impressive. A panoply of integrated courses is the equivalent of one great Text Book written by a wise Educator for "teachers" who are his mouthpieces. There is no such wisdom. The teachers do not teach it; it does not fit the students. In effect, the ideal curriculum becomes a format restricting the exchange between actual teachers and students in actual

* At a progressive school I taught at, we used the policy of "a cross-section of society," and had a Noah's ark of 2 Chinese, 2 Puerto Ricans, 2 children of bankers, 2 poor orphans, 2 children of the NMU, 2 children of the ILGWU, 2 children of Greenwich Village artists, etc. (I'm not kidding.) Fortunately, the woman in charge of recruiting had, like Socrates, a prejudice in favor of children who were beautiful or intelligent, so it was very well.

classes. E.g., since Professor McKeon's Aristotle is not the same as Professor Carnap's, it is useless to pretend that the student can stand on the one as "prerequisite" for the other. Interpretation is in fact a continuing debate and this is confusing for a youth; but unless he realizes it, his confusion is confounded.

The master Text Book does not exist. But since, as I have explained above, I think that *any* preconceived pattern is unviable and unnecessary, I do not need to pursue the details. Confusion and pressure can be reduced by simply dropping the whole rigmarole of credits and compulsory attendance, and by having free electives and guidance by a staff meeting of the student's actual teachers who know him. John Dewey's principle of an intrinsic organization of the studies: to learn something in such a way that it leads to wanting to learn more, seems to me quite sufficient.*

In this book I have rather scrupulously avoided discussing curriculum but have stuck to the relation of

---

* Unfortunately Dewey himself becomes panicky about it, and is swayed by the objection that students will only learn what they "enjoy," which is admittedly thin gruel. In the first place, a student can choose only those courses that some teacher is willing to teach. But also, people do not choose what "pleases" but what seems important, necessary, or exciting even though painful. I say "seems"—they are likely in error—but in such errors there is something important, if only to get rid of a conceit.

Instead, Dewey says, "The educator [!] must have a long look ahead; he must be aware of the potentialities for leading students into new fields . . . and must use this knowledge as his criterion for selection and arrangement" etc. This leads to the interminable administrative methodology of Progressive Schools. It is unnecessary. If the teacher and student stay in contact with each other and with the subject matter, in *both* enthusiasm and balkiness, rapidity and stupidity, the encounter will generate its own deep meaning and next attraction—or rejection.

teaching-and-learning. If a teacher wants to teach something, he must think it worth while; and students want either to learn something particular or to find out what it is that they want to learn. This is enough for a school. Within pretty wide limits of utter triviality, there can be good education that is "general" or "specialist," "liberal" or "useful," "humanist" or "technical." Put it this way: I can contemplate with equanimity a society in which the majority are well rounded or the majority are expert technicians; therefore I can accept an education that would lead to either. It is good in principle for a man to *know* literature and history, the workings of society, a natural science, and mathematics. But I am less and less convinced that *prescribing* these studies to undergraduates has any relation whatever to their mature use and knowledge of them. There is perhaps more hope in suggesting a new kind of experience to a youth when he seems to be starved for it, and so broadening *his* culture. Of course, like everybody else, I have my own view of what constitutes an ideal or "natural" curriculum; it means that this is what I myself would choose to teach, and it is probably what I myself learned or lacked. (It is hard for writers on education not to be guided by the satisfactions and aversions of their own education, which inevitably has a certain "rightness," since it has brought them to exactly where they are.) Furthermore, if there is real encounter in a *studium generale,* of teachers with teachers, students with students, and teachers and students, there is bound to be a kind of humanism. Communication, common language, comes from good will and encounter, not from all studying the same master Text Book. But naturally academics have a fetishism of curriculum. Even the crazy catch-all of big American state universities, with their degrees in hotel management, bee-keeping, and ceramics, has a democratic justification. As Lincoln said, "People who like that kind of thing find it just the kind of thing they like." Unless taught with willful stupidity and learned with apathetic obedience, no course is necessarily utterly trivial and divisive. If I am not mistaken, this is what the early Socratic dialogues are about: that you begin to guess at the idea of the good by becoming aware of what it is to be a good General, Actor, etc.; you do not get it by studying Philosophy.

The opposite error from the philosopher's is the administrator's curriculum, "planning for social needs." The philosopher tends to affirm that there is a special *subject matter* for college, e.g., theory, higher learning, well-rounded culture. The administration tends to deny that teaching-and-learning is even a special kind of *function*. "Social needs" can mean to fit the young into the adult world as it is, or—as with Dr. Conant's "new national needs"—to train them to meet an emergency that the adults have created but can't handle. The latter, narrower meaning is brute conscription, no different from ten years of selective service. The former, more democratic meaning is to make the school a pallid double of the outside world; in which case it would be better to stay in the solid city itself and apprentice oneself to its functions. Why go to college and get a watered-down version?

It is not necessary to plan for Society. Society is inevitably present in any school in how the children are, what the youth aspire to, what the teachers have mastered and can teach. This is the existing curriculum; *the problem is, by scholarship, to outgrow it.* And one is stuck with this curriculum, for—no matter what philosophers or administrators propose—nothing else will really be studied. A teacher may have something important for youth to hear, but there is no use in prescribing it. Either they gravitate to it, or they will not

learn it. Of course many things ought to be taught even
if nobody comes, *ad majorem Dei gloriam*. (Don't ask
me how to make a living out of that.)

vi

The crucial question is not what ought to be taught, but
whether the teaching-and-learning makes any difference. Is it committed or merely "academic"? If scholarship makes a difference in the soul and behavior,
studies will tend to integrate and focus by themselves,
for man is a unitary being, just as in *making* a book,
the research tends to integrate. The underlying then
comes to the fore, and this is the classical. It is not
grammar that is classical, but to find that one's speech
has a structure. The classic is not philosophy, but to
find that one's science has a method and limits. The humanities begin by finding that one's subject, whatever
it is, exists in time and place and is the work of men.
On the other hand, any abstract outline or ideal curriculum will in practice tend to divide, subdivide, and
go dead, like consulting a library catalogue.

Commitment, importance, integration, and the classical are the same thing. They are the underlying. Not
surprisingly, however, on the subject of the life-commit-
ment of what they are doing, academic critics have
been less fertile in inventive reforms. Many teachers are
very earnest as teachers, they love their subjects, and
they sweat to make the students learn the lesson; and
many students, who want to learn something, try very
hard to get the message. But it is astonishing how, except in the natural sciences and the professions, the
academic work is not even supposed to have consequences; it is considered as morally and even personally
useless. Perhaps it is simply that the teachers are impatient. They are rebuffed at the cold reception that

the students give so many beautiful arts and sciences, so they become cynical and trivial. But for many reasons, these students have lost touch with this tradition; its importance is not *prima facie* to them. They do not believe the studies, and so they do not believe in the teachers. However it is, it is certainly dismaying to go about the campuses and never hear, including the natural sciences and professions, a normal glorying in so many beautiful arts and sciences, nor hope in them, nor dedication to civilization.

There have been bold attempts to reform the academism of social sciences by teaching pragmatically, with a moral commitment to solve real problems. At Earlham, William Biddle's course in Community Dynamics was of this kind. Community Dynamics and the "Action Anthropology" of Sol Tax are grounded in the idea that the social sciences do not have, and really cannot have, a body of achieved truth that we can then "apply," but their truth is found in their use; and this must be taken into account also in teaching them. At the University of Pennsylvania, Karl Linn and his students in Landscape Architecture are carrying out a lovely dumb-bunny project of improving tax-delinquent properties in a slum area with the labor and improvisation of neighborhood kids. (They are just now, I am told, facing an interesting problem: shall they illegally knock down fences that obstruct use and beauty, since they cannot get in touch with the absentee landlords?) A few small schools, e.g., Goddard, consider themselves duty-bound to improve their local regions; some giant urban institutions, on the contrary, are charged with being slumlords. Especially at the richer schools, there is a good deal of field-tripping to Puerto Rico, etc.; but this idea would make more sense as education if the students would set up shop in the nearest 100 per cent segregated neighborhood and cope with the problem of acquaintanceship. Oscar Lewis tried this (among farm families) at the University of St. Louis. "Work periods," economic jobs in society, are now usual in the experimental colleges; the jobs become the subjects of unflattering analyses, but I do not know if, or how, this affects the career choices of the students. (I am told that, having analyzed a racket, the students either aspire to managerial jobs in it, or become beatniks.) Finally, one is struck that there is so little pragmatic sociology using small groups within the community itself; I know by experience that this is disturbing to deans, but that might be part of the hypothesis.

Society uses the schools for its purposes. By pragmatic sociology, the community of scholars returns on society and uses it for its own purposes.

The academic problem is the following: how to teach what is practical and yet not make the university a trade school. What is important is that the narrowly practical be what is practical according to the standard of a *studium generale*. For an elegant solution, let me quote from a study on Bail and the Indigent Accused: "Law schools have been concerned about the little opportunity for clinical work provided for their students. Fledgling lawyers are often disturbed to find that many of the lawyer's practical skills could not be taught in school. The students on the bail project are acquiring some of these skills. One need only watch these young men and women learning to talk to and gain trust of the poor, the illiterate, the frightened and the hostile, to be convinced that this experience is invaluable. It would do the law teacher good to listen to a student review a case with the project director and be forced to buttress his conclusion with verified facts. Lawyers make decisions and people's lives and property depend on those decisions. These students are getting a taste of the responsibilities of the lawyer and they can see the flesh-

and-blood results. They are learning to make decisions that count: their recommendations may determine whether a man remains in jail for weeks or months, or is returned to his family and his job."—Professor Charles Ares of New York University and Herbert Sturz of the Vera Foundation, a Project to further equal protection of the law for the poor.

This experiment, let me say, has a further dimension: The enrichment of society by the excursion of the University. To quote further: "The students are getting a clinical experience [incidentally, with pay] and an academic course related to that experience. If along the way an interest in the criminal law as a career is stimulated, the whole criminal process will be enriched. It has long been lamented that the 'good' lawyer shuns criminal law and applies himself to corporate affairs and the like. Only when the problem of an accused takes the form of an intriguing constitutional question does the 'respectable' lawyer pay much attention. Perhaps exposure will change this for some of these students."

The situation in the humanities, however, is pretty hopeless. There have been "reforms" but, by and large, they do more harm than good. There has been an immense increase in courses in creative art and writing and in courses in appreciation; and these must have their customary effect, since the teachers are often competent, of liberating feeling and fantasy. But they have certainly not had an important moral effect, except just in the cases of students who become disgusted with the community of scholars and leave it. (Mostly in such cases there is a good deal of conceit; I doubt that they will amount to much as artists and writers; nevertheless their excitement and their protest are real.) The same holds for the proliferation of artists and writers in residence that we have mentioned. They make conversation pieces but they are academically quarantined. Consider a good remark of Dewey's on Appreciation: "Appreciation, by enhancement of qualities which make an ordinary experience appealing, appropriable, capable of full assimilation, constitutes the prime function of literature, music, drawing, etc., in education. . . . They have the effect of fixing taste, forming standards for the worth of later experiences. They arouse discontent with conditions which fall below their measure, they create a demand for surroundings up to their own level. . . . They are not luxuries of education, but emphatic expressions of that which makes any education worth while." This is an excellent restatement of Matthew Arnold; it repeats the emphasis on the moral use of music in Greek and Chinese antiquity; it does not apply at all to the work of the fine arts in our present schools.

The same holds for the accurate distinctions of duty made in courses of moral philosophy; the here-and-now crisis taught in courses in existentialism; the recollection of past humanity in courses in history; the analysis of power and pattern in courses in sociology and anthropology. These evidently do not rouse effectual discontent or any demand on society, or even in the college community. They do not initiate character-change in the students or the teachers. What is worse, nobody proposes that they should! I have not read a single statement of the academic critics to this purpose. Instead, there is all along the line a double standard, the academic truth and the real truth. Milton and Racine are read with one aesthetic perception, but the newspaper and the movie are taken in by quite another. Socrates and Kant, I have been told, enjoyed the luxury of being able to choose the useful, the right, etc., but this is not for teachers and students in America

1962. The melancholy scene of history does not disturb the scholars as they create an even more melancholy history (some of them in Washington); the few human moments in history do not stir them to emulation.

Here is the arc of this book. We started with the University of Paris, embattled with the Double Truth of Averroes and Siger. At that time the Double Truth was a (conscious and unconscious) camouflage to enable the University to promulgate *its* unorthodox truth. We end with the two "truths" browsing peacefully side by side, in co-ordination.* And the new double standard has again been elevated to an official academic theology, thanks to Dr. Niebuhr!—there are spiritual values but with the institutions of man nothing good can be done. Taken at face value, this doctrine means that there is no practical reason to retain the humanities in the university; they should quietly be dropped. They were the first to come, in Paris and Oxford; they should be the first to be disposed of. For honorific reasons, nobody dares to propose this—aside from the fact that there are so many tenured jobs.

Let me make one simple counterproposal to teachers of writing that I myself have used in class. Since the college is a community and ought to have a culture, let the students write serious stories, plays, and essays about the persons and events in the community, the

---

* The situation is not restricted to universities. As a writer for the magazines, I am told that I can be as "far out" as I please, for the articles and stories are the nonsustaining part of the magazine—the sustaining part is the advertising. There must be some writing in order to keep up circulation and get second-class mailing; but it is not important whether I influence (or offend) readers. I ought not, of course, directly to offend advertisers, but they are pretty thick-skinned. I still seem to have a good knack of offending editors; yet as my reputation grows, even this is failing me.

other students, the teachers, the administrators; and publish the pieces that are imaginative, feelingful, and true. It is more or less what the writers-in-residence do after they have left but, as Mahatma Gandhi would have said, this is much less charming.

Chapter VIII

A SIMPLE PROPOSAL

i

For the near future the prospect of significant reform in the great majority of schools and especially in the most populous ones, is dim. In the nature of the case the very changes that are needed are the ones that administrations must resist, for they curtail administration's reason for being and jeopardize its security. Decentralizing control, splitting up rather than expanding, dispensing with credits, grading, and admissions, de-emphasizing buildings and grounds, being selective about contracting research—all these make pale the hectic flush. It would seem to be self-evident that the only purpose of educational administration is to expedite education, but this thought is entirely naïve and out-of-date. Worse, however, the reforms toward freedom, commitment, criticism, and inevitable social conflict, endanger the Image and indeed nullify the historical role of administration which has been not to protect its community but to pacify it. So let us propose to go outside the present collegiate framework. The simplest remedy is the historical one, for bands of scholars to secede and set up where they can teach and learn on their own simple conditions. Such a movement is difficult but not impractical. In my opinion, if it could succeed in a dozen cases—proving that there is a viable social alternative to what we have—the entire system would experience a profound and salutary jolt.

Secession is inevitably occurring in any case. But for want of thought it is occurring wrong. Briefly, as our present social system approaches a cultural crisis of meaninglessness, dissatisfied young people cannot/will not conform to it and they quit the schools. They group and try to find a culture or create it out of nothing. Even little academies are formed, led by tutors in their twenties and early thirties, e.g., Emerson, Blake, Pasternak. This is classical; but what is wrong is that they include few senior scholars who know something, and few veterans who undertake to teach professions in an objective and systematic way. This is because the seniors are a generation older and got their grasp when the situation was bad but not quite so desperate; therefore they are not now so completely at a loss. The young regard them—I have experienced it—with a mixture of superstitious respect and personal unbelief. The respect—sometimes envious, resentful, and hostile —is that these men have "made it," meaning that they have learned something, done something, or that they simply belong in the world in any reasonable and justified way whatever. The unbelief, because such a thing is for themselves impossible. The young have social, creative, intellectual experiences, and even a resurgence of religious impulses, but finally it is only big Society and big Culture that give meaning. The young know this not vaguely but acutely, and feel excluded, and of course magnify their difficulties to be overwhelming.

What is lacking as a bridge, of course, is just the objective culture and the professions that provide public identity and the ability to operate confidently, whether succeeding or failing, in society. But if this goes on a while longer, our culture and professions will be irrelevant; there will not even be "carriers" of them, except occasional dilettantes and dodos. By and large the present universities do not and cannot educate.

ii

A young fellow who cannot/will not learn in school may consult his benevolent senior scholars, and he might get the following responses:

At the worst, he will be referred to Guidance. For his case is a psychological one and needs help of that kind. The case surely is psychological or rapidly becomes so, for a youth can hardly remain in a conflict of pressure to perform, including his own pressure on himself, and dumb conviction that it is meaningless to perform, without soon suffering anxiety, depression, and various kinds of flight. But such an academic response by the senior merely pushes off the problem onto an administrator who is even less qualified to help, despite his battery of tests.

On the other hand, the senior scholar may rather quickly identify with the youth's woes and gripes. He does not see any reasons why the young man should not quit, strike out on his own with the teeming projects of his brain that the school is stifling, and eventually educate himself. This response lets the young fellow down, because if he practically had such projects, he would be engaged on them. I think it betrays a lack of imagination. The senior has "made it," and from this vantage point he sees, what is obvious, that the schools are worthless for the gifted and original who do not happen to have the knack to take *anything* and profit by it. But the young man has not "made it" and is suffering. And it is too hard to educate oneself. The few who have the determination and synthetic power to do so are not the ones who cannot/will not learn even in a modern university.

A middle response—the one that I myself tend to give—is to stick with it by becoming aware of the situation just as it is, taking stupid rules whence they come, refraining anger, not being too co-operative and, above all, refusing to perform in any positive way that is base or dishonest. This formula, I argue, is usually possible because the teachers are not malevolent, and of course the subjects are great subjects. Also, I explain how I came to smoke a pipe: when I used to explode in a certain class at Chicago and make a nuisance of myself, McKeon, who was my mentor in such matters, showed me his pipe, the stem full of deep tooth-marks, and advised me to get me a pipe. Also, college has this undoubted advantage: although the young man won't get much from a college education, he will at least know that there is not much to be gotten, he will have run the obstacle course; he won't have to reproach himself stupidly later. All this advice is honest on my part and no doubt supportive.

Yet it is craven advice. I would not give it in politics, where I would rather say, Protest, don't vote, prudently disregard the laws that are harmful. I would not advise an adult to keep a useless and depressing job. This advice belongs to a veteran who occasionally does the best he can and therefore can stoically endure or merrily endure (depending on his character) the usual frustrations. But for a young person it is spirit-breaking and probably even unhealthy—mononucleosis seems to be the current psychosomatic effect of student blues.

The realistic response has to be: "You exaggerate,

but you're essentially right. But then what? If you quit school as you are, any job you get will be worse, because you're not ready to make it better. You don't know anything." This is not supportive at all. The student doesn't know anything and the senior scholar doesn't know where he can learn anything. They look at one another.

iii

Secession has been, I have said, the historical remedy for disaffected communities of scholars. But of course there are never real historical parallels. For instance, the classical strikes and migrations during the thirteenth century occurred because of direct clashes with church and state on doctrine, behavior, politics, by banded scholars defending their freedom and privileges; and at the same time, the universities had both a moral authority and an economic importance in their towns that made strike and migration a powerful weapon. In our own time, we have a unique system of co-ordinative management and democracy-by-consent designed precisely to prevent direct clashes; there is plenty of freedom and the whittling away of privileges is slow and subtle; and dissenters have no authority or economic power whatever. But more hopefully, our democracy and affluence, and the present expansion and turmoil of the colleges in any case, are unusually open to experiment, including even a simple experiment.

In the English-speaking world, the most important academic precedent for setting up shop in the face of the Establishment is the dissenting Academies that sprang up after the Act of Uniformity in 1662. More than 2,000 rectors and vicars resigned, including teachers at Oxford and Cambridge. "One of the first resources of the ejected ministers was to take to teaching, partly in order to eke out a living but mainly that they might not see their sons and the sons of the likeminded deprived of university education." (H. McLachlan, *English Education Under the Test Acts.*) They started with tiny schools of one to four tutors and five to six to thirty students; and during more than a century they were outlaws, either because they were not allowed to teach at the university level outside of the two universities, or because they did not subscribe to the Articles. Nevertheless, the secession survived, new texts were written and exchanged, students went from one little school to another, and during the eighteenth century these academies gave the best education in England and were probably the chief influence on the early American colleges. Some of them, subsidized by church bodies, were simply dissenting seminaries, but others became centers of rationalism and even politically revolutionary thought, influencing both the American and French revolutions and the reform movement in England, developing modern science and letters, and producing major changes in educational theory and practice. Their dissent happened to be the tide of the future. Their tutors and senior students, "unlike men studying for holy orders in the universities, were sent out to preach to congregations far and near"—and these included radical students from Joseph Priestley's Warrington. It is said that Marat was a tutor at Warrington. And to tie our story together, let us recall that it was Priestley's son-in-law, Dr. Cooper, who was barred as an atheist from Jefferson's great faculty by the House of Burgesses.

In America, we have already noticed the secession in the Dartmouth College Case. Another interesting secession is described by Professor Metzger in *The Development of Academic Freedom in the United States.* "In 1833 an antislavery society was formed at

Lane Theological Seminary in Cincinnati by students and a number of the faculty. The board of trustees banned the society, stating that 'education must be completed before the young are fitted to engage in the collisions of active life.' . . . But the young in this case happened to be rather old—30 of the seminarians were over the age of twenty-six. 'Free discussion, being a duty,' they announced, 'is consequently a right. It is *our* right. It *was* before we entered Lane; privileges we might and did relinquish; advantages we might and did receive. But this *right* the institution could neither give nor take away.' After firing this broadside, the students removed in a body to Oberlin, where they won the concession that their faculty (which included a professor who had been dismissed from Lane) would supervise them without interference from the trustees." The case, Professor Metzger points out, was "unfortunately atypical. A mass boycott of this kind, reminiscent of the medieval universities, was never to be repeated."

More relevant to contemporary conditions was the founding of the New School for Social Research in 1919. This is best viewed as a secession of teachers, for some of its chief spirits—e.g., Beard, Veblen, Robinson—could not conform to the Stanfords and Columbias, and others were attracted who were restive in such places. Later the school was, not accidentally, spectacularly augmented by the refugees from Hitler, the "university in exile." Over the course of the years, to be sure, the New School has itself succumbed to expansion, buildings and grounds, etc., in the normal process of decay of the prophetic to the bureaucratic.

The secession that is most relevant for our purposes, since the nearest in time, is the founding of Black Mountain College by the teachers fired from Rollins because of the "academic freedom" case of John Rice.

What is especially relevant about Rice's case is that he did not seem to espouse any particular heresy: it was his general nonconformity and nuisance value in the local society and with prospective donors that was condemned. He and his friends formed, really, the first Beat school—and its graduates have been leaders in this kind of art and culture. The school certainly had a zeal of medieval poverty, its teachers often went unpaid; but they continued because the school was theirs, it had no trustees and no administration. (Rice himself was ostracized as a "leader.") I myself taught a summer at Black Mountain.* I found it very feeble in the universal culture, but on the other hand nobody hindered me from teaching more scholastically and trying to influence the others. There was a frantic effort for community, resulting in affectionate loyalty and fatal dissensions. It was a justified and significant boast that students who had dropped out of the Ivy League could still get some kind of education at Black Mountain College. The school lasted nearly twenty-five years and then, like a little magazine, folded. Its spirit survives.

iv

Now, in the sixties, a small secession from about twenty colleges and universities would be immensely profitable for American education. I propose that a core faculty of about five professors secede from a school, taking some of their students with them; attach to themselves an equal number of like-minded professionals in the region; collect a few more students; and set up a small unchartered university that would be nothing but an

---

* I was discontinued, against my wishes, because of my wicked ways. Not, however, because of my behavior as such but, oddly, because of my public claim of the right to it, which was apparently legally and otherwise dangerous.

association for teaching-and-learning. Ten teachers would constitute a sufficient faculty for such a *studium generale*. (For comparison, Jefferson's University of Virginia had eight teachers; Joseph Priestley's Warrington had a maximum of thirteen.) Instead of five professionals, there could be a few more, some teaching part-time. With a class size of twelve to fifteen for ten teachers, there would be 120 to 150 students.

I choose the class size of twelve to fifteen as a mean in my own not untypical experience. It gives a sufficient weight of thoughts, objections, and questions to oppose and activate the teacher. When the number falls below this, to seven or eight, I begin to feel that I am leading a group therapy; I am overly conscious of the individual personalities coping with the subject, rather than teaching the objective subject. When the number rises to between twenty and thirty, I begin to feel I am lecturing the subject, with a question-and-answer period, and perhaps leading a "discussion." But of course the mean number varies with the subject, the character of the persons, and how the subject is handled. E.g., in teaching a course in writing, I combine several approaches: Structural analyses of classical texts, and these are largely lectures, with questions, that could be given to a group of thirty-five; psychological unblocking exercises, and exercises on points of style and technique, for both of which I like the class of twelve to fifteen; reading and criticism of the students' own writing, which I prefer in groups of five or six and *not* in a classroom. There are similar variations in anything else I would teach; and I presume it is the same for other teachers.

Throughout this book I have explained the advantages of a strong weight of professionals on a faculty. It is especially important in a small school composed entirely of teachers and students in close relation and without administrative rules, for otherwise it can become clubby, like excellent progressive schools or like Black Mountain College. These are lovely intentional communities, but they are not small universities; they do not sharply turn to the world. Furthermore, if a small school purports to be a *studium generale* it must have resources available outside itself. Suppose that a teacher teaches an elementary and a more advanced course, taking two years; then he will want to take his students nearer to real practice in the city, and the professionals have access to such practice.

It is evident, I hope, that I am not thinking of any particular educational experiment or ideology, like Goddard, Antioch, Sarah Lawrence, etc., aiming at democracy, communal living, community service, individual development, creativity, and so forth. These are fine things. But I am proposing simply to take teaching-and-learning in its own terms, for the students and teachers to associate in the traditional way and according to their existing interest, but *entirely dispensing with the external control, administration, bureaucratic machinery, and other excrescences that have swamped our communities of scholars*. I have no doubt that many such faculties, of dissatisfied academics and professionals who would like to teach, are ready in existence. At present there is no dearth of students; but of course such academic and professional faculties would choose the students very strictly, perhaps unduly so.

v

Three problems immediately arise: (1) the economics of the community; (2) its plant, library, and equipment; and (3) its relation to the chartered academic world and the rest of society, that is, the need for accredited degrees.

(1) We are not thinking of a social experiment, so let us pitch our prices according to the current inflated national scale of living. This is psychologically quite unrealistic (and perhaps any merely economic discussion would be), for teachers who would engage in such an experiment would also be less interested in the current standards; and of course, psychologically committed to it, they would have to make the experiment succeed, even if it cost them heavily financially. The professionals would be the doctors, lawyers, reform politicians, etc., who work too hard for too little reward anyway. And such a faculty would find it hard to exclude serious youngsters who could not foot the inflated bill.

Nevertheless, since we are thinking precisely of acting in society and of preparing professionals, we have to take the world as it is. This is the irony of actuality: those who want to transform a system of society, rather than to withdraw from it or destroy it, must operate practically within it. Our economy is administrative and venal through and through, and *therefore* inflated; but it is only the academic administration that we propose withdrawing from!

The relevant comparative figures are:

Median College Salaries, 1961

Professor	$10,250
Associate Professor	8,200
Assistant Professor	6,900
Instructor	5,600
(Assistant Instructor, Preceptor, etc.)	2,000-3,000

Typical College Tuition (plus fees), 1961

Cornell	$1,600 plus 260
Dartmouth	1,550
Harvard	1,520
Columbia	1,450 plus 10
New York University	1,280 plus 100

Swarthmore	1,250 plus 150
Oberlin	1,150 plus 80
University of Chicago	1,140
Amherst	1,150 plus 110

State Colleges for Out-of-State Students, 1961

Michigan	$ 750
Rutgers	500
California	500
North Carolina	500

Let us fix the salaries for teachers in two opposite ways: as a guild of teachers, and as a guild of students. For the first, we can adopt the national median for full professor, $10,000. (This is, of course, lower than the top at the great Eastern schools.) Then, the expenses are:

Salaries	$100,000
Rent (10 rooms, urban	
middle-class)	4,000
	$104,000

Divided among 150 students, this comes to tuition of $685. Among 120 students, $850. This is $300-500 less than the good liberal arts colleges, and half of the Ivy League. It includes, of course, no extras whatever, importantly no Medical; and there are no endowed library, laboratories, gymnasium, stadium, which are usually, however, paid for by the special "fees," not as "tuition." No school provides books.

Conversely, we might assume that the students as a guild would be satisfied to pay the tuition of an average State university, $500 plus fees. Then,

Income from 150 students	$75,000
Rent	—4,000
	$71,000

Income from 120 students	$60,000
Rent	—4,000
	$56,000

This would pay each teacher $7,100, a little more than the median for Assistant Professor, or $5,600, the median for an Instructor.

Perhaps the teachers and students might compromise on the median for Associate Professor, $8,200! This is for forty weeks. And we must remember that especially the professionals would have subsidiary income.

(2) With regard to plant and equipment, let us envisage several possibilities. But we must keep in mind that this is a *community* of scholars. It would immediately have available for its use 10,000 to 20,000 carefully selected books and some apparatus. Its professional associations would give it some access to the laboratories and equipment that the teaching professionals would happen to be interested in.

It is simplest to think of such a little community as located in a large city, with a municipal library, a Y, and many available part-time professionals. On the other hand, there are obvious charms and advantages to location in a town and its region; nor need such places be lacking in excellent professionals with a lively local practice. (I do not much picture a school of this kind as isolated in the country.)

But another possibility for providing books and plant is to consider the small university as next to, and unofficially adjunct to, some great university which extends to it friendly services because it is a necessary experiment and a source of good graduate students. The economic independence of the community dissociates it from the great school; the administration of the great school has no responsibility for it whatever; yet the secession of a small faculty need *not* mean a rupture of friendly relations. That is, we can conceive of a free academy set up in the neighborhood of a great university to their mutual advantage.

Historically, this is *almost* familiar. In Germany,

our teachers paid directly by the students would be recognized as Private-Docents of the University, officially associated with it and teaching in its classrooms. What we propose is simply the secession and association of these Independents, so that they become again, what they were in the beginning, regent masters of their own guild.

(3) Finally, a major difficulty of any unchartered *ad hoc* association of scholars is that it cannot grant degrees leading to licenses. It is not to be expected, and *it is not desirable,* that young people spend their years and money in study that does not lead to careers in society.

An obvious possible solution is the European plan: to have the graduates matriculate for a term in an accredited school and pass the comprehensives. (E.g., the University of Chicago used to accept candidates for comprehensives after one Quarter, three months, of residence.) To my mind this solution has a theoretical drawback. The comprehensives of an accredited school must necessarily follow the curriculum of that school; and this cannot, of course, be a determining "goal" for the community of scholars which has been teaching-and-learning according to its implicit goals, without extrinsic "motivation." But it is likely—and perhaps I am sanguine—that for many of the students it would not be difficult, after several years of good education, to make up the usual requirements with a semester's cramming.

Far more attractive, however, would be a friendly arrangement whereby graduate and professional schools, that compete for good students, would accept these students on their merits. In this case their first accredited degree would be a master's or doctor's.

vi

How complicated this simple proposal is! We must bring together 150 persons, subject the young to considerable expense, and think of future arrangements that have no real relevance to the living present. Is there no easier way to grow up?

The *studium generale* is, finally, what we mean by the Western World. It *is* complicated, let's face it— but it is not necessarily absurd, it can be viable. Anyway, it is the way we have chosen, and we are committed to it! Our fundamental idea is that the growing social animals become free citizens. They grow into civilization in a way rational to themselves, they understand it, and therefore they continue to have initiative. They have also taken *on* the civilization; they are responsible for it. They are no longer simple social animals confronting God and the other people.*

We can think of two different (fictitious) extremes, and see that the *studium generale* is in the middle and is neither of them. Education can be regarded as socialization, to make the young conform harmoniously to society—and this can be a base or noble purpose, depending on the quality of society. Or it may be regarded as the effort to perfect people as such, perhaps giving them defenses against the existing, or any, society, in the interest of liberty. But the Western university rather regards society itself as a drama of persons, in which

---

* Let me repeat an anecdote of Buber's: An Eastern sage and a Western sage are climbing a mountain. But the Western sage is carrying a heavy box, drops it, falls backward, shoulders it again, struggles on. The Easterner easily races ahead to the top and is soon on his way down. "Why don't you throw away that box?" he says to the other, "then you could easily get up." "But what," says the Westerner, "if I have to get to the top just with my box? Otherwise it is nothing to me."

the educated understand the play and so can invent a new play. *Liberty is, essentially, the exercise of initiative in a mixed city.*

The tendency of contemporary society, collectivized, technocratic, managerial, is to impose a culture on its members, to train them to carry it and perform. Such a society is different from ancient despotism in that, ideally, it has no elite, though it may have top managers, for decisions are also made by a technological process to maximize the common good. The schools of society are, ideally, partly trade schools and partly finishing schools in conformity. Of course there is not, and probably cannot be, such an ideal social machine. In America, the need for personal co-ordination, democracy-by-consent, is a limit of management as well as a managerial triumph. Other more tyrannical technocracies have other limitations.

But there have been high cultures with a contrary tendency, psychical and cosmological, to by-pass as much as possible the objective tools and institutions of society and civilization, in order to attain holiness, beatitude, or wisdom as directly as possible. Since these are the goals that men seek in the end, other things are illusion, and it is the task of learning to see through them. Schools are then retreats, whose guru, monk, or therapist has the right soul to liberate the right disciples. But of course, every such religious culture is embedded in its civilization, believes its myths, conforms to its social structure, and partly has to be defined as an escape from its troubles.

By and large, we have to say that the city culture of the West is both moral and technical, personal and collective. Yet it is not, as some writers think, a dialectical process of the other two tendencies, for it has a different principle. The principle of the *studium generale* is that civilization has been a continual gift of the Creator Spirit; it consists of inventions, discoveries, insights, art works, highly theorized institutions, methods of workmanship. All of this has vastly accumulated over the ages and become very unwieldly, yet, in the spirit, it is always appropriable. As Socrates would have said, its meaning can be recalled. The advantage of recalling it is that we are then not enslaved to it, we are citizens, and we again have it available as our own. Consider. It is by losing himself in the objective, in inquiry, creation, and craft, that a man becomes something. It is as if a man "makes himself," but of course it is the spirit that makes him. On the other hand, he need not be submerged in the civilization that he inherits, that others made, for if he studies it he will surely find himself there; it is his.

The university, the *studium generale,* is the appropriable city. "Its proper end," said Coleridge, "is civilization with freedom." A city culture is a mixture of clashing influences, foreigners from all parts. The objective culture that we have inherited is by now total confusion; and certainly there is too much of it for anybody to cope with. As if this were not bad enough, the young are kept from learning, by rules, task-work, and extraneous distractions. They have no conversation and they meet no veterans. Nevertheless, there is no other way for them to grow up to be free citizens, to commence, except by discovering, in an earnest moment, that some portion of the objective culture is after all natively their own; it is usable by *them;* it is humane, comprehensible and practicable, and it communicates with everything else. The discovery flashes with spirit.